ABOUT THIS PUBLICATION

FOR SERVICE ASSISTANCE

Customer Service:
1.704.898.0770

North Carolina General Statues is published by The Muliti-Media Group of Greater Charlotte in Charlotte, North Carolina. Copyright 2015 by the Multi-Media Group of Greater Charlotte. This book or parts thereof may not be reproduced in any form, stored in a retrieval system, or transmitted in any form by any means—electronic, mechanical, photocopy, recording or otherwise—without prior written permission of the publisher, except as provided by United States of America copyright law.

The records required by U.S. Code 2257(a) through (c) and the pertinent regulations 28 C.F.R. Cli. 1, Part 75 with respect to this publication and all materials associated with such records are maintained by The Multi-Media Group of Greater Charlotte, Publisher and available for review by Attorney General.

www.visionbooks.org

Copyright © 2015 by MMGGC
All rights reserved!

TID: 5061728
ISBN (10) digit: 1502915367
ISBN (13) digit: 978-1502915368

123-4-56789-01239-Paperback
123-4-56789-01239-Hardback

First Edition

090520140547

Printed in the United States of America

2015 EDITION

North Carolina Criminal Law And Procedure-Pamphlet # 49

Printed In conjunction with the Administration of the Courts

North Carolina Criminal Law and Procedure
Pamphlet Reference Guide

Chapters	Pamphlet
Chapter 1 Civil Procedure	1
Chapter 1 Civil Procedure (Continue)	2
Chapter 1A Rules of Civil Procedure	2
Chapter 1B Contribution.	2
Chapter 1C Enforcement of Judgments.	2
Chapter 1D Punitive Damages.	2
Chapter 1E Eastern Band of Cherokee Indians.	2
Chapter 1F North Carolina Uniform Interstate Depositions and Discovery Act.	2
Chapter 2 - Clerk of Superior Court [Repealed and Transferred.]	3
Chapter 3 - Commissioners of Affidavits and Deeds [Repealed.]	3
Chapter 4 - Common Law	3
Chapter 5 - Contempt [Repealed.]	3
Chapter 5A - Contempt	3
Chapter 6 - Liability for Court Costs	3
Chapter 7 - Courts [Repealed and Transferred.]	3
Chapter 7A – Judicial Department	3
Chapter 7A – Continuation (Judicial Department)	4
Chapter 7A – Continuation (Judicial Department)	5
Chapter 7B - Juvenile Code	5
Chapter 8 - Evidence	6
Chapter 8A - Interpreters for Deaf Persons [Recodified.]	6
Chapter 8B - Interpreters for Deaf Persons	6
Chapter 8C - Evidence Code	6
Chapter 9 - Jurors	6
Chapter 10 - Notaries [Repealed.]	6
Chapter 10A - Notaries [Recodified.]	6
Chapter 10B - Notaries	6
Chapter 11 - Oaths	6
Chapter 12 - Statutory Construction	6
Chapter 13 - Citizenship Restored	6
Chapter 14 - Criminal Law	7
Chapter 14 –Criminal Law (Continuation)	8
Chapter 15 - Criminal Procedure	9
Chapter 15A - Criminal Procedure Act (Continuation)	10
Chapter 15A - Criminal Procedure Act (Continuation)	11
Chapter 15B - Victims Compensation	11
Chapter 15C - Address Confidentiality Program	11
Chapter 16 - Gaming Contracts and Futures	11
Chapter 17 - Habeas Corpus	11

Chapter 17A - Law-Enforcement Officers [Recodified.]	11
Chapter 17B - North Carolina Criminal Justice Education and Training System [Recodified.] Chapter 17C - North Carolina Criminal Justice Education and Training Standards Commission	11 11
Chapter 17D - North Carolina Justice Academy	11
Chapter 17E - North Carolina Sheriffs' Education and Training Standards Commission	11
Chapter 18 - Regulation of Intoxicating Liquors [Repealed.]	12
Chapter 18A - Regulation of Intoxicating Liquors [Repealed.]	12
Chapter 18B - Regulation of Alcoholic Beverages	12
Chapter 18C - North Carolina State Lottery	12
Chapter 19 - Offenses against Public Morals	12
Chapter 19A - Protection of Animals	12
Chapter 20 - Motor Vehicles	13
Chapter 20 - Motor Vehicles (Continuation)	14
Chapter 20 - Motor Vehicles (Continuation)	15
Chapter 20 - Motor Vehicles (Continuation)	16
Chapter 21 - Bills of Lading	17
Chapter 22 - Contracts Requiring Writing	17
Chapter 22A - Signatures	17
Chapter 22B - Contracts Against Public Policy	17
Chapter 22C - Payments to Subcontractors	17
Chapter 23 - Debtor and Creditor	17
Chapter 24 – Interest	17
Chapter 25 – Uniform Commercial Code	18
Chapter 25 – Uniform Commercial Code (Continuation)	19
Chapter 25A – Retail Installment Sales Act	20
Chapter 25B - Credit	20
Chapter 25C - Sales of Artwork	20
Chapter 26 - Suretyship	20
Chapter 27 - Warehouse Receipts [Repealed.]	20
Chapter 28 - Administration [Repealed.]	20
Chapter 28A - Administration of Decedents' Estates	20
Chapter 28B - Estates of Absentees in Military Service	20
Chapter 28C - Estates of Missing Persons	20
Chapter 29 - Intestate Succession	21
Chapter 30 - Surviving Spouses	21
Chapter 31 - Wills	21
Chapter 31A - Acts Barring Property Rights	21
Chapter 31B - Renunciation of Property and Renunciation of Fiduciary Powers Act	21
Chapter 31C - Uniform Disposition of Community Property Rights at Death Act	21
Chapter 32 - Fiduciaries	21
Chapter 32A - Powers of Attorney	21
Chapter 33 - Guardian and Ward [Repealed and Recodified.]	21

Chapter 33A - North Carolina Uniform Transfers to Minors Act	21
Chapter 33B - North Carolina Uniform Custodial Trust Act	21
Chapter 34 - Veterans' Guardianship Act	22
Chapter 35 - Sterilization Procedures	22
Chapter 35A - Incompetency and Guardianship	22
Chapter 36 - Trusts and Trustees [Repealed.]	22
Chapter 36A - Trusts and Trustees	22
Chapter 36B - Uniform Management of Institutional Funds Act [Repealed.]	22
Chapter 36C - North Carolina Uniform Trust Code	22
Chapter 36D - North Carolina Community Third Party Trusts, Pooled Trusts	23
Chapter 36E - Uniform Prudent Management of Institutional Funds Act	23
Chapter 37 - Allocation of Principal and Income [Repealed.]	23
Chapter 37A - Uniform Principal and Income Act	23
Chapter 38 - Boundaries	23
Chapter 38A - Landowner Liability	23
Chapter 39 - Conveyances	23
Chapter 39A - Transfer Fee Covenants Prohibited	23
Chapter 40 - Eminent Domain [Repealed.]	23
Chapter 40A - Eminent Domain	23
Chapter 41 - Estates	23
Chapter 41A - State Fair Housing Act	23
Chapter 42 - Landlord and Tenant	23
Chapter 42A - Vacation Rental Act	23
Chapter 43 - Land Registration	23
Chapter 44 - Liens	24
Chapter 44A - Statutory Liens and Charges	24
Chapter 45 - Mortgages and Deeds of Trust	24
Chapter 45A - Good Funds Settlement Act	24
Chapter 46 - Partition	24
Chapter 47 - Probate and Registration	25
Chapter 47A - Unit Ownership	25
Chapter 47B - Real Property Marketable Title Act	25
Chapter 47C - North Carolina Condominium Act	25
Chapter 47D - Notice of Settlement Act [Expired.]	25
Chapter 47E - Residential Property Disclosure Act	25
Chapter 47F - North Carolina Planned Community Act	25
Chapter 47G - Option to Purchase Contracts	25
Chapter 47H - Contracts for Deed	25
Chapter 48 - Adoptions +	26
Chapter 48A - Minors	26
Chapter 49 - Bastardy	26
Chapter 49A - Rights of Children	26
Chapter 50 - Divorce and Alimony	26
Chapter 50A - Uniform Child-Custody Jurisdiction and	

Enforcement Act	26
Chapter 50B - Domestic Violence	26
Chapter 50C - Civil No-Contact Orders	26
Chapter 51 - Marriage	26
Chapter 52 - Powers and Liabilities of Married Persons	27
Chapter 52A - Uniform Reciprocal Enforcement of Support Act [Repealed.]	27
Chapter 52B - Uniform Premarital Agreement Act	27
Chapter 52C - Uniform Interstate Family Support Act	27
Chapter 53 - Banks	27
Chapter 53A - Business Development Corporations and North Carolina Capital Resource Corporations	28
Chapter 53B - Financial Privacy Act	28
Chapter 54 - Cooperative Organizations	28
Chapter 54A - Capital Stock Savings and Loan Associations [Repealed.]	28
Chapter 54B - Savings and Loan Associations	29
Chapter 54C - Savings Banks	29
Chapter 55 - North Carolina Business Corporation Act	30
Chapter 55A - North Carolina Nonprofit Corporation Act	31
Chapter 55B - Professional Corporation Act	31
Chapter 55C - Foreign Trade Zones	31
Chapter 55D - Filings, Names, and Registered Agents for Corporations, Nonprofit Corporations, and Partnerships	31
Chapter 56 - Electric, Telegraph and Power Companies [Repealed.]	31
Chapter 57 - Hospital, Medical and Dental Service Corporations [Recodified.]	31
Chapter 57A - Health Maintenance Organization Act [Recodified.]	31
Chapter 57B - Health Maintenance Organization Act [Recodified.]	31
Chapter 57C - North Carolina Limited Liability Company Act.	31
Chapter 58 - Insurance.	32
Chapter 58A - North Carolina Health Insurance Trust Commission [Recodified.]	32
Chapter 58A - North Carolina Health Insurance Trust Commission [Recodified.] (Continuation)	33
Chapter 58A - North Carolina Health Insurance Trust Commission [Recodified.] (Continuation)	34
Chapter 58A - North Carolina Health Insurance Trust Commission [Recodified.] (Continuation)	35
Chapter 58A - North Carolina Health Insurance Trust Commission [Recodified.] (Continuation)	36
Chapter 58A - North Carolina Health Insurance Trust Commission [Recodified.] (Continuation)	37
Chapter 58A - North Carolina Health Insurance Trust	

Commission [Recodified.] (Continuation)	38
Chapter 59 - Partnership.	39
Chapter 59B - Uniform Unincorporated Nonprofit Association Act.	39
Chapter 60 - Railroads and Other Carriers [Repealed and Transferred.]	39
Chapter 61 - Religious Societies	39
Chapter 62 - Public Utilities	39
Chapter 62 - Public Utilities (Continuation)	40
Chapter 62A - Public Safety Telephone Service And Wireless Telephone Service	40
Chapter 63 - Aeronautics	40
Chapter 63A - North Carolina Global TransPark Authority	40
Chapter 64 - Aliens	40
Chapter 65 – Cemeteries	40
Chapter 66 - Commerce and Business	41
Chapter 67 - Dogs	41
Chapter 68 - Fences and Stock Law	41
Chapter 69 - Fire Protection	41
Chapter 70 - Indian Antiquities, Archaeological Resources and Unmarked Human Skeletal Remains Protection	42
Chapter 71 - Indians [Repealed.]	42
Chapter 71A - Indians	42
Chapter 72 - Inns, Hotels and Restaurants	42
Chapter 73 - Mills	42
Chapter 74 - Mines and Quarries	42
Chapter 74A - Company Police [Repealed.]	42
Chapter 74B - Private Protective Services Act [Repealed.]	42
Chapter 74C - Private Protective Services	42
Chapter 74D - Alarm Systems	42
Chapter 74E - Company Police Act	42
Chapter 74F - Locksmith Licensing Act	42
Chapter 74G - Campus Police Act	42
Chapter 75 - Monopolies, Trusts and Consumer Protection	42
Chapter 75A - Boating and Water Safety	43
Chapter 75B - Discrimination in Business	43
Chapter 75C - Motion Picture Fair Competition Act	43
Chapter 75D - Racketeer Influenced and Corrupt Organizations	43
Chapter 75E - Unlawful Activities in Connection With Certain Corporate Transactions	43
Chapter 76 - Navigation	43
Chapter 76A - Navigation and Pilotage Commissions	43
Chapter 77 - Rivers, Creeks, and Coastal Waters	43
Chapter 78 - Securities Law [Repealed.]	43
Chapter 78A - North Carolina Securities Act	43
Chapter 78B - Tender Offer Disclosure Act [Repealed.]	43
Chapter 78C - Investment Advisers	43
Chapter 78D - Commodities Act	43

Chapter 79 - Strays [Repealed.]	43
Chapter 80 - Trademarks, Brands, etc.	44
Chapter 81 - Weights and Measures [Recodified.]	44
Chapter 81A - Weights and Measures Act of 1975.	44
Chapter 82 - Wrecks [Repealed.]	44
Chapter 83 - Architects [Recodified.]	44
Chapter 83A - Architects	44
Chapter 84 - Attorneys-at-Law	44
Chapter 84A - Foreign Legal Consultants	44
Chapter 85 - Auctions and Auctioneers [Repealed.]	44
Chapter 85A - Bail Bondsmen and Runners [Recodified.]	44
Chapter 85B - Auctions and Auctioneers	44
Chapter 85C - Bail Bondsmen and Runners [Recodified.]	44
Chapter 86 - Barbers [Recodified.]	44
Chapter 86A - Barbers	44
Chapter 87 - Contractors	44
Chapter 88 - Cosmetic Art [Repealed.]	44
Chapter 88A - Electrolysis Practice Act	44
Chapter 88B - Cosmetic Art	45
Chapter 89 - Engineering and Land Surveying [Recodified.]	45
Chapter 89A - Landscape Architects	45
Chapter 89B - Foresters	45
Chapter 89C - Engineering and Land Surveying	45
Chapter 89D - Landscape Contractors	45
Chapter 89E - Geologists Licensing Act	45
Chapter 89F - North Carolina Soil Scientist Licensing Act	45
Chapter 89G - Irrigation Contractors	45
Chapter 90 - Medicine and Allied Occupations	45
Chapter 90 - Medicine and Allied Occupations (Continuation)	46
Chapter 90 - Medicine and Allied Occupations (Continuation)	47
Chapter 90 - Medicine and Allied Occupations (Continuation)	48
Chapter 90A - Sanitarians and Water and Wastewater Treatment Facility Operators	48
Chapter 90B - Social Worker Certification and Licensure Act	48
Chapter 90C - North Carolina Recreational Therapy Licensure Act	48
Chapter 90D - Interpreters and Transliterators	48
Chapter 91 - Pawnbrokers [Repealed.]	48
Chapter 91A - Pawnbrokers Modernization Act of 1989	48
Chapter 92 - Photographers [Deleted.]	48
Chapter 93 - Certified Public Accountants	48
Chapter 93A - Real Estate License Law	49
Chapter 93B - Occupational Licensing Boards	49
Chapter 93C - Watchmakers [Repealed.]	49
Chapter 93D - North Carolina State Hearing Aid Dealers and Fitters Board.	49
Chapter 93E - North Carolina Appraisers Act	49

Chapter 94 - Apprenticeship	49
Chapter 95 - Department of Labor and Labor Regulations	49
Chapter 95 - Department of Labor and Labor Regulations (Continuation)	50
Chapter 96 - Employment Security	50
Chapter 97 - Workers' Compensation Act	50
Chapter 97 - Workers' Compensation Act (Continuation)	51
Chapter 98 - Burnt and Lost Records	51
Chapter 99 - Libel and Slander	51
Chapter 99A - Civil Remedies for Criminal Actions	51
Chapter 99B - Products Liability	51
Chapter 99C - Actions Relating to Winter Sports Safety and Accidents	51
Chapter 99D - Civil Rights	51
Chapter 99E - Special Liability Provisions	51
Chapter 100 - Monuments, Memorials and Parks	51
Chapter 101 - Names of Persons	51
Chapter 102 - Official Survey Base	51
Chapter 103 - Sundays, Holidays and Special Days	51
Chapter 104 - United States Lands	51
Chapter 104A - Degrees of Kinship	51
Chapter 104B - Hurricanes or Other Acts of Nature	51
Chapter 104C - Atomic Energy, Radioactivity and Ionizing Radiation [Repealed and Recodified.]	51
Chapter 104D - Southern States Energy Compact	51
Chapter 104E - North Carolina Radiation Protection Act	51
Chapter 104F - Southeast Interstate Low-Level Radioactive Waste Management Compact [Repealed]	51
Chapter 104G - North Carolina Low-Level Radioactive Waste Management Authority Act of 1987 [Repealed]	51
Chapter 105 - Taxation	51
Chapter 105 - Taxation (Continuation)	52
Chapter 105 - Taxation (Continuation)	53
Chapter 105 - Taxation (Continuation)	54
Chapter 105A - Setoff Debt Collection Act	55
Chapter 105B - Defaulted Student Loan Recovery Act	55
Chapter 106 - Agriculture	55
Chapter 106 - Agriculture (Continue)	56
Chapter 106 - Agriculture (Continue)	57
Chapter 107 - Agricultural Development Districts [Repealed.]	57
Chapter 108 - Social Services [Repealed and Recodified.]	57
Chapter 108A - Social Services	57
Chapter 108B - Community Action Programs	58
Chapter 108C Medicaid and Health Choice Provider Requirements.	58
Chapter 108D Medicaid Managed Care for Behavioral Health Services.	58
Chapter 109 - Bonds [Recodified.]	58

Chapter 110 - Child Welfare	58
Chapter 111 - Aid to the Blind	58
Chapter 112 - Confederate Homes and Pensions [Repealed.]	58
Chapter 113 - Conservation and Development	58
Chapter 113 - Conservation and Development (Continuation)	59
Chapter 113A - Pollution Control and Environment	59
Chapter 113A - Pollution Control and Environment (Continuation)	60
Chapter 113B - North Carolina Energy Policy Act of 1975	60
Chapter 114 - Department of Justice	60
Chapter 115 - Elementary and Secondary Education [Repealed.]	60
Chapter 115A - Community Colleges, Technical Institutes, and Industrial Education Centers [Repealed.]	60
Chapter 115B - Tuition and Fee Waivers	60
Chapter 115C - Elementary and Secondary Education	60
Chapter 115C - Elementary and Secondary Education (Continuation)	61
Chapter 115C - Elementary and Secondary Education (Continuation)	62
Chapter 115C - Elementary and Secondary Education (Continuation)	63
Chapter 115D - Community Colleges	63
Chapter 115E - Private Educational Facilities Finance Act [Recodified]	63
Chapter 116 - Higher Education	63
Chapter 116 - Higher Education (Continuation)	63
Chapter 116A - Escheats and Abandoned Property [Repealed.]	64
Chapter 116B - Escheats and Abandoned Property	64
Chapter 116C - Continuum of Education Programs	64
Chapter 116D - Higher Education Bonds	64
Chapter 117 - Electrification	64
Chapter 118 - Firemen's and Rescue Squad Workers' Relief and Pension Funds [Recodified.]	64
Chapter 118A - Firemen's Death Benefit Act [Repealed.]	64
Chapter 118B - Members of a Rescue Squad Death Benefit Act [Repealed.]	64
Chapter 119 - Gasoline and Oil Inspection and Regulation	64
Chapter 120 - General Assembly	65
Chapter 120 - General Assembly (Continuation)	66
Chapter 120 - General Assembly (Continuation)	67
Chapter 120C - Lobbying	67
Chapter 121 - Archives and History	67
Chapter 122 - Hospitals for the Mentally Disordered [Repealed.]	67
Chapter 122A - North Carolina Housing Finance Agency	67
Chapter 122B - North Carolina Agricultural Facilities	

Finance Act [Repealed.]	67
Chapter 122C - Mental Health, Developmental Disabilities, and Substance Abuse Act of 1985	67
Chapter 122C - Mental Health, Developmental Disabilities, and Substance Abuse Act of 1985 (Continuation)	68
Chapter 122D - North Carolina Agricultural Finance Act	68
Chapter 122E - North Carolina Housing Trust and Oil Overcharge Act	68
Chapter 123 - Impeachment	69
Chapter 123A - Industrial Development [Repealed.]	69
Chapter 124 - Internal Improvements	69
Chapter 125 - Libraries	69
Chapter 126 - State Personnel System	69
Chapter 127 - Militia [Repealed.]	69
Chapter 127A - Militia	69
Chapter 127B - Military Affairs	69
Chapter 127C - Advisory Commission on Military Affairs	69
Chapter 128 - Offices and Public Officers	69
Chapter 128 - Offices and Public Officers (Continuation)	70
Chapter 129 - Public Buildings and Grounds	70
Chapter 130 - Public Health [Repealed.]	70
Chapter 130A - Public Health	70
Chapter 130A - Public Health (Continuation)	71
Chapter 130A - Public Health (Continuation)	72
Chapter 130B - Hazardous Waste Management Commission [Repealed.]	72
Chapter 131 - Public Hospitals [Repealed.]	72
Chapter 131A - Health Care Facilities Finance Act	72
Chapter 131B - Licensing of Ambulatory Surgical Facilities [Repealed.]	72
Chapter 131C - Charitable Solicitation Licensure Act [Repealed.]	72
Chapter 131D - Inspection and Licensing of Facilities	72
Chapter 131E - Health Care Facilities and Services	72
Chapter 131E - Health Care Facilities and Services (Continuation)	73
Chapter 131F - Solicitation of Contributions	73
Chapter 132 - Public Records	73
Chapter 133 - Public Works	74
Chapter 134 - Youth Development [Recodified.]	74
Chapter 134A - Youth Services [Repealed.]	74
Chapter 135 - Retirement System for Teachers and State Employees; Social Security; Health Insurance Program for Children	74
Chapter 135 - Retirement System for Teachers and State Employees; Social Security; Health Insurance Program for Children	75

Chapter 136 - Transportation	75
Chapter 136 - Transportation (Continuation)	76
Chapter 137 - Rural Rehabilitation [Repealed.]	76
Chapter 138 - Salaries, Fees and Allowances	76
Chapter 138A - State Government Ethics Act	76
Chapter 139 - Soil and Water Conservation Districts	76
Chapter 140 - State Art Museum; Symphony and Art Societies	76
Chapter 140A - State Awards System	76
Chapter 141 - State Boundaries	76
Chapter 142 - State Debt	76
Chapter 143 - State Departments, Institutions, and Commissions	77
Chapter 143 - State Departments, Institutions, and Commissions (Continuation)	78
Chapter 143 - State Departments, Institutions, and Commissions (Continuation)	79
Chapter 143 - State Departments, Institutions, and Commissions (Continuation)	80
Chapter 143A - State Government Reorganization	80
Chapter 143B - Executive Organization Act of 1973	80
Chapter 143B - Executive Organization Act of 1973 (Continuation)	81
Chapter 143B - Executive Organization Act of 1973 (Continuation)	82
Chapter 143C - State Budget Act	83
Chapter 143D - The State Governmental Accountability and Internal Control Act	83
Chapter 144 - State Flag, Official Governmental Flags, Motto, and Colors	83
Chapter 145 - State Symbols and Other Official Adoptions.	83
Chapter 146 - State Lands	83
Chapter 147 - State Officers	83
Chapter 148 - State Prison System	84
Chapter 149 - State Song and Toast	84
Chapter 150 - Uniform Revocation of Licenses [Repealed.]	84
Chapter 150A - Administrative Procedure Act [Recodified.]	84
Chapter 150B - Administrative Procedure Act	84
Chapter 151 - Constables [Repealed.]	84
Chapter 152 - Coroners	84
Chapter 152A - County Medical Examiner [Repealed.]	84
Chapter 152A - County Medical Examiner [Repealed.] (Continuation)	85
Chapter 153 - Counties and County Commissioners [Repealed.]	85
Chapter 153A - Counties	85

Chapter 153B - Mountain Resources Planning Act	85
Chapter 153C - Uwharrie Regional Resources Act	85
Chapter 154 - County Surveyor [Repealed.]	85
Chapter 155 - County Treasurer [Repealed.]	85
Chapter 156 - Drainage	85
Chapter 156 – Drainage (Continuation)	86
Chapter 157 - Housing Authorities and Projects	86
Chapter 157A - Historic Properties Commissions [Transferred.]	86
Chapter 158 - Local Development	86
Chapter 159 - Local Government Finance	86
Chapter 159 - Local Government Finance (Continuation)	87
Chapter 159A - Pollution Abatement and Industrial Facilities Financing Act [Unconstitutional.]	87
Chapter 159B - Joint Municipal Electric Power and Energy Act	87
Chapter 159C - Industrial and Pollution Control Facilities Financing Act	87
Chapter 159D - The North Carolina Capital Facilities Financing Act	87
Chapter 159E - Registered Public Obligations Act	87
Chapter 159F - North Carolina Energy Development Authority [Repealed.]	87
Chapter 159G - Water Infrastructure	87
Chapter 159H - [Reserved.]	87
Chapter 159I - Solid Waste Management Loan Program and Local Government Special Obligation Bonds	87
Chapter 160 - Municipal Corporations [Repealed And Transferred.]	87
Chapter 160A - Cities and Towns	88
Chapter 160A - Cities and Towns (Continuation)	89
Chapter 160B - Consolidated City-County Act	89
Chapter 160C - Baseball Park Districts [Repealed.]	90
Chapter 161 - Register of Deeds	90
Chapter 162 - Sheriff	90
Chapter 162A - Water and Sewer Systems	90
Chapter 162B Continuity of Local Government in Emergency.	90
Chapter 163 Elections and Election Laws.	90
Chapter 163 Elections and Election Laws. (Continuation)	91
Chapter 164 Concerning the General Statutes of North Carolina.	92
Chapter 165 Veterans.	92
Chapter 166 Civil Preparedness Agencies [Repealed.]	92
Chapter 166A North Carolina Emergency Management Act.	92
Chapter 167 State Civil Air Patrol [Repealed.]	92
Chapter 168 Persons with Disabilities.	92
Chapter 168A Persons With Disabilities Protection Act.	92

Chapter 93A.

Real Estate License Law.

Article 1.

Real Estate Brokers and Salespersons.

§ 93A-1. License required of real estate brokers.

From and after July 1, 1957, it shall be unlawful for any person, partnership, corporation, limited liability company, association, or other business entity in this State to act as a real estate broker, or directly or indirectly to engage or assume to engage in the business of real estate broker or to advertise or hold himself or herself or themselves out as engaging in or conducting such business without first obtaining a license issued by the North Carolina Real Estate Commission (hereinafter referred to as the Commission), under the provisions of this Chapter. A license shall be obtained from the Commission even if the person, partnership, corporation, limited liability company, association, or business entity is licensed in another state and is affiliated or otherwise associated with a licensed real estate broker in this State. (1957, c. 744, s. 1; 1969, c. 191, s. 1; 1983, c. 81, ss. 1, 2; 1995, c. 351, s. 19; 1999-229, s. 1; 2005-395, s. 1.)

§ 93A-2. Definitions and exceptions.

(a) A real estate broker within the meaning of this Chapter is any person, partnership, corporation, limited liability company, association, or other business entity who for a compensation or valuable consideration or promise thereof lists or offers to list, sells or offers to sell, buys or offers to buy, auctions or offers to auction (specifically not including a mere crier of sales), or negotiates the purchase or sale or exchange of real estate, or who leases or offers to lease, or who sells or offers to sell leases of whatever character, or rents or offers to rent any real estate or the improvement thereon, for others.

(a1) The term broker-in-charge within the meaning of this Chapter means a real estate broker who has been designated as the broker having responsibility for the supervision of brokers on provisional status engaged in real estate brokerage at a particular real estate office and for other administrative and supervisory duties as the Commission shall prescribe by rule.

(a2)   The term provisional broker within the meaning of this Chapter means a real estate broker who, pending acquisition and documentation to the Commission of the education or experience prescribed by either G.S. 93A-4(a1) or G.S. 93A-4.3, must be supervised by a broker-in-charge when performing any act for which a real estate license is required.

(b)   The term real estate salesperson within the meaning of this Chapter shall mean and include any person who was formerly licensed by the Commission as a real estate salesperson before April 1, 2006.

(c)   The provisions of G.S. 93A-1 and G.S. 93A-2 do not apply to and do not include:

(1)   Any partnership, corporation, limited liability company, association, or other business entity that, as owner or lessor, shall perform any of the acts aforesaid with reference to property owned or leased by them, where the acts are performed in the regular course of or as incident to the management of that property and the investment therein. The exemption from licensure under this subsection shall extend to officers and employees of an exempt corporation, the general partners of an exempt partnership, and the managers of an exempt limited liability company when said persons are engaged in acts or services for which the corporation, partnership, or limited liability company would be exempt hereunder.

(2)   Any person acting as an attorney-in-fact under a duly executed power of attorney from the owner authorizing the final consummation of performance of any contract for the sale, lease or exchange of real estate.

(3)   Acts or services performed by an attorney who is an active member of the North Carolina State Bar if the acts and services constitute the practice of law under Chapter 84 of the General Statutes.

(4)   Any person, while acting as a receiver, trustee in bankruptcy, guardian, administrator or executor or any person acting under order of any court.

(5)   Any person, while acting as a trustee under a written trust agreement, deed of trust or will, or that person's regular salaried employees. The trust agreement, deed of trust, or will must specifically identify the trustee, the beneficiary, the corpus of trust, and the trustee's authority over the corpus.

(6) Any salaried person employed by a licensed real estate broker, for and on behalf of the owner of any real estate or the improvements thereon, which the licensed broker has contracted to manage for the owner, if the salaried employee's employment is limited to: exhibiting units on the real estate to prospective tenants; providing the prospective tenants with information about the lease of the units; accepting applications for lease of the units; completing and executing preprinted form leases; and accepting security deposits and rental payments for the units only when the deposits and rental payments are made payable to the owner or the broker employed by the owner. The salaried employee shall not negotiate the amount of security deposits or rental payments and shall not negotiate leases or any rental agreements on behalf of the owner or broker. However, in a vacation rental transaction as defined by G.S. 42A-4(3), the employee may offer a prospective tenant a rental price and term from a schedule setting forth prices and terms and the conditions and limitations under which they may be offered. The schedule shall be written and provided by the employee's employing broker with the written authority of the landlord.

(7) Any individual owner who personally leases or sells the owner's own property.

(8) Any housing authority organized in accordance with the provisions of Chapter 157 of the General Statutes and any regular salaried employees of the housing authority when performing acts authorized in this Chapter with regard to the sale or lease of property owned by the housing authority or the subletting of property which the housing authority holds as tenant. This exception shall not apply to any person, partnership, corporation, limited liability company, association, or other business entity that contracts with a housing authority to sell or manage property owned or leased by the housing authority. (1957, c. 744, s. 2; 1967, c. 281, s. 1; 1969, c. 191, s. 2; 1975, c. 108; 1983, c. 81, ss. 4, 5; 1985, c. 535, s. 1; 1995, c. 351, s. 20; 1999-229, ss. 2, 3; 1999-409, s. 1; 2001-487, s. 23(a); 2005-395, ss. 2, 3; 2011-217, s. 1; 2011-235, s. 1.)

§ 93A-3. Commission created; compensation; organization.

(a) There is hereby created the North Carolina Real Estate Commission, hereinafter called the Commission. The Commission shall consist of nine members, seven members to be appointed by the Governor, one member to be appointed by the General Assembly upon the recommendation of the President Pro Tempore of the Senate in accordance with G.S. 120-121, and one member to be appointed by the General Assembly upon the recommendation of the Speaker of the House of Representatives in accordance with G.S. 120-121. At least three members of the Commission shall be licensed real estate brokers. At least two members of the Commission shall be persons who are not involved directly or indirectly in the real estate or real estate appraisal business. Members of the Commission shall serve three-year terms, so staggered that the terms of three members expire in one year, the terms of three members expire in the next year, and the terms of three members expire in the third year of each three-year period. The members of the Commission shall elect one of their members to serve as chairman of the Commission for a term of one year. The Governor may remove any member of the Commission for misconduct, incompetency, or willful neglect of duty. The Governor shall have the power to fill all vacancies occurring on the Commission, except vacancies in legislative appointments shall be filled under G.S. 120-122.

(b) The provisions of G.S. 93B-5 notwithstanding, members of the Commission shall receive as compensation for each day spent on work for the Commission a per diem in an amount established by the Commission by rule, and mileage reimbursement for transportation by privately owned automobile at the business standard mileage rate set by the Internal Revenue Service per mile of travel along with actual cost of tolls paid. The total expense of the administration of this Chapter shall not exceed the total income therefrom; and none of the expenses of said Commission or the compensation or expenses of any office thereof or any employee shall ever be paid or payable out of the treasury of the State of North Carolina; and neither the Commission nor any officer or employee thereof shall have any power or authority to make or incur any expense, debt or other financial obligation binding upon the State of North Carolina. After all expenses of operation, the Commission may set aside an expense reserve each year. The Commission may deposit moneys in accounts, certificates of deposit, or time deposits as the Commission may approve, in any bank, savings and loan association, or trust company. Moneys also may be invested in the same classes of securities referenced in G.S. 159-30(c).

(c) The Commission shall have power to make reasonable bylaws, rules and regulations that are not inconsistent with the provisions of this Chapter and the General Statutes; provided, however, the Commission shall not make rules or regulations regulating commissions, salaries, or fees to be charged by licensees under this Chapter.

(c1) The provisions of G.S. 93A-1 and G.S. 93A-2 notwithstanding, the Commission may adopt rules to permit a real estate broker to pay a fee or other valuable consideration to a travel agent for the introduction or procurement of tenants or potential tenants in vacation rentals as defined in G.S. 42A-4. Rules adopted pursuant to this subsection may include a definition of the term "travel agent", may regulate the conduct of permitted transactions, and may limit the amount of the fee or the value of the consideration that may be paid to the travel agent. However, the Commission may not authorize a person or entity not licensed as a broker to negotiate any real estate transaction on behalf of another.

(c2)   The Commission shall adopt a seal for its use, which shall bear thereon the words "North Carolina Real Estate Commission." Copies of all records and papers in the office of the Commission duly certified and authenticated by the seal of the Commission shall be received in evidence in all courts and with like effect as the originals.

(d)   The Commission may employ an Executive Director and professional and clerical staff as may be necessary to carry out the provisions of this Chapter and to put into effect the rules and regulations that the Commission may promulgate. The Commission shall fix salaries and shall require employees to make good and sufficient surety bond for the faithful performance of their duties. The Commission shall reimburse its employees for travel on official business. Mileage expenses for transportation by privately owned automobile shall be reimbursed at the business standard mileage set by the Internal Revenue Service per mile of travel along with the actual tolls paid. Other travel expenses shall be reimbursed in accordance with G.S. 138-6. The Commission may, when it deems it necessary or convenient, delegate to the Executive Director, legal counsel for the Commission, or other Commission staff, professional or clerical, the Commission's authority and duties under this Chapter, but the Commission may not delegate its authority to make rules or its duty to act as a hearing panel in accordance with the provisions of G.S. 150B-40(b).

(e)   The Commission shall be entitled to the services of the Attorney General of North Carolina, in connection with the affairs of the Commission, and may, with the approval of the Attorney General, employ attorneys to represent the Commission or assist it in the enforcement of this Chapter. The Commission may prefer a complaint for violation of this Chapter before any court of competent jurisdiction, and it may take the necessary legal steps through the proper legal offices of the State to enforce the provisions of this Chapter and collect the penalties provided therein.

(f) The Commission is authorized to acquire, hold, convey, rent, encumber, alienate, and otherwise deal with real property in the same manner as a private person or corporation, subject only to the approval of the Governor and Council of State. The rents, proceeds, and other revenues and benefits of the ownership of real property shall inure to the Commission. Collateral pledged by the Commission for any encumbrance of real property shall be limited to the assets, income, and revenues of the Commission. Leases, deeds, and other instruments relating to the Commission's interest in real property shall be valid when executed by the executive director of the Commission. The Commission may create and conduct education and information programs relating to the real estate business for the information, education, guidance and protection of the general public, licensees, and applicants for license. The education and information programs may include preparation, printing and distribution of publications and articles and the conduct of conferences, seminars, and lectures. The Commission may claim the copyright to written materials it creates and may charge fees for publications and programs. (1957, c. 744, s. 3; 1967, c. 281, s. 2; c. 853, s. 1; 1971, c. 86, s. 1; 1979, c. 616, ss. 1, 2; 1983, c. 81, ss. 1, 2, 6-8; 1989, c. 563, s. 1; 1993, c. 419, s. 9; 1999-229, s. 4; 1999-405, s. 2; 1999-431, s. 3.4(a); 2000-140, s. 19(a); 2001-293, ss. 1, 2; 2002-168, s. 3; 2005-374, s. 1; 2005-395, s. 4; 2007-366, s. 1; 2011-217, s. 2.)

§ 93A-4. Applications for licenses; fees; qualifications; examinations; privilege licenses; renewal or reinstatement of license; power to enforce provisions.

(a) Any person, partnership, corporation, limited liability company, association, or other business entity hereafter desiring to enter into business of and obtain a license as a real estate broker shall make written application for such license to the Commission in the form and manner prescribed by the Commission. Each applicant for a license as a real estate broker shall be at least 18 years of age. Each applicant for a license as a real estate broker shall, within three years preceding the date the application is made, have satisfactorily completed, at a school approved by the Commission, an education program consisting of at least 75 hours of classroom instruction in subjects determined by the Commission, or shall possess real estate education or experience in real estate transactions which the Commission shall find equivalent to the education program. Each applicant for a license as a real estate broker shall be required to pay a fee, fixed by the Commission but not to exceed thirty dollars ($30.00).

(a1) Each person who is issued a real estate broker license on or after April 1, 2006, shall initially be classified as a provisional broker and shall, within three years following initial licensure, satisfactorily complete, at a school approved by the Commission, a postlicensing education program consisting of 90 hours of classroom instruction in subjects determined by the Commission or shall possess real estate education or experience in real estate transactions which the Commission shall find equivalent to the education program. The Commission may, by rule, establish a schedule for completion of the prescribed postlicensing education that requires provisional brokers to complete portions of the 90-hour postlicensing education program in less than three years, and provisional brokers must comply with this schedule in order to be entitled to actively engage in real estate brokerage. Upon completion of the postlicensing education program, the provisional status of the broker's license shall be terminated. When a provisional broker fails to complete all 90 hours of required postlicensing education within three years following initial licensure, the broker's license shall be placed on inactive status. The broker's license shall not be returned to active status until he or she has satisfied such requirements as the Commission may by rule require. Every license cancelled after April 1, 2009, because the licensee failed to complete postlicensing education shall be reinstated on inactive status until such time as the licensee satisfies the requirements for returning to active status as the Commission may by rule require.

(a2) An approved school shall pay a fee of ten dollars ($10.00) per licensee to the Commission for each licensee completing a postlicensing education course conducted by the school, provided that these fees shall not be charged to a community college, junior college, college, or university located in this State and accredited by the Southern Association of Colleges and Schools.

(b) Except as otherwise provided in this Chapter, any person who submits an application to the Commission in proper manner for a license as real estate broker shall be required to take an examination. The examination may be administered orally, by computer, or by any other method the Commission deems appropriate. The Commission may require the applicant to pay the Commission or a provider contracted by the Commission the actual cost of the examination and its administration. The cost of the examination and its administration shall be in addition to any other fees the applicant is required to pay under subsection (a) of this section. The examination shall determine the applicant's qualifications with due regard to the paramount interests of the public as to the applicant's competency. A person who fails the license examination shall be entitled to know the result and score. A person who passes the exam shall be notified only that the person passed the examination. Whether a person passed or failed the examination shall be a matter of public record; however, the scores for license examinations shall not be considered public records. Nothing in this subsection shall limit the rights granted to any person under G.S. 93B-8.

An applicant for licensure under this Chapter shall satisfy the Commission that he or she possesses the competency, honesty, truthfulness, integrity, good moral character, and general fitness, including mental and emotional fitness, necessary to protect the public interest and promote public confidence in the real estate brokerage business. The Commission may investigate the moral character and fitness, including the mental and emotional fitness, of each applicant for licensure as the applicant's character and fitness may generally relate to the real estate brokerage business, the public interest, and the public's confidence in the real estate brokerage business. The Commission may also require an applicant to provide the Commission with a criminal record report. All applicants shall obtain criminal record reports from one or more reporting services designated by the Commission to provide criminal record reports. Applicants are required to pay the designated reporting service for the cost of these reports. Criminal record reports, credit reports, and reports relating to an applicant's mental and emotional fitness obtained in connection with the application process shall not be considered public records under Chapter 132 of the General Statutes. If the results of any required competency examination and investigation of the applicant's moral character and fitness shall be satisfactory to the Commission, then the Commission shall issue to the applicant a license, authorizing the applicant to act as a real estate broker in the State of North Carolina, upon the payment of any privilege taxes required by law.

Notwithstanding G.S. 150B-38(c), in a contested case commenced upon the request of a party applying for licensure regarding the question of the moral character or fitness of the applicant, if notice has been reasonably attempted, but cannot be given to the applicant personally or by certified mail in accordance with G.S. 150B-38(c), the notice of hearing shall be deemed given to the applicant when a copy of the notice is deposited in an official depository of the United States Postal Service addressed to the applicant at the latest mailing address provided by the applicant to the Commission or by any other means reasonably designed to achieve actual notice to the applicant.

(b1) The Department of Justice may provide a criminal record check to the Commission for a person who has applied for a license through the Commission. The Commission shall provide to the Department of Justice, along with the request, the fingerprints of the applicant, any additional information required by the Department of Justice, and a form signed by the applicant consenting to the check of the criminal record and to the use of the fingerprints and other identifying information required by the State or national repositories. The applicant's fingerprints shall be forwarded to the State Bureau of Investigation for a search of the State's criminal history record file, and the State Bureau of Investigation shall forward a set of the fingerprints to the Federal Bureau of Investigation for a national criminal history check. The Commission shall keep all information pursuant to this subsection privileged, in accordance with applicable State law and federal guidelines, and the information shall be confidential and shall not be a public record under Chapter 132 of the General Statutes.

The Department of Justice may charge each applicant a fee for conducting the checks of criminal history records authorized by this subsection.

(b2) Records, papers, and other documentation containing personal information collected or compiled by the Commission in connection with an application for examination, licensure, certification, or renewal or reinstatement, or the subsequent update of information shall not be considered public records within the meaning of Chapter 132 of the General Statutes unless admitted into evidence in a hearing held by the Commission.

(c) All licenses issued by the Commission under the provisions of this Chapter shall expire on the 30th day of June following issuance or on any other date that the Commission may determine and shall become invalid after that date unless reinstated. A license may be renewed 45 days prior to the expiration date by filing an application with and paying to the Executive Director of the Commission the license renewal fee. The license renewal fee is thirty dollars ($30.00) unless the Commission sets the fee at a higher amount. The Commission may set the license renewal fee at an amount that does not exceed fifty dollars ($50.00). The license renewal fee may not increase by more than five dollars ($5.00) during a 12-month period. The Commission may adopt rules establishing a system of license renewal in which the licenses expire annually with varying expiration dates. These rules shall provide for prorating the annual fee to cover the initial renewal period so that no licensee shall be charged an amount greater than the annual fee for any 12-month period. The fee for reinstatement of an expired license shall be fifty-five dollars ($55.00). In the event a licensee fails to obtain a reinstatement of such license within six months after the expiration date thereof, the Commission may, in its discretion, consider such person as not having been previously licensed, and thereby subject to the provisions of this Chapter relating to the issuance of an original license, including the examination requirements set forth herein. Duplicate licenses may be issued by the Commission upon payment of a fee of five dollars ($5.00) by the licensee. Commission certification of a licensee's license history shall be made only after the payment of a fee of ten dollars ($10.00).

(d)   The Commission is expressly vested with the power and authority to make and enforce any and all reasonable rules and regulations connected with license application, examination, renewal, and reinstatement as shall be deemed necessary to administer and enforce the provisions of this Chapter. The Commission is further authorized to adopt reasonable rules and regulations necessary for the approval of real estate schools, instructors, and textbooks and rules that prescribe specific requirements pertaining to instruction, administration, and content of required education courses and programs.

(e)   Nothing contained in this Chapter shall be construed as giving any authority to the Commission nor any licensee of the Commission as authorizing any licensee to engage in the practice of law or to render any legal service as specifically set out in G.S. 84-2.1 or any other legal service not specifically referred to in said section. (1957, c. 744, s. 4; 1967, c. 281, s. 3; c. 853, s. 2; 1969, c. 191, s. 3; 1973, c. 1390; 1975, c. 112; 1979, c. 614, ss. 2, 3, 6; c. 616, ss. 2-5; 1983, c. 81, ss. 2, 9, 11; c. 384; 1985, c. 535, ss. 2-5; 1995, c. 22, s. 1; 1999-200, s. 1.; 2000-140, s. 19(b); 2002-147, s. 11; 2002-168, s. 4; 2003-361, s. 1; 2005-395, s. 5; 2007-366, s. 2; 2011-217, s. 3; 2013-280, s. 1.)

§ 93A-4.1. Continuing education.

(a)   The Commission shall establish a program of continuing education for real estate brokers. An individual licensed as a real estate broker is required to complete continuing education requirements in an amount not to exceed eight classroom hours of instruction a year during any license renewal period in subjects and at times the Commission deems appropriate. Any licensee who fails to complete continuing education requirements pursuant to this section shall not actively engage in the business of real estate broker.

(a1)   The Commission may, as part of the broker continuing education requirements, require real estate brokers-in-charge to complete during each annual license period a special continuing education course consisting of not more than four classroom hours of instruction in subjects prescribed by the Commission.

(b) The Commission shall establish procedures allowing for a deferral of continuing education for brokers while they are not actively engaged in real estate brokerage.

(c) The Commission may adopt rules not inconsistent with this Chapter to give purpose and effect to the continuing education requirement, including rules that govern:

(1) The content and subject matter of continuing education courses.

(2) The curriculum of courses required.

(3) The criteria, standards, and procedures for the approval of courses, course sponsors, and course instructors.

(4) The methods of instruction.

(5) The computation of course credit.

(6) The ability to carry forward course credit from one year to another.

(7) The deferral of continuing education for brokers not engaged in brokerage.

(8) The waiver of or variance from the continuing education requirement for hardship or other reasons.

(9) The procedures for compliance and sanctions for noncompliance.

(d) The Commission may establish a nonrefundable course application fee to be charged to a course sponsor for the review and approval of a proposed continuing education course. The fee shall not exceed one hundred twenty-five dollars ($125.00) per course. The Commission may charge the sponsor of an approved course a nonrefundable fee not to exceed seventy-five dollars ($75.00) for the annual renewal of course approval.

An approved course sponsor shall pay a fee of ten dollars ($10.00) per licensee to the Commission for each licensee completing an approved continuing education course conducted by the sponsor.

The Commission shall not charge a course application fee, a course renewal fee, or any other fee for a continuing education course sponsored by a community college, junior college, college, or university located in this State and accredited by the Southern Association of Colleges and Schools.

(e) The Commission may award continuing education credit for an unapproved course or related educational activity. The Commission may prescribe procedures for a licensee to submit information on an unapproved course or related educational activity for continuing education credit. The Commission may charge a fee to the licensee for each course or activity submitted. The fee shall not exceed fifty dollars ($50.00). (1993, c. 492, s. 1; 1999-229, s. 5; 2003-361, s. 2; 2005-395, s. 6; 2011-217, s. 4.)

§ 93A-4.2. Broker-in-charge qualification.

To be qualified to serve as a broker-in-charge of a real estate office, a real estate broker shall possess at least two years of full-time real estate brokerage experience or equivalent part-time real estate brokerage experience within the previous five years or real estate education or experience in real estate transactions that the Commission finds equivalent to such experience and shall complete, within a time prescribed by the Commission, a course of study prescribed by the Commission for brokers-in-charge not to exceed 12 classroom hours of instruction. A provisional broker may not be designated as a broker-in-charge. (2005-395, s. 7.)

§ 93A-4.3. Elimination of salesperson license; conversion of salesperson licenses to broker licenses.

(a) Effective April 1, 2006, the Commission shall discontinue issuing real estate salesperson licenses. Also effective April 1, 2006, all salesperson licenses shall become broker licenses, and each person holding a broker license that was changed from salesperson to broker on that date shall be classified as a provisional broker as defined in G.S. 93A-2(a2).

(b) A provisional broker as contemplated in subsection (a) of this section who was issued a salesperson license prior to October 1, 2005, shall, not later than April 1, 2008, complete a broker transition course prescribed by the

Commission, not to exceed 24 classroom hours of instruction, or shall demonstrate to the Commission that he or she possesses four years' full-time real estate brokerage experience or equivalent part-time real estate brokerage experience within the previous six years. If the provisional broker satisfies this requirement by April 1, 2008, the provisional status of his or her broker license will be terminated, and the broker will not be required to complete the 90-classroom-hour broker postlicensing education program prescribed by G.S. 93A-4(a1). If the provisional broker fails to satisfy this requirement by April 1, 2008, his or her license will be placed on inactive status, if not already on inactive status, and he or she must complete the 90-classroom-hour broker postlicensing education program prescribed by G.S. 93A-4(a1) in order to terminate the provisional status of the broker license and to be eligible to return his or her license to active status.

(c) An approved school or sponsor shall pay a fee of ten dollars ($10.00) per licensee to the Commission for each licensee completing a broker transition course conducted by the school or sponsor, provided that these fees shall not be charged to a community college, junior college, college, or university located in this State and accredited by the Southern Association of Colleges and Schools.

(d) A provisional broker as contemplated in subsection (a) of this section, who was issued a salesperson license between October 1, 2005, and March 31, 2006, shall, not later than April 1, 2009, satisfy the requirements of G.S. 93A-4(a1). Upon satisfaction of the requirements of G.S. 93A-4(a1), the provisional status of the broker's license will be terminated. If the provisional broker fails to satisfy the requirements of G.S. 93A-4(a1) by April 1, 2009, the broker's license shall be cancelled, and the person will be subject to the requirements for licensure reinstatement prescribed by G.S. 93A-4(a1).

(e) A broker who was issued a broker license prior to April 1, 2006, shall not be required to complete either the 90-classroom-hour broker postlicensing education program prescribed by G.S. 93A-4(a1) or the broker transition course prescribed by subsection (b) of this section.

(f) For the purpose of determining a licensee's status, rights, and obligations under this section, the Commission may treat a person who is issued a license on or after the October 1, 2005, or April 1, 2006, dates cited in subsections (a), (b), (d), or (e) of this section as though the person had been issued a license prior to those dates if the only reason the person's license was not issued prior to those dates was that the person's application was pending a determination by the Commission as to whether the applicant possessed the requisite moral character for licensure. If a license application is pending on April 1, 2006, for any reason other than a determination by the Commission as to the applicant's moral character for licensure, and if the applicant has not satisfied all education and examination requirements for licensing in effect on April 1, 2006, the applicant's application shall be cancelled and the application fee refunded.

(g)   No applications for a real estate salesperson license shall be accepted by the Commission between September 1, 2005, and September 30, 2005. (2005-395, s. 7.)

§ 93A-4A: Recodified as G.S. 93A-4.1 by Session Laws 2005-395, s. 6.

§ 93A-5. Register of applicants and roster of brokers.

(a)   The Executive Director of the Commission shall keep a register of all applicants for license, showing for each the date of application, name, place of residence, and whether the license was granted or refused. Said register shall be prima facie evidence of all matters recorded therein.

(b)   The Executive Director of the Commission shall also keep a current roster showing the names and places of business of all licensed real estate brokers, which roster shall be kept on file in the office of the Commission and be open to public inspection.

(c)   The Commission shall file reports annually as required by G.S. 93B-2. (1957, c. 744, s. 5; 1969, c. 191, s. 4; 1983, c. 81, ss. 2, 9, 12.; 2000-140, s. 19(b); 2005-395, s. 8; 2011-217, s. 5.)

§ 93A-6. Disciplinary action by Commission.

(a)   The Commission has power to take disciplinary action. Upon its own initiative, or on the complaint of any person, the Commission may investigate the actions of any person or entity licensed under this Chapter, or any other person or entity who shall assume to act in such capacity. If the Commission finds probable cause that a licensee has violated any of the provisions of this Chapter, the Commission may hold a hearing on the allegations of misconduct.

The Commission has power to suspend or revoke at any time a license issued under the provisions of this Chapter, or to reprimand or censure any licensee, if, following a hearing, the Commission adjudges the licensee to be guilty of:

(1) Making any willful or negligent misrepresentation or any willful or negligent omission of material fact.

(2) Making any false promises of a character likely to influence, persuade, or induce.

(3) Pursuing a course of misrepresentation or making of false promises through agents, advertising or otherwise.

(4) Acting for more than one party in a transaction without the knowledge of all parties for whom he or she acts.

(5) Accepting a commission or valuable consideration as a real estate broker on provisional status for the performance of any of the acts specified in this Article or Article 4 of this Chapter, from any person except his or her broker-in-charge or licensed broker by whom he or she is employed.

(6) Representing or attempting to represent a real estate broker other than the broker by whom he or she is engaged or associated, without the express knowledge and consent of the broker with whom he or she is associated.

(7) Failing, within a reasonable time, to account for or to remit any monies coming into his or her possession which belong to others.

(8) Being unworthy or incompetent to act as a real estate broker in a manner as to endanger the interest of the public.

(9) Paying a commission or valuable consideration to any person for acts or services performed in violation of this Chapter.

(10) Any other conduct which constitutes improper, fraudulent or dishonest dealing.

(11)   Performing or undertaking to perform any legal service, as set forth in G.S. 84-2.1, or any other acts constituting the practice of law.

(12)   Commingling the money or other property of his or her principals with his or her own or failure to maintain and deposit in a trust or escrow account in a bank as provided by subsection (g) of this section all money received by him or her as a real estate licensee acting in that capacity, or an escrow agent, or the custodian or manager of the funds of another person or entity which relate to or concern that person's or entity's interest or investment in real property, provided, these accounts shall not bear interest unless the principals authorize in writing the deposit be made in an interest bearing account and also provide for the disbursement of the interest accrued.

(13)   Failing to deliver, within a reasonable time, a completed copy of any purchase agreement or offer to buy and sell real estate to the buyer and to the seller.

(14)   Failing, at the time a sales transaction is consummated, to deliver to the broker's client a detailed and accurate closing statement showing the receipt and disbursement of all monies relating to the transaction about which the broker knows or reasonably should know. If a closing statement is prepared by an attorney or lawful settlement agent, a broker may rely on the delivery of that statement, but the broker must review the statement for accuracy and notify all parties to the closing of any errors.

(15)   Violating any rule adopted by the Commission.

(b)   The Commission may suspend or revoke any license issued under the provisions of this Chapter or reprimand or censure any licensee when:

(1)   The licensee has obtained a license by false or fraudulent representation;

(2)   The licensee has been convicted or has entered a plea of guilty or no contest upon which final judgment is entered by a court of competent jurisdiction in this State, or any other state, of any misdemeanor or felony that involves false swearing, misrepresentation, deceit, extortion, theft, bribery, embezzlement, false pretenses, fraud, forgery, larceny, misappropriation of funds or property, perjury, or any other offense showing professional unfitness or involving moral turpitude which would reasonably affect the licensee's performance in the real estate business;

(3) The licensee has violated any of the provisions of G.S. 93A-6(a) when selling, leasing, or buying the licensee's own property;

(4) The broker's unlicensed employee, who is exempt from the provisions of this Chapter under G.S. 93A-2(c)(6), has committed, in the regular course of business, any act which, if committed by the broker, would constitute a violation of G.S. 93A-6(a) for which the broker could be disciplined; or

(5) The licensee, who is also licensed as an appraiser, attorney, home inspector, mortgage broker, general contractor, or member of another licensed profession or occupation, has been disciplined for an offense under any law involving fraud, theft, misrepresentation, breach of trust or fiduciary responsibility, or willful or negligent malpractice.

(c) The Commission may appear in its own name in superior court in actions for injunctive relief to prevent any person from violating the provisions of this Chapter or rules adopted by the Commission. The superior court shall have the power to grant these injunctions even if criminal prosecution has been or may be instituted as a result of the violations, or whether the person is a licensee of the Commission.

(d) Each broker shall maintain complete records showing the deposit, maintenance, and withdrawal of money or other property owned by the broker's principals or held in escrow or in trust for the broker's principals. The Commission may inspect these records periodically, without prior notice and may also inspect these records whenever the Commission determines that they are pertinent to an investigation of any specific complaint against a licensee.

(e) When a person or entity licensed under this Chapter is accused of any act, omission, or misconduct which would subject the licensee to disciplinary action, the licensee, with the consent and approval of the Commission, may surrender the license and all the rights and privileges pertaining to it for a period of time established by the Commission. A person or entity who surrenders a license shall not thereafter be eligible for or submit any application for licensure as a real estate broker during the period of license surrender.

(f) In any contested case in which the Commission takes disciplinary action authorized by any provision of this Chapter, the Commission may also impose reasonable conditions, restrictions, and limitations upon the license, registration, or approval issued to the disciplined person or entity. In any contested case concerning an application for licensure, time share project registration, or school, sponsor, instructor, or course approval, the Commission may impose reasonable conditions, restrictions, and limitations on any license, registration, or approval it may issue as a part of its final decision.

(g) A broker's trust or escrow account shall be a demand deposit account in a federally insured depository institution lawfully doing business in this State which agrees to make its records of the broker's account available for inspection by the Commission's representatives.

(h) The Executive Director shall transmit a certified copy of all final orders of the Commission suspending or revoking licenses issued under this Chapter to the clerk of superior court of the county in which the licensee maintains his or her principal place of business. The clerk shall enter the order upon the judgment docket of the county. (1957, c. 744, s. 6; 1967, c. 281, s. 4; c. 853, s. 3; 1969, c. 191, s. 5; 1971, c. 86, s. 2; 1973, c. 1112; c. 1331, s. 3; 1975, c. 28; 1979, c. 616, ss. 6, 7; 1981, c. 682, s. 15; 1983, c. 81, s. 13; 1987, c. 516, ss. 1, 2; 1989, c. 563, s. 2; 1993, c. 419, s. 10; 1999-229, s. 6; 2000-149, s. 19(b); 2001-487, s. 23(b); 2002-168, s. 5; 2005-374, s. 2; 2005-395, s. 9; 2011-217, s. 6.)

§ 93A-6.1. Commission may subpoena witnesses, records, documents, or other materials.

(a) The Commission, Executive Director, or other representative designated by the Commission may issue a subpoena for the appearance of witnesses deemed necessary to testify concerning any matter to be heard before or investigated by the Commission. The Commission may issue a subpoena ordering any person in possession of records, documents, or other materials, however maintained, that concern any matter to be heard before or investigated by the Commission to produce the records, documents, or other materials for inspection or deliver the same into the custody of the Commission's authorized representatives. Upon written request, the Commission shall revoke a subpoena if it finds that the evidence, the production of which is required, does not relate to a matter in issue, or if the subpoena does not describe with sufficient particularity the evidence, the production of which is required, or if for any other reason in law the subpoena is invalid. If any person shall fail to fully and promptly comply with a subpoena issued under this section, the Commission may apply to any judge of the superior court resident in any county where the person to whom the subpoena is issued maintains a residence or place of business for an order compelling the person to show cause why he or she should not be held in contempt of the Commission and its processes. The court shall have the power to impose punishment for acts that would constitute direct or indirect contempt if the acts occurred in an action pending in superior court.

(b)   The Commission shall be exempt from the requirements of Chapter 53B of the General Statutes with regard to subpoenas issued to compel the production of a licensee's trust account records held by any financial institution. Notwithstanding the exemption, whenever the Commission issues a subpoena under this subsection, the Commission shall send a copy to the licensee at his or her address of record by regular mail. (1999-229, s. 7; 2005-395, s. 10; 2011-217, s. 7.)

§ 93A-7. Power of courts to revoke.

Whenever any person, partnership, association or corporation claiming to have been injured or damaged by the gross negligence, incompetency, fraud, dishonesty or misconduct on the part of any licensee following the calling or engaging in the business herein described and shall file suit upon such claim against such licensee in any court of record in this State and shall recover judgment thereon, such court may as part of its judgment or decree in such case, if it deem it a proper case in which so to do, order a written copy of the transcript of record in said case to be forwarded by the clerk of court to the chairman of the said Commission with a recommendation that the licensee's certificate of license be revoked. (1957, c. 744, s. 7; 1983, c. 81, s. 2.)

§ 93A-8. Penalty for violation of Chapter.

Any person violating the provisions of this Chapter shall upon conviction thereof be deemed guilty of a Class 1 misdemeanor. (1957, c. 744, s. 8; 1993, c. 539, s. 657; 1994, Ex. Sess., c. 24, s. 14(c).)

§ 93A-9. Licensing foreign brokers.

(a) The Commission may issue a broker license to an applicant licensed in a foreign jurisdiction who has satisfied the requirements for licensure set out in G.S. 93A-4 or such other requirements as the Commission in its discretion may by rule require.

(b) The Commission may issue a limited broker's license to a person or an entity from another state or territory of the United States without regard to whether that state or territory offers similar licensing privileges to residents in North Carolina if the person or entity satisfies all of the following:

(1) Is of good moral character and licensed as a real estate broker or salesperson in good standing in another state or territory of the United States.

(2) Only engages in business as a real estate broker in North Carolina in transactions involving commercial real estate and while the person or entity is affiliated with a resident North Carolina real estate broker.

(3) Complies with the laws of this State regulating real estate brokers and rules adopted by the Commission.

The Commission may require an applicant for licensure under this subsection to pay a fee not to exceed three hundred dollars ($300.00). All licenses issued under this subsection shall expire on June 30 of each year following issuance or on a date that the Commission deems appropriate unless the license is renewed pursuant to the requirements of G.S. 93A-4. A person or entity licensed under this subsection may be disciplined by the Commission for violations of this Chapter as provided in G.S. 93A-6 and G.S. 93A-54.

Any person or entity licensed under this subsection shall be affiliated with a resident North Carolina real estate broker, and the resident North Carolina real estate broker shall actively and personally supervise the licensee in a manner that reasonably assures that the licensee complies with the requirements of this Chapter and rules adopted by the Commission. A person or entity licensed under this subsection shall not, however, be affiliated with a resident North Carolina real estate provisional broker. The Commission may exempt applicants for licensure under this subsection from examination and the other licensing requirements under G.S. 93A-4. The Commission may adopt rules as it deems necessary to give effect to this subsection, including rules establishing: (i) qualifications for licensure; (ii) licensure and renewal procedures; (iii) requirements for continuing education; (iv) conduct of persons and entities licensed under this subsection and their affiliated resident real estate brokers;

(v) a definition of commercial real estate; and (vi) any requirements or limitations on affiliation between resident real estate brokers and persons or entities seeking licensure under this subsection. (1957, c. 744, s. 9; 1967, c. 281, s. 5; 1969, c. 191, s. 6; 1971, c. 86, s. 3; 1983, c. 81, s. 2.; 2000-140, s. 19(b); 2003-361, s. 3; 2005-395, s. 11; 2011-217, s. 8.)

§ 93A-10. Nonresident licensees; filing of consent as to service of process and pleadings.

Every nonresident applicant shall file an irrevocable consent that suits and actions may be commenced against such applicant in any of the courts of record of this State, by the service of any process or pleading authorized by the laws of this State in any county in which the plaintiff may reside, by serving the same on the Executive Director of the Commission, said consent stipulating and agreeing that such service of such process or pleadings on said Executive Director shall be taken and held in all courts to be valid and binding as if due service had been made personally upon the applicant in this State. This consent shall be duly acknowledged, and, if made by a corporation, shall be executed by an officer of the corporation. The signature of the officer on the consent to service instrument shall be sufficient to bind the corporation and no further authentication is necessary. An application from a corporation or other business entity shall be signed by an officer of the corporation or entity or by an individual designated by the Commission. In all cases where process or pleadings shall be served, under the provisions of this Chapter, upon the Executive Director of the Commission, such process or pleadings shall be served in duplicate, one of which shall be filed in the office of the Commission and the other shall be forwarded immediately by the Executive Director of the Commission, by registered mail, to the last known business address of the nonresident licensee against which such process or pleadings are directed. (1957, c. 744, s. 10; 1983, c. 81, ss. 3, 10; 2003-361, s. 4.)

§ 93A-11. Reimbursement by real estate independent contractor of brokers' workers' compensation.

(a) Notwithstanding the provisions of G.S. 97-21 or any other provision of law, a real estate broker may include in the governing contract with a real estate broker on provisional status whose nonemployee status is recognized pursuant to section 3508 of the United States Internal Revenue Code, 26 U.S.C. § 3508, an agreement for the broker on provisional status to reimburse the broker for the cost of covering that broker on provisional status under the broker's workers' compensation coverage of the broker's business.

(b) Nothing in this section shall affect a requirement under any other law to provide workers' compensation coverage or in any manner exclude from coverage any person, firm, or corporation otherwise subject to the provisions of Article 1 of Chapter 97 of the General Statutes. (1995, c. 127, s. 1.; 2000-140, s. 19(b); 2011-217, s. 9.)

§ 93A-12. Disputed monies.

(a) A real estate broker licensed under this Chapter or an attorney licensed to practice law in this State may deposit with the clerk of court in accordance with this section monies, other than a residential security deposit, the ownership of which are in dispute and that the real estate broker or attorney received while acting in a fiduciary capacity.

(b) The disputed monies shall be deposited with the clerk of court in the county in which the property for which the disputed monies are being held is located. At the time of depositing the disputed monies, the real estate broker or attorney shall certify to the clerk of court that the persons who are claiming ownership of the disputed monies have been notified in accordance with subsection (c) of this section that the disputed monies are to be deposited with the clerk of court and that the persons may initiate a special proceeding with the clerk of court to recover the disputed monies.

(c) Notice to the persons who are claiming ownership to the disputed monies required under subsection (b) of this section shall be provided by delivering a copy of the notice to the person or by mailing it to the person by first-class mail, postpaid, properly addressed to the person at the person's last known address.

(d) A real estate broker or attorney shall not deposit disputed monies with the clerk of court until 90 days following notification of the persons claiming ownership of the disputed monies.

(e) Upon the filing of a special proceeding to recover the disputed monies, the clerk shall determine the rightful ownership of the monies and distribute the disputed monies accordingly. If no special proceeding is filed with the clerk of court within one year of the disputed monies being deposited with the clerk of court, the disputed monies shall be deemed unclaimed and shall be delivered by the clerk of court to the State Treasurer in accordance with the provisions of Article 4 of Chapter 116B of the General Statutes. (2005-395, s. 12.; 2011-350, s. 1.)

§ 93A-13. Contracts for broker services.

No action between a broker and the broker's client for recovery under an agreement for broker services is valid unless the contract is reduced to writing and signed by the party to be charged or by some other person lawfully authorized by the party to sign. (2011-165, s. 2.)

§ 93A-14: Reserved for future codification purposes.

§ 93A-15: Reserved for future codification purposes.

Article 2.

Real Estate Education and Recovery Fund.

§ 93A-16. Real Estate Education and Recovery Fund created; payment to fund; management.

(a) There is hereby created a special fund to be known as the "Real Estate Education and Recovery Fund" which shall be set aside and maintained by the North Carolina Real Estate Commission. The fund shall be used in the manner provided under this Article for the payment of unsatisfied judgments where the aggrieved person has suffered a direct monetary loss by reason of certain acts committed by any real estate broker. The Commission may also expend money from the fund to create books and other publications, courses, forms, seminars, and other programs and materials to educate licensees and the public in real estate subjects. However, the Commission shall make no expenditures from the fund for educational purposes if the expenditure will reduce the balance of the fund to an amount less than two hundred thousand dollars ($200,000).

(b)   On September 1, 1979, the Commission shall transfer the sum of one hundred thousand dollars ($100,000) from its expense reserve fund to the Real Estate Education and Recovery Fund. Thereafter, the Commission may transfer to the Real Estate Education and Recovery Fund additional sums of money from whatever funds the Commission may have, provided that, if on December 31 of any year the amount remaining in the fund is less than fifty thousand dollars ($50,000), the Commission may determine that each person or entity licensed under this Chapter, when renewing a license, shall pay in addition to the license renewal fee, a fee not to exceed ten dollars ($10.00) per broker as shall be determined by the Commission for the purpose of replenishing the fund.

(c)   The Commission shall invest and reinvest the monies in the Real Estate Education and Recovery Fund in the same manner as provided by law for the investment of funds by the clerk of superior court. The proceeds from such investments shall be deposited to the credit of the fund.

(d)   The Commission shall have the authority to adopt rules and procedures not inconsistent with the provisions of this Article, to provide for the orderly, fair and efficient administration and payment of monies held in the Real Estate Education and Recovery Fund. (1979, c. 614, s. 1; 1983, c. 81, ss. 1, 2; 1987, c. 516, ss. 3-5.; 2000-140, s. 19(b); 2001-487, s. 23(c); 2005-395, s. 13; 2011-217, s. 10.)

§ 93A-17. Grounds for payment; notice and application to Commission.

(a)   An aggrieved person who has suffered a direct monetary loss by reason of the conversion of trust funds by any licensed real estate broker shall be eligible to recover, subject to the limitations of this Article, the amount of trust funds converted and which is otherwise unrecoverable provided that:

(1)   The act or acts of conversion which form the basis of the claim for recovery occurred on or after September 1, 1979;

(2)   The aggrieved person has sued the real estate broker in a court of competent jurisdiction and has filed with the Commission written notice of such lawsuit within 60 days after its commencement unless the claim against the

Real Estate Education and Recovery Fund is for an amount less than three thousand dollars ($3,000), excluding attorneys' fees, in which case the notice may be filed within 60 days after the termination of all judicial proceedings including appeals;

(3)   The aggrieved person has obtained final judgment in a court of competent jurisdiction against the real estate broker on grounds of conversion of trust funds arising out of a transaction which occurred when such broker was licensed and acting in a capacity for which a license is required; and

(4)   Execution of the judgment has been attempted and has been returned unsatisfied in whole or in part.

Upon the termination of all judicial proceedings including appeals, and for a period of one year thereafter, a person eligible for recovery may file a verified application with the Commission for payment out of the Real Estate Education and Recovery Fund of the amount remaining unpaid upon the judgment which represents the actual and direct loss sustained by reason of conversion of trust funds. A copy of the judgment and return of execution shall be attached to the application and filed with the Commission.

(b)   For the purposes of this Article, the term "trust funds" shall include all earnest money deposits, down payments, sales proceeds, tenant security deposits, undisbursed rents and other such monies which belong to another or others and are held by a real estate broker acting in that capacity. Trust funds shall also include all time share purchase monies which are required to be held in trust by G.S. 93A-45(c) during the time they are, in fact, so held. Trust funds shall not include, however, any funds held by an independent escrow agent under G.S. 93A-42 or any funds which the court may find to be subject to an implied, constructive or resulting trust.

(c)   For the purposes of this Article, the terms "licensee" and "broker" shall include only individual persons licensed under this Chapter as brokers. The terms "licensee" and "broker" shall not include a time share developer, time share project, independent escrow agent, corporation or other entity licensed under this Chapter. (1979, c. 614, s. 1; 1983, c. 81, ss. 2, 14; 1987, c. 516, s. 6; 1999-229, s. 8.; 2000-140, s. 19(b); 2005-395, s. 14; 2011-217, s. 11.)

§ 93A-18. Hearing; required showing.

Upon application by an aggrieved person, the Commission shall conduct a hearing and the aggrieved person shall be required to show that the aggrieved person:

(1) Is not a spouse of the judgment debtor or a person representing the spouse;

(2) Is making application not more than one year after termination of all judicial proceedings, including appeals, in connection with the judgment;

(3) Has complied with all requirements of this Article;

(4) Has obtained a judgment as described in G.S. 93A-17, stating the amount owing thereon at the date of application;

(5) Has made all reasonable searches and inquiries to ascertain whether the judgment debtor is possessed of real or personal property or other assets liable to be sold or applied in satisfaction of the judgment;

(6) After searching as described in subdivision (5) of this section, has discovered no real or personal property or other assets liable to be sold or applied, or has discovered certain of them, describing them, but the amount so realized was insufficient to satisfy the judgment, stating the amount realized and the balance remaining due on the judgment after application of the amount realized;

(7) Has diligently pursued the aggrieved person's remedies, which include attempting execution on the judgment against all the judgment debtors, which execution has been returned unsatisfied; and

(8) Knows of no assets of the judgment debtor and has attempted collection from all other persons who may be liable for the transaction for which the aggrieved person seeks payment from the Real Estate Education and Recovery Fund if there be any such other persons. (1979, c. 614, s. 1; 1987, c. 516, s. 7; 2001-487, s. 23(d); 2011-217, s. 12.)

§ 93A-19. Response and defense by Commission and judgment debtor; proof of conversion.

(a) Whenever the Commission proceeds upon an application as set forth in this Article, counsel for the Commission may defend such action on behalf of the fund and shall have recourse to all appropriate means of defense, including the examination of witnesses. The judgment debtor may defend such action on his or her own behalf and shall have recourse to all appropriate means of defense, including the examination of witnesses. Counsel for the Commission and the judgment debtor may file responses to the application, setting forth answers and defenses. Responses shall be filed with the Commission and copies shall be served upon every party by the filing party. If at any time it appears there are no triable issues of fact and the application for payment from the fund is without merit, the Commission shall dismiss the application. A motion to dismiss may be supported by affidavit of any person or persons having knowledge of the facts and may be made on the basis that the application or the judgment referred to therein do not form a basis for meritorious recovery within the purview of G.S. 93A-17, that the applicant has not complied with the provisions of this Article, or that the liability of the fund with regard to the particular licensee or transaction has been exhausted; provided, however, notice of the motion shall be given at least 10 days prior to the time fixed for hearing. If the applicant or judgment debtor fails to appear at the hearing after receiving notice of the hearing, the applicant or judgment debtor waives the person's rights unless the absence is excused by the Commission.

(b) Whenever the judgment obtained by an applicant is by default, stipulation, or consent, or whenever the action against the licensee was defended by a trustee in bankruptcy, the applicant, for purposes of this Article, shall have the burden of proving the cause of action for conversion of trust funds. Otherwise, the judgment shall create a rebuttable presumption of the conversion of trust funds. This presumption is a presumption affecting the burden of producing evidence. (1979, c. 614, s. 1; 1983, c. 81, s. 2; 1987, c. 516, s. 8; 1999-229, s. 9; 2001-487, s. 23(e).)

§ 93A-20. Order directing payment out of fund; compromise of claims.

Applications for payment from the Real Estate Education and Recovery Fund shall be heard and decided by a majority of the members of the Commission. If, after a hearing, the Commission finds the claim should be paid from the fund, the Commission shall enter an order requiring payment from the fund of whatever sum the Commission shall find to be payable upon the claim in accordance with the limitations contained in this Article.

Subject to Commission approval, a claim based upon the application of an aggrieved person may be compromised; however, the Commission shall not be bound in any way by any compromise or stipulation of the judgment debtor. If a claim appears to be otherwise meritorious, the Commission may waive procedural defects in the application for payment. (1979, c. 614, s. 1; 1983, c. 81, s. 2; 1987, c. 516, s. 9; 1999-229, s. 10; 2011-217, s. 13.)

§ 93A-21. Limitations; pro rata distribution; attorney fees.

(a)   Payments from the Real Estate Education and Recovery Fund shall be subject to the following limitations:

(1)   The right to recovery under this Article shall be forever barred unless application is made within one year after termination of all proceedings including appeals, in connection with the judgment.

(2)   The fund shall not be liable for more than fifty thousand dollars ($50,000) per transaction regardless of the number of persons aggrieved or parcels of real estate involved in such transaction.

(3)   Payment from the fund shall not exceed in the aggregate twenty-five thousand dollars ($25,000) for any one licensee within a single calendar year, and in no event shall it exceed in the aggregate seventy-five thousand dollars ($75,000) for any one licensee.

(4)   The fund shall not be liable for payment of any judgment awards of consequential damages, multiple or punitive damages, civil penalties, incidental damages, special damages, interest, costs of court or action or other similar awards.

(b)   If the maximum liability of the fund is insufficient to pay in full the valid claims of all aggrieved persons whose claims relate to the same transaction or to the same licensee, the amount for which the fund is liable shall be distributed among the claimants in a ratio that their respective claims bear to the total of such valid claims or in such manner as the Commission, in its discretion, deems equitable. Upon petition of counsel for the Commission, the Commission may require all claimants and prospective claimants to be joined in one proceeding to the end that the respective rights of all such claimants to the Real Estate

Education and Recovery Fund may be equitably resolved. A person who files an application for payment after the maximum liability of the fund for the licensee or transaction has been exhausted shall not be entitled to payment and may not seek judicial review of the Commission's award of payment to any party except upon a showing that the Commission abused its discretion.

(c) In the event an aggrieved person is entitled to payment from the fund in an amount which is equal to or less than the maximum amount of money which may be awarded in small claims court under G.S. 7A-210, the Commission may allow such person to recover from the fund reasonable attorney's fees incurred in effecting such recovery. Reimbursement for attorney's fees shall be limited to those fees incurred in effecting recovery from the fund and shall not include any fee incurred in obtaining judgment against the licensee. (1979, c. 614, s. 1; 1983, c. 81, ss. 2, 15; 1987, c. 516, ss. 10-13; 1999-229, s. 11; 2011-217, s. 14.)

§ 93A-22. Repayment to fund; automatic suspension of license.

Should the Commission pay from the Real Estate Education and Recovery Fund any amount in settlement of a claim or toward satisfaction of a judgment against a licensed real estate broker, any license issued to the broker shall be automatically suspended upon the effective date of the order authorizing payment from the fund. No such broker shall be granted a reinstatement until the fund has been repaid in full, including interest at the legal rate as provided for in G.S. 24-1. (1979, c. 614, s. 1; 1983, c. 81, s. 2; 1987, c. 516, s. 14.; 2000-140, s. 19(b); 2001-487, s. 23(f); 2005-395, s. 15; 2011-217, s. 15.)

§ 93A-23. Subrogation of rights.

When the Commission has paid from the Real Estate Education and Recovery Fund any sum to the judgment creditor, the Commission shall be subrogated to all of the rights of the judgment creditor to the extent of the amount so paid and the judgment creditor shall assign all right, title, and interest in the judgment to the extent of the amount so paid to the Commission and any amount and interest so recovered by the Commission on the judgment shall be deposited in the Real Estate Education and Recovery Fund. (1979, c. 614, s. 1; 1983, c. 81, s. 2; 1987, c. 516, s. 15; 2001-487, s. 23(g); 2011-217, s. 16.)

§ 93A-24. Waiver of rights.

The failure of an aggrieved person to comply with this Article shall constitute a waiver of any rights hereunder. (1979, c. 614, s. 1.)

§ 93A-25. Persons ineligible to recover from fund.

No real estate broker who suffers the loss of any commission from any transaction in which he or she was acting in the capacity of a real estate broker shall be entitled to make application for payment from the Real Estate Education and Recovery Fund for the loss. (1979, c. 614, s. 1.; 2000-140, s. 19(b); 2001-487, s. 23(h); 2011-217, s. 17.)

§ 93A-26. Disciplinary action against licensee.

Nothing contained in this Article shall limit the authority of the Commission to take disciplinary action against any licensee under this Chapter, nor shall the repayment in full of all obligations to the fund by any licensee nullify or modify the effect of any other disciplinary proceeding brought under this Chapter. (1979, c. 614, s. 1; 1983, c. 81, s. 2.)

§§ 93A-27 through 93A-31. Reserved for future codification purposes.

Article 3.

Private Real Estate Schools.

§ 93A-32. Definitions.

As used in this Article:

(1)   "Commission" means the North Carolina Real Estate Commission.

(2)   "Private real estate school" means any real estate educational entity which is privately owned and operated by an individual, partnership, corporation, limited liability company, or association, and which conducts, for a profit or tuition charge, real estate broker prelicensing or postlicensing courses prescribed by G.S. 93A-4(a) or (a1), provided that a proprietary business or trade school licensed by the State Board of Community Colleges under G.S. 115D-90 to conduct courses other than those real estate courses described herein shall not be considered to be a private real estate school. (1979, 2nd Sess., c. 1193, s. 1; 1983, c. 81, ss. 1, 2; 1989, c. 563, s. 3; 1993, c. 419, s. 11; c. 553, s. 29.1.; 2000-140, s. 19(b); 2005-395, s. 16.)

§ 93A-33. Commission to administer Article; authority of Commission to conduct investigations, issue licenses, and promulgate regulations.

The Commission shall have authority to administer and enforce this Article and to issue licenses to private real estate schools as defined herein which have complied with the requirements of this Article and regulations promulgated by the Commission. Through licensing applications, periodic reports required of licensed schools, periodic investigations and inspections of schools, and appropriate regulations, the Commission shall exercise general supervisory authority over private real estate schools, the object of such supervision being to protect the public interest and to assure the conduct of quality real estate education programs. To this end the Commission is authorized and directed to promulgate such regulations as it deems necessary which are not inconsistent with the provisions of this Article and which relate to the subject areas set out in G.S. 93A-34(c). (1979, 2nd Sess., c. 1193, s. 1; 1983, c. 81, s. 2.)

§ 93A-34. License required; application for license; fees; requirements for issuance of license.

(a)   No person, partnership, corporation or association shall operate or maintain or offer to operate in this State a private real estate school as defined herein unless a license is first obtained from the Commission in accordance with the provisions of this Article and the rules and regulations promulgated by the Commission under this Article. For licensing purposes, each branch location where a school conducts courses shall be considered a separate school requiring a separate license.

(b) Application for a license shall be filed in the manner and upon the forms prescribed by the Commission for that purpose. The Commission may by rule set nonrefundable application fees not to exceed two hundred fifty dollars ($250.00) for each school location and fifty dollars ($50.00) for each real estate broker prelicensing or postlicensing course. The application for a license shall be accompanied by the appropriate fees and shall contain the following:

(1) Name and address of the applicant and the school;

(2) Names, biographical data, and qualifications of director, administrators and instructors;

(3) Description of school facilities and equipment;

(4) Description of course(s) to be offered and instructional materials to be utilized;

(5) Information on financial resources available to equip and operate the school;

(6) Information on school policies and procedures regarding administration, record keeping, entrance requirements, registration, tuition and fees, grades, student progress, attendance, and student conduct;

(7) Copies of bulletins, catalogues and other official publications;

(8) Copy of bond required by G.S. 93A-36;

(9) Such additional information as the Commission may deem necessary to enable it to determine the adequacy of the instructional program and the ability of the applicant to operate a school in such a manner as would best serve the public interest.

(c) After due investigation and consideration by the Commission, a license shall be issued to the applicant when it is shown to the satisfaction of the Commission that the applicant and school are in compliance with the following standards, as well as the requirements of any supplemental regulations of the Commission regarding these standards:

(1) The program of instruction is adequate in terms of quality, content and duration.

(2) The director, administrators and instructors are adequately qualified by reason of education and experience.

(3) There are adequate facilities, equipment, instructional materials and instructor personnel to provide instruction of good quality.

(4) The school has adopted adequate policies and procedures regarding administration, instruction, record keeping, entrance requirements, registration, tuition and fees, grades, student progress, attendance, and student conduct.

(5) The school publishes and provides to all students upon enrollment a bulletin, catalogue or similar official publication which is certified as being true and correct in content and policy by an authorized school official, and which contains the following information:

a. Identifying data and publication date;

b. Name(s) of school and its full-time officials and faculty;

c. School's policies and procedures relating to entrance requirements, registration, grades, student progress, attendance, student conduct and refund of tuition and fees;

d. Detailed schedule of tuition and fees;

e. Detailed course outline of all courses offered.

(6) Adequate records as prescribed by the Commission are maintained in regard to grades, attendance, registration and financial operations.

(7) Institutional standards relating to grades, attendance and progress are enforced in a satisfactory manner.

(8) The applicant is financially sound and capable of fulfilling educational commitments made to students.

(9) The school's owner(s), director, administrators and instructors are of good reputation and character.

(10) The school's facilities and equipment comply with all applicable local, State and federal laws and regulations regarding health, safety, and welfare,

including the Americans with Disabilities Act and other laws relating to accessibility standards for places of public accommodation.

(11)   The school does not utilize advertising of any type which is false or misleading, either by actual statement, omission or intimation.

(12)   Such additional standards as may be deemed necessary by the Commission to assure the conduct of adequate instructional programs and the operation of schools in a manner which will best serve the public interest. (1979, 2nd Sess., c. 1193, s. 1; 1983, c. 81, ss. 1, 2; 1989, c. 563, s. 4; 1993, c. 419, s. 12.; 2000-140, s. 19(b); 2005-395, s. 17.)

§ 93A-35. Duration and renewal of licenses; transfer of school ownership.

(a)   All licenses issued shall expire on June 30 following the date of issuance.

(b)   Licenses shall be renewable annually on July 1, provided that a renewal application accompanied by the appropriate renewal fees has been filed not later than June 1 in the form and manner prescribed by the Commission, and provided further that the applicant and school are found to be in compliance with the standards established for issuance of an original license. The Commission may by rule set nonrefundable renewal fees not to exceed one hundred twenty-five dollars ($125.00) for each school location and twenty-five dollars ($25.00) for each real estate broker prelicensing and postlicensing course.

(c)   In the event a school is sold or ownership is otherwise transferred, the license issued to the original owner is not transferable to the new owner. Such new owner must make application for an original license as prescribed by this Article and Commission regulations. (1979, 2nd Sess., c. 1193, s. 1; 1983, c. 81, ss. 1, 2; 1989, c. 563, s. 5; 1993, c. 419, s. 13.; 2000-140, s. 19(b); 2011-217, s. 18.)

§ 93A-36. Execution of bond required; applicability to branch schools; actions upon bond.

(a) Before the Commission shall issue a license the applicant shall execute a bond in the sum of five thousand dollars ($5,000), payable to the State of North Carolina, signed by a solvent guaranty company authorized to do business in the State of North Carolina, and conditioned that the principal in said bond will carry out and comply with each and every contract or agreement, written or verbal, made and entered into by the applicant's school acting by and through its officers and agents with any student who desires to enter such school and to take any courses offered therein and that said principal will refund to such students all amounts collected in tuition and fees in case of failure on the part of the party obtaining a license from the Commission to open and operate a private real estate school or to provide the instruction agreed to or contracted for. Such bond shall be required for each school for which a license is required and shall be first approved by the Commission and then filed with the clerk of superior court of the county in which the school is located, to be recorded by such clerk in a book provided for that purpose. A separate bond shall not be required for each branch of a licensed school.

(b) In any and all cases where the party licensed by the Commission fails to fulfill its obligations under any contract or agreement, written or verbal, made and entered into with any student, then the State of North Carolina, upon the relation of the student(s) entering into said contract or agreement, shall have a cause of action against the principal and surety on the bond herein required for the full amount of payments made to such party, plus court costs and six percent (6%) interest from the date of payment of said amount. Such suits shall be brought in Wake County Superior Court within one year of the alleged default. (1979, 2nd Sess., c. 1193, s. 1; 1983, c. 81, s. 2; 1999-229, s. 12.)

§ 93A-37. Contracts with unlicensed schools and evidences of indebtedness made null and void.

All contracts or agreements entered into on or after October 1, 1980, by private real estate schools, as defined in this Article, with students or prospective students, and all promissory notes or other evidence of indebtedness taken on or after October 1, 1980, in lieu of cash payments by such schools, shall be null and void unless such schools are duly licensed as required by this Article on the date of such contract or agreement or taking of any promissory note or other evidence of indebtedness. (1979, 2nd Sess., c. 1193, s. 1.)

§ 93A-38. Suspension, revocation or denial of license.

The Commission shall have the power to suspend, revoke, deny issuance, or deny renewal of license to operate a private real estate school. In all proceedings to suspend, revoke or deny a license, the provisions of Chapter 150B of the General Statutes shall be applicable. The Commission may suspend, revoke, or deny such license when it finds:

(1) That the applicant for or holder of such license has refused or failed to comply with any of the provisions of this Article or the rules or regulations promulgated thereunder;

(2) That the applicant for or holder of such license has knowingly presented to the Commission false or misleading information relating to matters within the purview of the Commission under this Article;

(3) That the applicant for or holder of such license has presented to its students or prospective students false or misleading information relating to its instructional program, to the instructional programs of other institutions or to employment opportunities;

(4) That the applicant for or holder of such license has failed to comply with the provisions of any contract or agreement entered into with a student;

(5) That the applicant for or holder of such license has at any time refused to permit authorized representatives of the Commission to inspect the school, or failed to make available to them upon request full information relating to matters within the purview of the Commission under the provisions of this Article or the rules or regulations promulgated thereunder; or

(6) That the applicant for or holder of such license or any officer of a corporate licensee or corporation applying for a license, any partner of a partnership licensee or partnership applying for a license, or any member of a limited liability company licensee or limited liability company applying for a license has pleaded guilty, entered a plea of nolo contendere or been found guilty of a crime involving moral turpitude in any state or federal court. (1979, 2nd Sess., c. 1193, s. 1; 1983, c. 81, s. 2; 1987, c. 827, s. 1; 2005-395, s. 18.)

Article 4.

Time Shares.

§ 93A-39. Title.

This Article shall be known and may be cited as the "North Carolina Time Share Act." (1983, c. 814, s. 1.)

§ 93A-40. Registration required of time share projects; real estate license required.

(a) It shall be unlawful for any person in this State to engage or assume to engage in the business of a time share salesperson without first obtaining a real estate broker license issued by the North Carolina Real Estate Commission under the provisions of Article 1 of this Chapter, and it shall be unlawful for a time share developer to sell or offer to sell a time share located in this State without first obtaining a certificate of registration for the time share project to be offered for sale issued by the North Carolina Real Estate Commission under the provisions of this Article.

(b) A person responsible as general partner, corporate officer, joint venturer or sole proprietor who intentionally acts as a time share developer, allowing the offering of sale or the sale of time shares to a purchaser, without first obtaining registration of the time share project under this Article shall be guilty of a Class I felony. (1983, c. 814, s. 1; 1987, c. 516, s. 16.; 2000-140, s. 19(b); 2005-395, s. 19.)

§ 93A-41. Definitions.

When used in this Article, unless the context otherwise requires, the term:

(1) "Commission" means the North Carolina Real Estate Commission;

(2) "Developer" means any person or entity which creates a time share or a time share project or program, purchases a time share for purpose of resale, or is engaged in the business of selling its own time shares and shall include any person or entity who controls, is controlled by, or is in common control with the developer which is engaged in creating or selling time shares for the developer,

but a person who purchases a time share for his or her occupancy, use, and enjoyment shall not be deemed a developer;

(3) "Enrolled" means paid membership in exchange programs or membership in an exchange program evidenced by written acceptance or confirmation of membership;

(4) "Exchange company" means any person operating an exchange program;

(5) "Exchange program" means any opportunity or procedure for the assignment or exchange of time shares among purchasers in the same or other time share project;

(5a) "Independent escrow agent" means a licensed attorney located in this State or a financial institution located in this State;

(6) "Managing agent" means a person who undertakes the duties, responsibilities, and obligations of the management of a time share program;

(7) "Person" means one or more natural persons, corporations, partnerships, associations, trusts, other entities, or any combination thereof;

(7a) "Project broker" means a natural person licensed as a real estate broker and designated by the developer to supervise brokers at the time share project;

(8) "Purchaser" means any person other than a developer or lender who owns or acquires an interest or proposes to acquire an interest in a time share;

(9) "Time share" means a right to occupy a unit or any of several units during five or more separated time periods over a period of at least five years, including renewal options, whether or not coupled with a freehold estate or an estate for years in a time share project or a specified portion of a time share project. "Time share" shall also include a vacation license, prepaid hotel reservation, club membership, limited partnership, vacation bond, or a plan or system where the right to use a time share unit or units for periods of time is awarded or apportioned on the basis of points, vouchers, split, divided, or floating use, even if on a competitive basis with other purchasers;

(9a) "Time share instrument" means an instrument transferring a time share or any interest, legal or beneficial, in a time share to a purchaser, including a contract, installment contract, lease, deed, or other instrument;

(10) "Time share program" means any arrangement for time shares whereby real property has been made subject to a time share;

(11) "Time share project" means any real property that is subject to a time share program;

(11a) "Time share registrar" means a natural person who is designated by the developer to record or cause time share instruments and lien releases to be recorded and to fulfill the other duties imposed by this Article;

(12) "Time share salesperson" means a person who sells or offers to sell on behalf of a developer a time share to a purchaser; and

(13) "Time share unit" or "unit" means the real property or real property improvement in a project which is divided into time shares and designated for separate occupancy and use. (1983, c. 814, s. 1; 1985, c. 578, s. 1; 1999-229, ss. 13, 14.; 2000-140, s. 19(b); 2005-395, s. 20; 2011-217, s. 19.)

§ 93A-42. Time shares deemed real estate.

(a) A time share which in whole or in part burdens or pertains to real property in this State is deemed to be an interest in real estate, and shall be governed by the law of this State relating to real estate.

(b) A purchaser of a time share which burdens or pertains to real property located in the State may in accordance with G.S. 47-18 register the time share instrument by which the purchaser acquired the interest and upon such registration shall be entitled to the protection provided by Chapter 47 of the General Statutes for the recordation of other real property instruments. A time share instrument transferring or encumbering a time share shall not be rejected for recordation because of the nature or duration of that estate, provided all other requirements necessary to make an instrument recordable are complied with. An instrument concerning a time share which burdens or pertains to no real property located in this State shall not be recorded in the office of the register of deeds in any county in this State.

(c)   The developer shall record or cause to be recorded a time share instrument:

(1)   Not less than six days nor more than 45 days following the execution of the contract of sale by the purchaser; or

(2)   Not later than 180 days following the execution of the contract of sale by the purchaser, provided that all payments made by the purchaser shall be placed by the developer with an independent escrow agent upon the expiration of the 10-day escrow period provided by G.S. 93A-45(c).

(d)   The independent escrow agent provided by G.S. 93A-42(c)(2) shall deposit and maintain the purchaser's payments in an insured trust or escrow account in a bank or savings and loan association located in this State. The trust or escrow account may be interest-bearing and the interest earned shall belong to the developer, if agreed upon in writing by the purchaser; provided, however, if the time share instrument is not recorded within the time periods specified in this section, then the interest earned shall belong to the purchaser. The independent escrow agent shall return all payments to the purchaser at the expiration of 180 days following the execution of the contract of sale by the purchaser, unless prior to that time the time share instrument has been recorded. However, if prior to the expiration of 180 days following the execution of the contract of sale, the developer and the purchaser provide their written consent to the independent escrow agent, the developer's obligation to record the time share instrument and the escrow period may be extended for an additional period of 120 days. Upon recordation of the time share instrument, the independent escrow agent shall pay the purchaser's funds to the developer. Upon request by the Commission, the independent escrow agent shall promptly make available to the Commission inspection of records of money held by the independent escrow agent.

(e)   In no event shall the developer be required to record a time share instrument if the purchaser is in default of the purchaser's obligations.

(f)   Recordation under the provisions of this section of the time share instrument shall constitute delivery of that instrument from the developer to the purchaser. (1983, c. 814, s. 1; 1985, c. 578, ss. 2, 3; 1989, c. 302; 2001-487, s. 23(i); 2011-217, s. 20.)

§ 93A-43. Partition.

When a time share is owned by two or more persons as tenants in common or as joint tenants either may seek a partition by sale of that interest but no purchaser of a time share may maintain an action for partition by sale or in kind of the unit in which such time share is held. (1983, c. 814, s. 1.)

§ 93A-44. Public offering statement.

Each developer shall fully and conspicuously disclose in a public offering statement:

(1) The total financial obligation of the purchaser, which shall include the initial purchase price and any additional charges to which the purchaser may be subject;

(2) Any person who has or may have the right to alter, amend or add to charges to which the purchaser may be subject and the terms and conditions under which such charges may be imposed;

(3) The nature and duration of each agreement between the developer and the person managing the time share program or its facilities;

(4) The date of availability of each amenity and facility of the time share program when they are not completed at the time of sale of a time share;

(5) The specific term of the time share;

(6) The purchaser's right to cancel within five days of execution of the contract and how that right may be exercised under G.S. 93A-45;

(7) A statement that under North Carolina law an instrument conveying a time share must be recorded in the Register of Deeds Office to protect that interest; and

(8) Any other information which the Commission may by rule require.

The public offering statement shall also contain a one page cover containing a summary of the text of the statement. (1983, c. 814, s. 1.)

§ 93A-45. Purchaser's right to cancel; escrow; violation.

(a) A developer shall, before transfer of a time share and no later than the date of any contract of sale, provide a prospective purchaser with a copy of a public offering statement containing the information required by G.S. 93A-44. The contract of sale is voidable by the purchaser for five days after the execution of the contract. The contract shall conspicuously disclose the purchaser's right to cancel under this subsection and how that right may be exercised. The purchaser may not waive this right of cancellation. Any oral or written declaration or instrument that purports to waive this right of cancellation is void.

(b) A purchaser may elect to cancel within the time period set out in subsection (a) by hand delivering or by mailing notice to the developer or the time share salesperson. Cancellation under this section is without penalty and upon receipt of the notice all payments made prior to cancellation must be refunded immediately.

(c) Any payments received by a time share developer or time share salesperson in connection with the sale of the time share shall be immediately deposited by such developer or salesperson in a trust or escrow account in an insured bank or savings and loan association in North Carolina and shall remain in such account for 10 days or cancellation by the purchaser, whichever occurs first. Payments held in such trust or escrow accounts shall be deemed to belong to the purchaser and not the developer. In lieu of such escrow requirements, the Commission shall have the authority to accept, in its discretion, alternative financial assurances adequate to protect the purchaser's interest during the contract cancellation period, including but not limited to a surety bond, corporate bond, cash deposit or irrevocable letter of credit in an amount equal to the escrow requirements.

(d) If a developer fails to provide a purchaser to whom a time share is transferred with the statement as required by subsection (a), the purchaser, in addition to any rights to damages or other relief, is entitled to receive from the developer an amount equal to ten percent (10%) of the sales price of the time share not to exceed three thousand dollars ($3,000). A receipt signed by the purchaser stating that the purchaser has received the statement required by subsection (a) is prima facie evidence of delivery of the statement. (1983, c. 814, s. 1; 1985, c. 578, s. 4.; 2000-140, s. 19(b); 2001-487, s. 23(j).)

§ 93A-46. Prizes.

An advertisement of a time share which includes the offer of a prize or other inducement shall fully comply with the provisions of Chapter 75 of the General Statutes. (1983, c. 814, s. 1.)

§ 93A-47. Time shares proxies.

No proxy, power of attorney or similar device given by the purchaser of a time share regarding the management of the time share program or its facilities shall exceed one year in duration, but the same may be renewed from year to year. (1983, c. 814, s. 1.)

§ 93A-48. Exchange programs.

(a)   If a purchaser is offered the opportunity to subscribe to any exchange program, the developer shall, except as provided in subsection (b), deliver to the purchaser, prior to the execution of (i) any contract between the purchaser and the exchange company, and (ii) the sales contract, at least the following information regarding the exchange program:

(1)   The name and address of the exchange company;

(2)   The names of all officers, directors, and shareholders owning five percent (5%) or more of the outstanding stock of the exchange company;

(3)   Whether the exchange company or any of its officers or directors has any legal or beneficial interest in any developer or managing agent for any time share project participating in the exchange program and, if so, the name and location of the time share project and the nature of the interest;

(4)   Unless the exchange company is also the developer a statement that the purchaser's contract with the exchange company is a contract separate and distinct from the sales contract;

(5) Whether the purchaser's participation in the exchange program is dependent upon the continued affiliation of the time share project with the exchange program;

(6) Whether the purchaser's membership or participation, or both, in the exchange program is voluntary or mandatory;

(7) A complete and accurate description of the terms and conditions of the purchaser's contractual relationship with the exchange company and the procedure by which changes thereto may be made;

(8) A complete and accurate description of the procedure to qualify for and effectuate exchanges;

(9) A complete and accurate description of all limitations, restrictions, or priorities employed in the operation of the exchange program, including, but not limited to, limitations on exchanges based on seasonality, unit size, or levels of occupancy, expressed in boldfaced type, and, in the event that such limitations, restrictions, or priorities are not uniformly applied by the exchange program, a clear description of the manner in which they are applied;

(10) Whether exchanges are arranged on a space available basis and whether any guarantees of fulfillment of specific requests for exchanges are made by the exchange program;

(11) Whether and under what circumstances an owner, in dealing with the exchange company, may lose the use and occupancy of the owner's time share in any properly applied for exchange without being provided with substitute accommodations by the exchange company;

(12) The expenses, fees or range of fees for participation by owners in the exchange program, a statement whether any such fees may be altered by the exchange company, and the circumstances under which alterations may be made;

(13) The name and address of the site of each time share project or other property which is participating in the exchange program;

(14) The number of units in each project or other property participating in the exchange program which are available for occupancy and which qualify for

participation in the exchange program, expressed within the following numerical groupings, 1-5, 6-10, 11-20, 21-50 and 51, and over;

(15) The number of owners with respect to each time share project or other property which are eligible to participate in the exchange program expressed within the following numerical groupings, 1-100, 101-249, 250-499, 500-999, and 1,000 and over, and a statement of the criteria used to determine those owners who are currently eligible to participate in the exchange program;

(16) The disposition made by the exchange company of time shares deposited with the exchange program by owners eligible to participate in the exchange program and not used by the exchange company in effecting exchanges;

(17) The following information which, except as provided in subsection (b) below, shall be independently audited by a certified public accountant in accordance with the standards of the Accounting Standards Board of the American Institute of Certified Public Accountants and reported for each year no later than July 1, of the succeeding year:

a. The number of owners enrolled in the exchange program and such numbers shall disclose the relationship between the exchange company and owners as being either fee paying or gratuitous in nature;

b. The number of time share projects or other properties eligible to participate in the exchange program categorized by those having a contractual relationship between the developer or the association and the exchange company and those having solely a contractual relationship between the exchange company and owners directly;

c. The percentage of confirmed exchanges, which shall be the number of exchanges confirmed by the exchange company divided by the number of exchanges properly applied for, together with a complete and accurate statement of the criteria used to determine whether an exchange requested was properly applied for;

d. The number of time shares or other intervals for which the exchange company has an outstanding obligation to provide an exchange to an owner who relinquished a time share or interval during the year in exchange for a time share or interval in any future year; and

e. The number of exchanges confirmed by the exchange company during the year; and

(18) A statement in boldfaced type to the effect that the percentage described in sub-subdivision c. of subdivision (17) of this subsection is a summary of the exchange requests entered with the exchange company in the period reported and that the percentage does not indicate a purchaser's/owner's probabilities of being confirmed to any specific choice or range of choices, since availability at individual locations may vary.

The purchaser shall certify in writing to the receipt of the information required by this subsection and any other information which the Commission may by rule require.

(b) The information required by subdivisions (a)(2), (3), (13), (14), (15), and (17) shall be accurate as of December 31 of the year preceding the year in which the information is delivered, except for information delivered within the first 180 days of any calendar year which shall be accurate as of December 31 of the year two years preceding the year in which the information is delivered to the purchaser. The remaining information required by subsection (a) shall be accurate as of a date which is no more than 30 days prior to the date on which the information is delivered to the purchaser.

(c) In the event an exchange company offers an exchange program directly to the purchaser or owner, the exchange company shall deliver to each purchaser or owner, concurrently with the offering and prior to the execution of any contract between the purchaser or owner and the exchange company the information set forth in subsection (a) above. The requirements of this paragraph shall not apply to any renewal of a contract between an owner and an exchange company.

(d) All promotional brochures, pamphlets, advertisements, or other materials disseminated by the exchange company to purchasers in this State which contain the percentage of confirmed exchanges described in (a)(17)c. must include the statement set forth in (a)(18). (1983, c. 814, s. 1; 2001-487, s. 23(k).)

§ 93A-49. Service of process on exchange company.

Any exchange company offering an exchange program to a purchaser shall be deemed to have made an irrevocable appointment of the Commission to receive service of lawful process in any proceeding against the exchange company arising under this Article. (1983, c. 814, s. 1.)

§ 93A-50. Securities laws apply.

The North Carolina Securities Act, Chapter 78A, shall also apply, in addition to the laws relating to real estate, to time shares deemed to be investment contracts or to other securities offered with or incident to a time share; provided, in the event of such applicability of the North Carolina Securities Act, any offer or sale of time shares registered under this Article shall not be subject to the provisions of G.S. 78A-24 and any real estate broker registered under Article 1 of this Chapter shall not be subject to the provisions of G.S. 78A-36. (1983, c. 814, s. 1.; 2000-140, s. 19(b); 2005-395, s. 21.)

§ 93A-51. Rule-making authority.

The Commission shall have the authority to adopt rules and regulations that are not inconsistent with the provisions of this Article and the General Statutes of North Carolina. The Commission may prescribe forms and procedures for submitting information to the Commission. (1983, c. 814, s. 1.)

§ 93A-52. Application for registration of time share project; denial of registration; renewal; reinstatement; and termination of developer's interest.

(a)   Prior to the offering in this State of any time share located in this State, the developer of the time share project shall make written application to the Commission for the registration of the project. The application shall be accompanied by a fee in an amount fixed by the Commission but not to exceed one thousand five hundred dollars ($1,500), and shall include a description of the project, copies of proposed time share instruments including public offering statements, sale contracts, deeds, and other documents referred to therein, information pertaining to any marketing or managing entity to be employed by the developer for the sale of time shares in a time share project or the management of the project, information regarding any exchange program available to the purchaser, an irrevocable appointment of the Commission to receive service of any lawful process in any proceeding against the developer or the developer's time share salespersons arising under this Article, and such other information as the Commission may by rule require.

Upon receipt of a properly completed application and fee and upon a determination by the Commission that the sale and management of the time shares in the time share project will be directed and conducted by persons of good moral character, the Commission shall issue to the developer a certificate of registration authorizing the developer to offer time shares in the project for sale. The Commission shall within 15 days after receipt of an incomplete application, notify the developer by mail that the Commission has found specified deficiencies, and shall, within 45 days after the receipt of a properly completed application, either issue the certificate of registration or notify the developer by mail of any specific objections to the registration of the project. The certificate shall be prominently displayed in the office of the developer on the site of the project.

The developer shall promptly report to the Commission any and all changes in the information required to be submitted for the purpose of the registration. The developer shall also immediately furnish the Commission complete information regarding any change in its interest in a registered time share project. In the event a developer disposes of, or otherwise terminates its interest in a time share project, the developer shall certify to the Commission in writing that its interest in the time share project is terminated and shall return to the Commission for cancellation the certificate of registration.

(b) In the event the Commission finds that there is substantial reason to deny the application for registration as a time share project, the Commission shall notify the applicant that such application has been denied and shall afford the applicant an opportunity for a hearing before the Commission to show cause why the application should not be denied. In all proceedings to deny a certificate of registration, the provisions of Chapter 150B of the General Statutes shall be applicable.

(c) The acceptance by the Commission of an application for registration shall not constitute the approval of its contents or waive the authority of the Commission to take disciplinary action as provided by this Article.

(d) All certificates of registration granted and issued by the Commission under the provisions of this Article shall expire on the 30th day of June following issuance thereof, and shall become invalid after such date unless reinstated. Renewal of such certificate may be effected at any time during the month of June preceding the date of expiration of such registration upon proper application to the Commission and by the payment of a renewal fee fixed by the Commission but not to exceed one thousand five hundred dollars ($1,500) for each time share project. The developer shall, when making application for renewal, also provide a copy of the report required in G.S. 93A-48. Each certificate reinstated after the expiration date thereof shall be subject to a fee of fifty dollars ($50.00) in addition to the required renewal fee. In the event a time share developer fails to reinstate the registration within 12 months after the expiration date thereof, the Commission may, in its discretion, consider the time share project as not having been previously registered, and thereby subject to the provisions of this Article relating to the issuance of an original certificate. Duplicate certificates may be issued by the Commission upon payment of a fee of one dollar ($1.00) by the registrant developer. Except as prescribed by Commission rules, all fees paid pursuant to this Article shall be nonrefundable. (1983, c. 814, s. 1; 1985, c. 578, s. 5; 1987, c. 827, s. 1; 1999-229, s. 15.; 2000-140, s. 19(b); 2005-395, s. 22.)

§ 93A-53. Register of applicants; roster of registrants; registered projects; financial report to Secretary of State.

(a) The Executive Director of the Commission shall keep a register of all applicants for certificates of registration, showing for each the date of application, name, business address, and whether the certificate was granted or refused.

(b) The Executive Director of the Commission shall also keep a current roster showing the name and address of all time share projects registered with the Commission. The roster shall be kept on file in the office of the Commission and be open to public inspection.

(c) The Commission shall include a copy of the roster of time share projects current on the preceding June 30 and a statement of the income received by the Commission in connection with the registration of time share projects during the fiscal year ending on June 30 with the report required by G.S. 93B-2. (1983, c. 814, s. 1; 2011-217, s. 21.)

§ 93A-54. Disciplinary action by Commission.

(a) The Commission has power to take disciplinary action. Upon its own motion, or on the verified complaint of any person, the Commission may investigate the actions of any time share salesperson, developer, or project broker of a time share project registered under this Article, or any other person or entity who shall assume to act in such capacity. If the Commission finds probable cause that a time share salesperson, developer, or project broker has violated any of the provisions of this Article, the Commission may hold a hearing on the allegations of misconduct.

The Commission has the power to suspend or revoke at any time a real estate license issued to a time share salesperson or project broker, or a certificate of registration of a time share project issued to a developer; or to reprimand or censure such salesperson, developer, or project broker; or to fine such developer in the amount of five hundred dollars ($500.00) for each violation of this Article, if, after a hearing, the Commission adjudges either the salesperson, developer, or project broker to be guilty of:

(1) Making any willful or negligent misrepresentation or any willful or negligent omission of material fact about any time share or time share project;

(2) Making any false promises of a character likely to influence, persuade, or induce;

(3) Pursuing a course of misrepresentation or making of false promises through agents, salespersons, advertising or otherwise;

(4) Failing, within a reasonable time, to account for all money received from others in a time share transaction, and failing to remit such monies as may be required in G.S. 93A-45 of this Article;

(5) Acting as a time share salesperson or time share developer in a manner as to endanger the interest of the public;

(6) Paying a commission, salary, or other valuable consideration to any person for acts or services performed in violation of this Article;

(7) Any other conduct which constitutes improper, fraudulent, or dishonest dealing;

(8) Performing or undertaking to perform any legal service as set forth in G.S. 84-2.1, or any other acts not specifically set forth in that section;

(9) Failing to deposit and maintain in a broker's trust or escrow account as defined by G.S. 93A-6(g) all money received from others in a time share transaction as may be required in G.S. 93A-45 of this Article or failing to place with an independent escrow agent the funds of a time share purchaser when required by G.S. 93A-42(c);

(10) Failing to deliver to a purchaser a public offering statement containing the information required by G.S. 93A-44 and any other disclosures that the Commission may by regulation require;

(11) Failing to comply with the provisions of Chapter 75 of the General Statutes in the advertising or promotion of time shares for sale, or failing to assure such compliance by persons engaged on behalf of a developer;

(12) Failing to comply with the provisions of G.S. 93A-48 in furnishing complete and accurate information to purchasers concerning any exchange program which may be offered to such purchaser;

(13) Making any false or fraudulent representation on an application for registration;

(14) Violating any rule or regulation promulgated by the Commission;

(15) Failing to record or cause to be recorded a time share instrument as required by G.S. 93A-42(c), or failing to provide a purchaser the protection against liens required by G.S. 93A-57(a); or

(16) Failing as a time share project broker to exercise reasonable and adequate supervision of the conduct of sales at a project or location by the brokers and salespersons under the time share project broker's control.

(a1) The clear proceeds of fines collected pursuant to subsection (a) of this section shall be remitted to the Civil Penalty and Forfeiture Fund in accordance with G.S. 115C-457.2.

(b) Following a hearing, the Commission shall also have power to suspend or revoke any certificate of registration issued under the provisions of this Article or to reprimand or censure any developer when the registrant has been convicted or has entered a plea of guilty or no contest upon which final judgment is entered by a court of competent jurisdiction in this State, or any other state, of the criminal offenses of: embezzlement, obtaining money under false pretense, fraud, forgery, conspiracy to defraud, or any other offense involving moral turpitude which would reasonably affect the developer's performance in the time share business.

(c)   The Commission may appear in its own name in superior court in actions for injunctive relief to prevent any person or entity from violating the provisions of this Article or rules promulgated by the Commission. The superior court shall have the power to grant these injunctions even if criminal prosecution has been or may be instituted as a result of the violations, or regardless of whether the person or entity has been registered by the Commission.

(d)   Each developer shall maintain or cause to be maintained complete records of every time share transaction including records pertaining to the deposit, maintenance, and withdrawal of money required to be held in a trust or escrow account, or as otherwise required by the Commission, under G.S. 93A-45 of this Article. The Commission may inspect these records periodically without prior notice and may also inspect these records whenever the Commission determines that they are pertinent to an investigation of any specific complaint against a registrant.

(e)   When a licensee is accused of any act, omission, or misconduct under this Article which would subject the licensee to disciplinary action, the licensee may, with the consent and approval of the Commission, surrender the licensee's license and all the rights and privileges pertaining to it for a period of time to be established by the Commission. A licensee who surrenders a license shall not be eligible for, or submit any application for, licensure as a real estate broker or registration of a time share project during the period of license surrender. For the purposes of this section, the term licensee shall include a time share developer. (1983, c. 814, s. 1; 1985, c. 578, ss. 6-10; 1987, c. 516, ss. 17, 18; 1998-215, s. 138.; 2000-140, s. 19(b); 2001-487, s. 23(l); 2005-395, s. 23; 2011-217, s. 22.)

§ 93A-55. Private enforcement.

The provisions of the Article shall not be construed to limit in any manner the right of a purchaser or other person injured by a violation of this Article to bring a private action. (1983, c. 814, s. 1.)

§ 93A-56. Penalty for violation of Article.

Except as provided in G.S. 93A-40(b) and G.S. 93A-58, any person violating the provisions of this Article shall be guilty of a Class 1 misdemeanor. (1983, c. 814, s. 1; 1985, c. 578, s. 11; 1987, c. 516, s. 19; 1993, c. 539, s. 658; 1994, Ex. Sess., c. 24, s. 14(c).)

§ 93A-57. Release of liens.

(a)   Prior to any recordation of the instrument transferring a time share, the developer shall record and furnish notice to the purchaser of a release or subordination of all liens affecting that time share, or shall provide a surety bond or insurance against the lien from a company acceptable to the Commission as provided for liens on real estate in this State, or such underlying lien document shall contain a provision wherein the lienholder subordinates its rights to that of a time share purchaser who fully complies with all of the provisions and terms of the contract of sale.

(b)   Unless a time share owner or a time share owner who is his predecessor in title agree otherwise with the lienor, if a lien other than a mortgage or deed of trust becomes effective against more than one time share in a time share project, any time share owner is entitled to a release of his time share from a lien upon payment of the amount of the lien attributable to his time share. The amount of the payment must be proportionate to the ratio that the time share owner's liability bears to the liabilities of all time share owners whose interests are subject to the lien. Upon receipt of payment, the lien holder shall promptly deliver to the time share owner a release of the lien covering that time share. After payment, the managing agent may not assess or have a lien against that time share for any portion of the expenses incurred in connection with that lien. (1983, c. 814, s. 1; 1985, c. 578, s. 12.)

§ 93A-58. Registrar required; criminal penalties; project broker.

(a) Every developer of a registered project shall, by affidavit filed with the Commission, designate a natural person to serve as time share registrar for its registered projects. The registrar shall be responsible for the recordation of time share instruments and the release of liens required by G.S. 93A-42(c) and G.S. 93A-57(a). A developer may, from time to time, change the designated time share registrar by proper filing with the Commission and by otherwise complying with this subsection. No sales or offers to sell shall be made until the registrar is designated for a time share project.

The registrar has the duty to ensure that the provisions of this Article are complied with in a time share project for which the person is registrar. No registrar shall record a time share instrument except as provided by this Article.

(b) A time share registrar is guilty of a Class I felony if he or she knowingly or recklessly fails to record or cause to be recorded a time share instrument as required by this Article.

A person responsible as general partner, corporate officer, joint venturer or sole proprietor of the developer of a time share project is guilty of a Class I felony if the person intentionally allows the offering for sale or the sale of time share to purchasers without first designating a time share registrar.

(c) The developer shall designate for each project and other locations where time shares are sold or offered for sale a project broker. The project broker shall act as supervising broker for all time share salespersons at the project or other location and shall directly, personally, and actively supervise all such persons at the project or other location in a manner to reasonably ensure that the sale of time shares will be conducted in accordance with the provisions of this Chapter. (1985, c. 578, s. 13; 1987, c. 516, s. 20; 1993, c. 539, s. 1289; 1994, Ex. Sess., c. 24, s. 14(c).; 2000-140, s. 19(b); 2001-487, s. 23(m); 2005-395, s. 24.)

§ 93A-59. Preservation of time share purchaser's claims and defenses.

(a) For one year following the execution of an instrument of indebtedness for the purchase of a time share, the purchaser of a time share may assert against the seller, assignee of the seller, or other holder of the instrument of indebtedness, any claims or defenses available against the developer or the original seller, and the purchaser may not waive the right to assert these claims or defenses in connection with a time share purchase. Any recovery by the purchaser on a claim asserted against an assignee of the seller or other holder of the instrument of indebtedness shall not exceed the amount paid by the purchaser under the instrument. A holder shall be the person or entity with the rights of a holder as set forth in G.S. 25-3-301.

(b)   Every instrument of indebtedness for the purchase of a time share shall set forth the following provision in a clear and conspicuous manner:

"NOTICE

FOR A PERIOD OF ONE YEAR FOLLOWING THE EXECUTION OF THIS INSTRUMENT OF INDEBTEDNESS, ANY HOLDER OF THIS INSTRUMENT OF INDEBTEDNESS IS SUBJECT TO ALL CLAIMS AND DEFENSES WHICH THE PURCHASER COULD ASSERT AGAINST THE SELLER OF THE TIME SHARE. RECOVERY BY THE PURCHASER SHALL NOT EXCEED AMOUNTS PAID BY THE PURCHASER UNDER THIS INSTRUMENT."

(1985, c. 578, s. 13.)

§§ 93A-60 through 93A-69. Reserved for future codification purposes.

Article 5.

Real Estate Appraisers.

§§ 93A-70 through 93A-81: Repealed by Session Laws 1993, c. 419, s. 7.

Article 6.

Broker Price Opinions and Comparative Market Analyses.

§ 93A-82. Definitions.

As used in this Article, the terms "broker price opinion" and "comparative market analysis" mean an estimate prepared by a licensed real estate broker that details the probable selling price or leasing price of a particular parcel of or interest in property and provides a varying level of detail about the property's condition, market, and neighborhood, and information on comparable properties, but does not include an automated valuation model. (2012-163, s. 2.)

§ 93A-83. Broker price opinions and comparative market analyses for a fee.

(a)   Authorized. - A person licensed under this Chapter, other than a provisional broker, may prepare a broker price opinion or comparative market analysis and charge and collect a fee for the opinion if:

(1)   The license of that licensee is active and in good standing; and

(2)   The broker price opinion or comparative market analysis meets the requirements of subsection (c) of this section.

(3)   The requirements of this Article shall not apply to any broker price opinion or comparative market analysis performed by a licensee for no fee or consideration.

(b)   For Whom Opinion May Be Prepared. - Notwithstanding any provision to the contrary, a person licensed under this Chapter may prepare a broker price opinion or comparative market analysis for any of the following:

(1)   An existing or potential seller of a parcel of real property.

(2)   An existing or potential buyer of a parcel of real property.

(3)   An existing or potential lessor of a parcel of or interest in real property.

(4)   An existing or potential lessee of a parcel of or interest in real property.

(5) A third party making decisions or performing due diligence related to the potential listing, offering, sale, option, lease, or acquisition price of a parcel of or interest in real property.

(6) An existing or potential lienholder or other third party for any purpose other than as the basis to determine the value of a parcel of or interest in property, for a mortgage loan origination, including first and second mortgages, refinances, or equity lines of credit.

(7) The provisions of this subsection do not preclude the preparation of a broker price opinion or comparative market analysis to be used in conjunction with or in addition to an appraisal.

(c) Required Contents of a Broker Price Opinion or Comparative Market Analysis. - A broker price opinion or comparative market analysis shall be in writing and conform to the standards provided in this Article that shall include, but are not limited to, the following:

(1) A statement of the intended purpose of the broker price opinion or comparative market analysis.

(2) A brief description of the subject property and property interest to be priced.

(3) The basis of reasoning used to reach the conclusion of the price, including the applicable market data or capitalization computation.

(4) Any assumptions or limiting conditions.

(5) A disclosure of any existing or contemplated interest of the broker issuing the broker price opinion, including the possibility of representing the landlord/tenant or seller/buyer.

(6) The effective date of the broker price opinion.

(7) The name and signature of the broker issuing the broker price opinion and broker license number.

(8) The name of the real estate brokerage firm for which the broker is acting.

(9) The signature date.

(10) A disclaimer stating that "This opinion is not an appraisal of the market value of the property, and may not be used in lieu of an appraisal. If an appraisal is desired, the services of a licensed or certified appraiser shall be obtained. This opinion may not be used by any party as the primary basis to determine the value of a parcel of or interest in real property for a mortgage loan origination, including first and second mortgages, refinances, or equity lines of credit."

(11) A copy of the assignment request for the broker price opinion or comparative market analysis.

(d) Rules. - The North Carolina Real Estate Commission shall have the power to adopt rules that are not inconsistent with the provisions in this Article.

(e) Additional Requirements for Electronic or Form Submission. - In addition to the requirement of subsection (c) of this section, if a broker price opinion is submitted electronically or on a form supplied by the requesting party, the following provisions apply:

(1) A signature required by subdivision (7) of subsection (c) of this section may be an electronic signature, as defined in G.S. 47-16.2.

(2) A signature required by subdivision (7) of subsection (c) of this section and the disclaimer required by subdivision (10) of subsection (c) of this section may be transmitted in a separate attachment if the electronic format or form supplied by the requesting party does not allow additional comments to be written by the licensee. The electronic format or form supplied by the requesting party shall do the following:

a. Reference the existence of a separate attachment.

b. Include a statement that the broker price opinion or comparative market analysis is not complete without the attachment.

(f) Restrictions. - Notwithstanding any provisions to the contrary, a person licensed pursuant to this Chapter may not knowingly prepare a broker price opinion or comparative market analysis for any purpose in lieu of an appraisal when an appraisal is required by federal or State law. A broker price opinion or comparative market analysis that estimates the value of or worth a parcel of or interest in real estate rather than sales or leasing price shall be deemed to be an appraisal and may not be prepared by a licensed broker under the authority of this Article, but may only be prepared by a duly licensed or certified appraiser, and shall meet the regulations adopted by the North Carolina Appraisal Board. A broker price opinion or comparative market analysis shall not under any circumstances be referred to as a valuation or appraisal.

(g) No Report of Predetermined Result. - A broker price opinion or comparative market analysis shall not include the reporting of a predetermined result. (2012-163, s. 2; 2012-194, s. 61.)

Chapter 93B.

Occupational Licensing Boards.

§ 93B-1. Definitions.

As used in this Chapter:

"License" means any license (other than a privilege license), certificate, or other evidence of qualification which an individual is required to obtain before he may engage in or represent himself to be a member of a particular profession or occupation.

"Occupational licensing board" means any board, committee, commission, or other agency in North Carolina which is established for the primary purpose of regulating the entry of persons into, and/or the conduct of persons within, a particular profession or occupation, and which is authorized to issue licenses; "occupational licensing board" does not include State agencies, staffed by full-time State employees, which as a part of their regular functions may issue licenses. (1957, c. 1377, s. 1.)

§ 93B-2. Annual reports required; contents; open to inspection; sanction for failure to report.

(a) No later than October 31 of each year, each occupational licensing board shall file with the Secretary of State, the Attorney General, and the Joint

Regulatory Reform Committee an annual report containing all of the following information:

(1)   The address of the board, and the names of its members and officers.

(2)   The number of persons who applied to the board for examination.

(3)   The number who were refused examination.

(4)   The number who took the examination.

(5)   The number to whom initial licenses were issued.

(6)   The number who applied for license by reciprocity or comity.

(7)   The number who were granted licenses by reciprocity or comity.

(7a)   The number of official complaints received involving licensed and unlicensed activities.

(7b)   The number of disciplinary actions taken against licensees, or other actions taken against nonlicensees, including injunctive relief.

(8)   The number of licenses suspended or revoked.

(9)   The number of licenses terminated for any reason other than failure to pay the required renewal fee.

(10)   The substance of any anticipated request by the occupational licensing board to the General Assembly to amend statutes related to the occupational licensing board.

(11)   The substance of any anticipated change in rules adopted by the occupational licensing board or the substance of any anticipated adoption of new rules by the occupational licensing board.

(b)   No later than October 31 of each year, each occupational licensing board shall file with the Secretary of State, the Attorney General, the Office of State Budget and Management, and the Joint Regulatory Reform Committee a financial report that includes the source and amount of all funds credited to the occupational licensing board and the purpose and amount of all funds disbursed by the occupational licensing board during the previous fiscal year.

(c) The reports required by this section shall be open to public inspection.

(d) Failure of a board to comply with the reporting requirements of this section by October 31 of each year shall result in a suspension of the board's authority to expend any funds until such time as the board files the required reports. Suspension of a board's authority to expend funds under this subsection shall not affect the board's duty to issue and renew licenses or the validity of any application or license for which fees have been tendered in accordance with law. Each board shall adopt rules establishing a procedure for implementing this subsection and shall maintain an escrow account into which any fees tendered during a board's period of suspension under this subsection shall be deposited. (1957, c. 1377, s. 2; 1969, c. 42; 2006-70, s. 1; 2007-323, s. 23.2; 2009-125, s. 2; 2011-291, ss. 2.19, 2.20.)

§ 93B-3. Register of persons licensed; information as to licensed status of individuals.

Each occupational licensing board shall prepare a register of all persons currently licensed by the board and shall supplement said register annually by listing the changes made in it by reason of new licenses issued, licenses revoked or suspended, death, or any other cause. The board shall, upon request of any citizen of the State, inform the requesting person as to the licensed status of any individual. (1957, c. 1377, s. 3.)

§ 93B-4. Audit of Occupational Licensing Boards; payment of costs.

(a) The State Auditor shall audit occupational licensing boards from time to time to ensure their proper operation. The books, records, and operations of each occupational licensing board shall be subject to the oversight of the State Auditor pursuant to Article 5A of Chapter 147 of the General Statutes. In accordance with G.S. 147-64.7(b), the State Auditor may contract with independent professionals to meet the requirements of this section.

(b)   Each occupational licensing board with a budget of at least fifty thousand dollars ($50,000) shall conduct an annual financial audit of its operations and provide a copy to the State Auditor. (1957, c. 1377, s. 4; 1965, c. 661; 1973, c. 1301; 1983, c. 913, s. 11; 2009-125, s. 3; 2012-142, s. 17.1.)

§ 93B-5. Compensation, employment, and training of board members.

(a)   Board members shall receive as compensation for their services per diem not to exceed one hundred dollars ($100.00) for each day during which they are engaged in the official business of the board.

(b)   Board members shall be reimbursed for all necessary travel expenses in an amount not to exceed that authorized under G.S. 138-6(a) for officers and employees of State departments. Actual expenditures of board members in excess of the maximum amounts set forth in G.S. 138-6(a) for travel and subsistence may be reimbursed if the prior approval of the State Director of Budget is obtained and such approved expenditures are within the established and published uniform standards and criteria of the State Director of Budget authorized under G.S. 138-7 for extraordinary charges for hotels, meals, and convention registration for State officers and employees, whenever such charges are the result of required official business of the Board.

(c)   Repealed by Session Laws 1981, c. 757, s. 2.

(d)   Except as provided herein board members shall not be paid a salary or receive any additional compensation for services rendered as members of the board.

(e)   Board members shall not be permanent, salaried employees of said board.

(f)   Repealed by Session Laws 1975, c. 765, s. 1.

(g)   Within six months of a board member's initial appointment to the board, and at least once within every two calendar years thereafter, a board member shall receive training, either from the board's staff, including its legal advisor, or from an outside educational institution such as the School of Government of the University of North Carolina, on the statutes governing the board and rules adopted by the board, as well as the following State laws, in order to better understand the obligations and limitations of a State agency:

(1)   Chapter 150B, The Administrative Procedure Act.

(2)   Chapter 132, The Public Records Law.

(3)   Article 33C of Chapter 143, The Open Meetings Act.

(4)   Articles 31 and 31A of Chapter 143, The State Tort Claims Act and The Defense of State Employees Law.

(5)   Chapter 138A, The State Government Ethics Act.

(6)   Chapter 120C, Lobbying.

Completion of the training requirements contained in Chapter 138A and Chapter 120C of the General Statutes satisfies the requirements of subdivisions (5) and (6) of this subsection. (1957, c. 1377, s. 5; 1973, c. 1303, s. 1; c. 1342, s. 1; 1975, c. 765, s. 1; 1981, c. 757, ss. 1, 2; 1991 (Reg. Sess., 1992), c. 1011, s. 1; 2009-125, s. 4.)

§ 93B-6. Use of funds for lobbying prohibited.

Occupational licensing boards shall not use any funds to promote or oppose in any manner the passage by the General Assembly of any legislation. (1973, c. 1302.)

§ 93B-7. Rental of state-owned office space.

Any occupational licensing board, which financially operates on the licensing fees charged and also occupies state-owned office space, shall pay rent, in a reasonable amount to be determined by the Governor, to the State for the occupancy of such space. (1973, c. 1300.)

§ 93B-8. Examination procedures.

(a) Each applicant for an examination given by any occupational licensing board shall be informed in writing or print of the required grade for passing the examination prior to the taking of such examination.

(b) Each applicant for an examination given by any occupational licensing board shall be identified, for purposes of the examination, only by number rather than by name.

(c) Each applicant who takes an examination given by any occupational licensing board, and does not pass such examination, shall have the privilege to review his examination in the presence of the board or a representative of the board. Except as provided in this subsection, an occupational licensing board shall not be required to disclose the contents of any examination or of any questions which have appeared thereon, or which may appear thereon in the future.

(d) Notwithstanding the provisions of this section, under no circumstances shall an occupational licensing board be required to disclose to an applicant questions or answers to tests provided by recognized testing organizations pursuant to contracts which prohibit such disclosures. (1973, c. 1334, s. 1; 1991, c. 360, s. 1.)

§ 93B-8.1. Use of criminal history records.

(a) The following definitions apply in this section:

(1) Applicant. - A person who makes application for licensure from an occupational licensing board.

(2) Board. - An occupational licensing board as defined in G.S. 93B-1.

(3) Criminal history record. - A State or federal history of conviction of a crime, whether a misdemeanor or felony, that bears upon an applicant's or a licensee's fitness to be licensed or disciplined.

(4) Licensee. - A person who has obtained a license to engage in or represent himself or herself to be a member of a particular profession or occupation.

(b) Unless the law governing a particular occupational licensing board provides otherwise, a board shall not automatically deny licensure on the basis of an applicant's criminal history. If the board is authorized to deny a license to an applicant on the basis of conviction of any crime or for commission of a crime involving fraud or moral turpitude, and the applicant's verified criminal history record reveals one or more convictions of any crime, the board may deny the license if it finds that denial is warranted after consideration of the following factors:

(1) The level and seriousness of the crime.

(2) The date of the crime.

(3) The age of the person at the time of the crime.

(4) The circumstances surrounding the commission of the crime, if known.

(5) The nexus between the criminal conduct and the prospective duties of the applicant as a licensee.

(6) The prison, jail, probation, parole, rehabilitation, and employment records of the applicant since the date the crime was committed.

(7) The subsequent commission of a crime by the applicant.

(8) Any affidavits or other written documents, including character references.

(c) The board may deny licensure to an applicant who refuses to consent to a criminal history record check or use of fingerprints or other identifying information required by the State or National Repositories of Criminal Histories.

(d) This section does not apply to The North Carolina Criminal Justice Education and Training Standards Commission and the North Carolina Sheriffs' Education and Training Standards Commission. (2013-24, s. 1.)

§ 93B-9. Age requirements.

Except certifications issued by the North Carolina Criminal Justice Education and Training Standards Commission and the North Carolina Sheriffs' Education and Training Standards Commission pursuant to Chapters 17C, 17E, 74E, and 74G of the General Statutes, no occupational licensing board may require that an individual be more than 18 years of age as a requirement for receiving a license with the following exceptions: the North Carolina Criminal Justice Education and Training Standards Commission and the North Carolina Sheriffs' Education and Training Standards Commission may establish a higher age as a requirement for holding certification through either Commission. (1973, c. 1356; 2010-97, s. 8; 2010-122, s. 27.)

§ 93B-10. Expiration of term of appointment of board member.

A board member serving on an occupational and professional licensing board whose term of appointment has expired shall continue to serve until a successor is appointed and qualified. (1973, c. 1373, s. 1.)

§ 93B-11. Interest from State Treasurer's Investment Program.

Any interest earned by an occupational licensing board under G.S. 147-69.3(d) may be used only for the following purposes:

(1)   To reduce fees;

(2)   Improve services offered to licensees and the public; or

(3)   For educational purposes to benefit licensees or the public. (1983, c. 515, s. 2.)

§ 93B-12. Information from licensing boards having authority over health care providers.

(a) Every occupational licensing board having authority to license physicians, physician assistants, nurse practitioners, and nurse midwives in this State shall modify procedures for license renewal to include the collection of information specified in this section for each board's regular renewal cycle. The purpose of this requirement is to assist the State in tracking the availability of health care providers to determine which areas in the State suffer from inequitable access to specific types of health services and to anticipate future health care shortages which might adversely affect the citizens of this State. Occupational licensing boards shall collect, report, and update the following information:

(1) Area of health care specialty practice;

(2) Address of all locations where the licensee practices; and

(3) Other information the occupational licensing board deems relevant to assisting the State in achieving the purpose set out in this section, including social security numbers for research purposes only in matching other data sources.

(b) Every occupational licensing board required to collect information pursuant to subsection (a) of this section shall report and update the information on an annual basis to the Department of Health and Human Services. The Department shall provide this information to programs preparing primary care physicians, physicians assistants, and nurse practitioners upon request by the program and by the Board of Governors of The University of North Carolina. Information provided by the occupational licensing board pursuant to this subsection may be provided in such form as to omit the identity of the health care licensee. (1995, c. 507, s. 23A.4; 1996, 2nd Ex. Sess., c. 17, s. 16.4; 1997-443, s. 11A.118(a).)

§ 93B-13. Revocation when licensing privilege forfeited for nonpayment of child support or for failure to comply with subpoena.

(a) Upon receipt of a court order, pursuant to G.S. 50-13.12 and G.S. 110-142.1, revoking the occupational license of a licensee under its jurisdiction, an occupational licensing board shall note the revocation in its records, report the action within 30 days to the Department of Health and Human Services, and follow the normal postrevocation rules and procedures of the board as if the revocation had been ordered by the board. The revocation shall remain in effect until the board receives certification by the clerk of superior court or the Department of Health and Human Services in an IV-D case that the licensee is no longer delinquent in child support payments, or, as applicable, that the licensee is in compliance with or is no longer subject to the subpoena that was the basis for the revocation.

(b)   Upon receipt of notification from the Department of Health and Human Services that a licensee under an occupational licensing board's jurisdiction has forfeited the licensee's occupational license pursuant to G.S. 110-142.1, then the occupational licensing board shall send a notice of intent to revoke or suspend the occupational license of that licensee as provided by G.S. 110-142.1(d). If the license is revoked as provided by the provisions of G.S. 110-142.1, the revocation shall remain in effect until the board receives certification by the designated representative or the child support enforcement agency that the licensee is no longer delinquent in child support payments, or, as applicable, that the licensee is in compliance with or no longer subject to a subpoena that was the basis for the revocation.

(c)   If at the time the court revokes a license pursuant to subsection (a) of this section, or if at the time the occupational licensing board revokes a license pursuant to subsection (b) of this section, the occupational licensing board has revoked the same license under the licensing board's disciplinary authority over licensees under its jurisdiction, and that revocation period is greater than the revocation period resulting from forfeiture pursuant to G.S. 50-13.12 or G.S. 110-142.1 then the revocation period imposed by the occupational licensing board applies.

(d)   Immediately upon certification by the clerk of superior court or the child support enforcement agency that the licensee whose license was revoked pursuant to subsection (a) or (b) of this section is no longer delinquent in child support payments, the occupational licensing board shall reinstate the license. Immediately upon certification by the clerk of superior court or the child support enforcement agency that the licensee whose license was revoked because of failure to comply with a subpoena is in compliance with or no longer subject to the subpoena, the occupational licensing board shall reinstate the license. Reinstatement of a license pursuant to this section shall be made at no additional cost to the licensee. (1995, c. 538, s. 1.3; 1997-433, s. 5.4; 1997-443, s. 11A.118(a); 1998-17, s. 1; 2003-288, s. 2.)

§ 93B-14. Information on applicants for licensure.

Every occupational licensing board shall require applicants for licensure to provide to the Board the applicant's social security number. This information shall be treated as confidential and may be released only as follows:

(1) To the State Child Support Enforcement Program of the Department of Health and Human Services upon its request and for the purpose of enforcing a child support order.

(2) To the Department of Revenue for the purpose of administering the State's tax laws. (1997-433, s. 4.6; 1997-443, s. 11A-122; 1998-17, s. 1; 1998-162, s. 9.)

§ 93B-15. Payment of license fees by members of the Armed Forces; board waiver rules.

(a) An individual who is serving in the Armed Forces of the United States and to whom G.S. 105-249.2 grants an extension of time to file a tax return is granted an extension of time to pay any license fee charged by an occupational licensing board as a condition of retaining a license granted by the board. The extension is for the same period that would apply if the license fee were a tax.

(b) Occupational licensing boards shall adopt rules to postpone or waive continuing education, payment of renewal and other fees, and any other requirements or conditions relating to the maintenance of licensure by an individual who is currently licensed by and in good standing with the board, is serving in the Armed Forces of the United States, and to whom G.S. 105-249.2 grants an extension of time to file a tax return. (1998-95, s. 8; 1999-337, s. 12; 2009-458, s. 1; 2011-183, s. 68.)

§ 93B-15.1. Licensure for individuals with military training and experience; licensure by endorsement for military spouses; temporary license.

(a) Notwithstanding any other provision of law, an occupational licensing board, as defined in G.S. 93B-1, shall issue a license, certification, or registration to a military-trained applicant to allow the applicant to lawfully practice the applicant's occupation in this State if, upon application to an occupational licensing board, the applicant satisfies the following conditions:

(1) Has been awarded a military occupational specialty and has done all of the following at a level that is substantially equivalent to or exceeds the requirements for licensure, certification, or registration of the occupational licensing board from which the applicant is seeking licensure, certification, or registration in this State: completed a military program of training, completed testing or equivalent training and experience as determined by the board, and performed in the occupational specialty.

(2) Has engaged in the active practice of the occupation for which the person is seeking a license, certification, or permit from the occupational licensing board in this State for at least two of the five years preceding the date of the application under this section.

(3) Has not committed any act in any jurisdiction that would have constituted grounds for refusal, suspension, or revocation of a license to practice that occupation in this State at the time the act was committed.

(4) Pays any fees required by the occupational licensing board for which the applicant is seeking licensure, certification, or registration in this State.

(b) Notwithstanding any other provision of law, an occupational licensing board, as defined in G.S. 93B-1, shall issue a license, certification, or registration to a military spouse to allow the military spouse to lawfully practice the military spouse's occupation in this State if, upon application to an occupational licensing board, the military spouse satisfies the following conditions:

(1) Holds a current license, certification, or registration from another jurisdiction, and that jurisdiction's requirements for licensure, certification, or registration are substantially equivalent to or exceed the requirements for licensure, certification, or registration of the occupational licensing board for which the applicant is seeking licensure, certification, or registration in this State.

(2) Can demonstrate competency in the occupation through methods as determined by the Board, such as having completed continuing education units or having had recent experience for at least two of the five years preceding the date of the application under this section.

(3)   Has not committed any act in any jurisdiction that would have constituted grounds for refusal, suspension, or revocation of a license to practice that occupation in this State at the time the act was committed.

(4)   Is in good standing and has not been disciplined by the agency that had jurisdiction to issue the license, certification, or permit.

(5)   Pays any fees required by the occupational licensing board for which the applicant is seeking licensure, certification, or registration in this State.

(c)   All relevant experience of a military service member in the discharge of official duties or, for a military spouse, all relevant experience, including full-time and part-time experience, regardless of whether in a paid or volunteer capacity, shall be credited in the calculation of years of practice in an occupation as required under subsection (a) or (b) of this section.

(d)   A nonresident licensed, certified, or registered under this section shall be entitled to the same rights and subject to the same obligations as required of a resident licensed, certified, or registered by an occupational licensing board in this State.

(e)   Nothing in this section shall be construed to apply to the practice of law as regulated under Chapter 84 of the General Statutes.

(f)   An occupational licensing board may issue a temporary practice permit to a military-trained applicant or military spouse licensed, certified, or registered in another jurisdiction while the military-trained applicant or military spouse is satisfying the requirements for licensure under subsection (a) or (b) of this section if that jurisdiction has licensure, certification, or registration standards substantially equivalent to the standards for licensure, certification, or registration of an occupational licensing board in this State. The military-trained applicant or military spouse may practice under the temporary permit until a license, certification, or registration is granted or until a notice to deny a license, certification, or registration is issued in accordance with rules adopted by the occupational licensing board.

(g)   An occupational licensing board may adopt rules necessary to implement this section.

(h)   Nothing in this section shall be construed to prohibit a military-trained applicant or military spouse from proceeding under the existing licensure, certification, or registration requirements established by an occupational licensing board in this State.

(i)   For the purposes of this section, the State Board of Education shall be considered an occupational licensing board when issuing teacher licenses under G.S. 115C-296.

(j)   For the purposes of this section, the North Carolina Medical Board shall not be considered an occupational licensing board. (2012-196, s. 1.)

§ 93B-16. Occupational board liability for negligent acts.

(a)   An occupational licensing board may purchase commercial insurance of any kind to cover all risks or potential liability of the board, its members, officers, employees, and agents, including the board's liability under Articles 31 and 31A of Chapter 143 of the General Statutes.

(b)   Occupational licensing boards shall be deemed State agencies for purposes of Articles 31 and 31A of Chapter 143 of the General Statutes, and board members and employees of occupational licensing boards shall be considered State employees for purposes of Articles 31 and 31A of Chapter 143 of the General Statutes. To the extent an occupational licensing board purchases commercial liability insurance coverage in excess of one hundred fifty thousand dollars ($150,000) per claim for liability arising under Article 31 or 31A of Chapter 143 of the General Statutes, the provisions of G.S. 143-299.4 shall not apply. To the extent that an occupational licensing board purchases commercial insurance coverage for liability arising under Article 31 or 31A of Chapter 143 of the General Statutes, the provisions of G.S. 143-300.6(c) shall not apply.

(c)   The purchase of insurance by an occupational licensing board under this section shall not be construed to waive sovereign immunity or any other defense available to the board, its members, officers, employees, or agents in an action or contested matter in any court, agency, or tribunal. The purchase of insurance by an occupational licensing board shall not be construed to alter or expand the limitations on claims or payments established in G.S. 143-299.2 or limit the right of board members, officers, employees, or agents to defense by the State as provided by G.S. 143-300.3. (2002-168, s. 1.)

Chapter 93C.

Watchmakers.

§§ 93C-1 through 93C-18. Repealed by Session Laws 1977, c. 712, s. 2.

Chapter 93D.

North Carolina State Hearing Aid Dealers and Fitters Board.

§ 93D-1. Definitions.

For the purposes of this Chapter:

(1) "Board" shall mean the North Carolina State Hearing Aid Dealers and Fitters Board.

(2) "Fitting and selling hearing aids" shall mean the evaluation or measurement of the powers or range of human hearing by means of an audiometer or by other means and the consequent selection or adaptation or sale or rental of hearing aids intended to compensate for hearing loss including the making of an impression of the ear.

(3) "Hearing aid" shall mean any instrument or device designed for or represented as aiding, improving or compensating for defective human hearing and any parts, attachments or accessories of such an instrument or device.

(4) "Hearing Aid Specialist" shall mean a person licensed by the Board to engage in the activities within the scope of practice of a hearing aid specialist in North Carolina.

(5) "Registered Sponsor" shall mean a person with a permanent license as an audiologist under Article 22 of Chapter 90 of the General Statutes who is registered in accordance with G.S. 93D-3(c)(16), or a licensee of the Board who has been approved as a sponsor of an apprentice. (1969, c. 999; 2011-311, s. 1; 2013-410, s. 32.5(a).)

§ 93D-1.1. Hearing aid specialist; scope of practice.

The scope of practice of a hearing aid specialist regulated pursuant to this Chapter shall include the following activities:

(1)   Fitting and selling hearing aids.

(2)   Eliciting patient histories.

(3)   Performing hearing evaluations.

(4)   Administering and interpreting tests of human hearing.

(5)   Referring, as appropriate, for cochlear implant evaluation or other clinical, rehabilitative, or medical intervention.

(6)   Determining candidacy for hearing aids, tinnitus management devices, and other assistive listening devices.

(7)   Providing hearing aid, tinnitus management device, and assistive device recommendations and selection.

(8)   Performing hearing aid fittings, programming, and adjustments.

(9)   Assessing hearing aid efficacy utilizing appropriate fitting verification methodology.

(10)   Performing hearing aid repairs.

(11)   Administering cerumen management in the course of examining ears.

(12)   Taking ear impressions, and preparing, designing, and modifying ear molds.

(13)   Providing counseling and rehabilitation services related to hearing aids.

(14)   Providing supervision and in-service training for those entering the hearing aid dispensing profession.

(15)   Providing hearing health education.

(16)   Providing community services for individuals with hearing loss and the deaf. (2013-410, s. 32.5(b).)

§ 93D-2. Practice without license unlawful.

It shall be unlawful for any person to engage in any activity within the scope of practice of a hearing aid specialist, unless the person has first obtained a license from the North Carolina State Hearing Aid Dealers and Fitters Board, is an apprentice working under the supervision of a Registered Sponsor, or is otherwise authorized by law to engage in the activity within the scope of practice of another regulated profession. (1969, c. 999; 1981, c. 601, s. 1; 2011-311, s. 2; 2013-410, s. 32.5(c).)

§ 93D-3. North Carolina State Hearing Aid Dealers and Fitters Board; composition, organization, duties and compensation.

(a) There is hereby created a board whose duty it shall be to carry out the purposes and enforce the provisions of this Chapter, and which shall be known as the "North Carolina State Hearing Aid Dealers and Fitters Board." The Board shall be composed of seven members. Four members who have been a licensed Hearing Aid Specialist for at least the preceding three years prior to appointment, shall be appointed by the Governor. These initial appointments are for the following terms: one for one year, one for two years, one for three years and one for four years. All appointments made on or after July 1, 1981, shall be for terms of three years.

One member shall be appointed by the Governor who shall be a physician practicing in North Carolina, preferably specializing in the field of otolaryngology. All appointments shall be for terms of three years.

One member, who shall be a person with hearing loss, shall be appointed by the Governor to represent the interest of hearing aid consumers. This initial appointment shall be for a term ending June 30, 2013. All appointments made on or after July 1, 2013, shall be for a term of three years.

One member shall be appointed by the Governor to represent the interest of the public at large. This member shall have no ties to the hearing aid business nor shall he be an audiologist. The Governor shall appoint the public member not later than July 1, 1981, to serve a term of three years.

All Board members serving on June 30, 1981, shall be eligible to complete their respective terms. No member appointed to a term on or after July 1, 1981, shall serve more than two complete consecutive terms.

Vacancies on the Board shall be filled by appointment of the Governor. Appointees shall serve the unexpired term of their predecessor in office and must be appointed from the same category as their predecessor in office. The members of the Board, before entering their duties, shall respectively take all oaths taken and prescribed for other State officers, in the manner provided by law, which oaths shall be filed in the office of the Secretary of State, and the Board shall have a common seal.

(b)   The Board shall choose, at the first regular meeting and annually thereafter, one of its members to serve as president and one as secretary and treasurer. A majority of the Board shall constitute a quorum. The Board shall meet at least once a year, the time and place of the annual meeting and any special meetings to be designated by the president. The secretary and treasurer of the Board shall keep a full record of its proceedings, including a current list of all licensees, which shall at all reasonable times be open to public inspection. The Board is authorized to employ an executive secretary and to provide such assistance as may be required to enable said Board to properly perform its duties.

(c)   The Board shall:

(1)   Authorize all disbursements necessary to carry out the provisions of this Chapter;

(2)   Supervise and administer qualifying examinations to test and determine the knowledge and proficiency of applicants for licenses;

(3)   Issue licenses to qualified persons who apply to the Board;

(4)   Obtain audiometric equipment and facilities necessary to carry out the examination of applicants for licenses;

(5)   Suspend or revoke licenses pursuant to this Chapter;

(6)   Make and publish rules, including a code of ethics, that are necessary and proper to regulate hearing aid specialists and to carry out the provisions of this Chapter;

(7) Exercise jurisdiction over the hearing of complaints, charges of malpractice including corrupt or unprofessional conduct, and allegations of violations of the Board's rules that are made against any fitter and seller of hearing aids in North Carolina;

(8) Require the periodic inspection and calibration of audiometric testing equipment of persons who are fitting and selling hearing aids;

(9) In connection with any matter within the jurisdiction of the Board, summon and subpoena and examine witnesses under oath and to compel their attendance and the production of books, papers, or other documents or writings deemed by the Board to be necessary or material to the inquiry. Each summons or subpoena shall be issued under the hand of the secretary and treasurer or the president of the Board and shall have the force and effect of a summons or subpoena issued by a court of record. Any witness who shall refuse or neglect to appear in obedience thereto or to testify or produce books, papers, or other documents or writings required shall be liable to contempt charges. The Board shall pay to any witness subpoenaed before it the fees and per diem as paid witnesses in civil actions in the superior court of the county where such hearing is held;

(10) Inform the Attorney General of any information or knowledge it acquires regarding any "price-fixing" activity whatsoever in connection with the sales and service of hearing aids;

(11) Establish and enforce rules to guarantee that a full refund will be made by the seller of a hearing aid to the purchaser when presented with a written medical opinion of an otolaryngologist that the purchaser's hearing cannot be improved by the use of a hearing aid;

(12) Fund, establish, conduct, approve and sponsor instructional programs for registered apprentices and for persons who hold a license as well as for persons interested in obtaining adequate instruction or programs of study to qualify them for registration to the extent that the Board deems such instructional programs to be beneficial or necessary;

(13) Register persons serving as apprentices as set forth in G.S. 93D-9;

(14) Have the power to set and collect fees in accordance with Chapter 150B of the General Statutes for the items listed in this subdivision and for other items for which this Chapter gives the Board the authority to set a fee:

a. For a continuing education make-up class provided by the Board, a fee not to exceed fifty dollars ($50.00) per person for each day of instruction. The Board may not offer a make-up class that is longer than two days;

b. For a license examination preparation course provided by the Board, a fee not to exceed fifty dollars ($50.00) per person for each day of instruction. The Board may not offer an examination preparation course that is longer than three days;

c. For approval of a continuing education program provider, a fee not to exceed forty dollars ($40.00);

d. For verifying and recording attendance at a continuing education program not provided by the Board, a fee not to exceed fifteen dollars ($15.00) per licensee per program;

e. For providing a voluntary two-day apprentice training workshop, a fee not to exceed one hundred dollars ($100.00) per person, and for providing a three-day voluntary apprentice training workshop, a fee not to exceed one hundred fifty dollars ($150.00) per person;

f. For administering an examination, a fee of three hundred dollars ($300.00); and

g. For the registration of a Registered Sponsor not otherwise licensed under this Chapter, a fee of one hundred fifty dollars ($150.00) per annum;

(15) Adopt annually a balanced budget prior to the beginning of its fiscal year, against which expenditures shall be reviewed throughout the fiscal year to ensure that expenditures during the year do not exceed receipts for that year plus amounts held by the Board in reserve. Except for monies from charges for photocopying and similar charges, the Board's receipts shall consist of and be limited to funds derived from fees expressly authorized by law; and

(16) Register any person holding a valid permanent license as an audiologist under Article 22 of Chapter 90 of the General Statutes, who holds a doctoral degree in Audiology and who makes an application to serve as a Registered Sponsor to apprentice as set forth in G.S. 93D-9, but who is not otherwise subject to licensure by the Board.

(d) Members of the Board shall be entitled to travel, per diem, and other expenses authorized by G.S. 93B-5. The expenses shall be paid from the fees and assessments received by the Board under the provisions of this Chapter. No part of these expenses or any other expenses of the Board, in any manner whatsoever, shall be paid out of the State treasury. All moneys received in excess of expense allowance and mileage, as above provided, shall be held by the secretary-treasurer as a special fund for meeting other expenses of the Board and carrying out the provisions of this Chapter.

The Board shall make an annual report of its proceedings in accordance with G.S. 93B-2. (1969, c. 999; 1973, c. 1331, s. 3; c. 1345, ss. 1, 2; 1975, c. 550, s. 1; 1981, c. 601, ss. 2-5; 1987, c. 827, s. 80; 1991, c. 592, s. 1; 2007-406, ss. 1, 2; 2011-311, ss. 3, 4; 2013-410, s. 32.5(d).)

§ 93D-4. Board may enjoin illegal practices.

The Board may, if it finds that any person is violating any of the provisions of this Chapter, apply to superior court for a temporary or permanent restraining order or injunction to restrain such persons from continuing such illegal practices. If upon application, it appears to the court that such person has violated or is violating the provisions of this Chapter, the court shall issue an order restraining the sale or fitting of hearing aids or other conduct in violation of this Chapter. All such actions by the Board for injunctive relief shall be governed by the Rules of Civil Procedure and Article 37, Chapter 1 of the General Statutes; provided, that injunctive relief may be granted regardless of whether criminal prosecution has been or may be instituted under the provisions of this Chapter. Actions under this section shall be commenced in the superior court district or set of districts as defined in G.S. 7A-41.1 in which the respondent resides or has his principal place of business. (1969, c. 999; 1981, c. 601, s. 6; 1987 (Reg. Sess., 1988), c. 1037, s. 105.)

§ 93D-5. Requirements for registration; examinations; licenses.

(a) No person shall undertake any activity within the scope of practice of a hearing aid specialist in this State unless the person first has been issued a license by the Board or is an apprentice working under the supervision of a Registered Sponsor. Except as hereinafter provided, each applicant for a license shall pay a fee set by the Board, not to exceed five hundred dollars ($500.00), which fee may be prorated by the Board, and shall show to the satisfaction of the Board that the applicant:

(1)   Is a person of good moral character.

(2)   Is 18 years of age or older.

(3)   Has an education equivalent to a four-year course in an accredited high school.

(4)   Repealed by Session Laws 2007-406, s. 3, effective August 21, 2007.

(b)   Except as hereinafter provided, no license shall be issued to a person until he has successfully passed a qualifying examination administered by the Board.

(c)   No license shall be issued to any person until the person has served as an apprentice as set forth in G.S. 93D-9 for a period of at least one year; provided, that the one-year apprenticeship requirement shall be waived for the following:

(1)   Persons qualified under G.S. 93D-6.

(2)   Persons holding a permanent license as an audiologist under Article 22 of Chapter 90 of the General Statutes.

(3)   Persons holding a temporary license as an audiologist under Article 22 of Chapter 90 of the General Statutes who have undergone 250 hours of supervised activity fitting or selling hearing aids under the direct supervision of a Registered Sponsor.

(4)   Persons continuously licensed to fit or sell hearing aids in another state or jurisdiction for the preceding three years.

(5)   Persons who have worked full-time for one year in the office of and under the direct supervision of an otolaryngologist fitting or selling hearing aids. (1969, c. 999; 1975, c. 550, s. 2; 1981, c. 601, ss. 7, 8; c. 990, s. 1; 1991, c. 592, s. 2; 2007-406, s. 3; 2011-311, s. 5; 2012-194, s. 66; 2013-296, s. 2; 2013-410, s. 32.5(e).)

§ 93D-6. Hearing aid specialists licensed in other States.

Whenever the Board determines that another state or jurisdiction has requirements at least equivalent to those in effect pursuant to this Chapter for engaging in activities within the scope of practice of a hearing aid specialist and that such state or jurisdiction has a program at least equivalent to the program for determining whether applicants pursuant to this Chapter are qualified to engage in activities within the scope of practice of a hearing aid specialist, the Board may issue, but is not compelled to issue, licenses to applicants therefor who hold current, unsuspended and unrevoked certificates or licenses to engage in activities within the scope of practice of a hearing aid specialist in such other state or jurisdiction. No such applicant shall be required to submit to any examination or other procedure required by G.S. 93D-5, but shall be required to pay an application fee to the Board in an amount set by the Board, not to exceed one hundred fifty dollars ($150.00). Such applicant must have one full year of experience satisfactory to the Board before issuance of the license. (1969, c. 999; 1971, c. 1093, s. 2; 1981, c. 990, s. 2; 1991, c. 592, s. 3; 1991 (Reg. Sess., 1992), c. 1030, s. 24; 2013-410, s. 32.5(f).)

§ 93D-7. Statements of sale.

Every person fitting and selling a hearing aid, be it new or used, in the State of North Carolina, at or before the time of delivery of the hearing aid shall render to the user and/or purchaser a statement of sale to include the following:

(1)   Date of delivery

(2)   Condition of hearing aid; new, used, reconditioned

(3)   Hearing aid identification number

(4)   Name of manufacturer

(5)   Price of hearing aid

(6)   Charge for fitting and service

(7)   Name of dealer and/or fitter

(8)   Signature of customer. (1969, c. 999; 1973, c. 1345, s. 3; 2011-311, s. 6.)

§ 93D-8. Examination of applicants; issue of license certificate.

(a)   Every applicant for a license who is notified by the Board that he has fulfilled the requirements of G.S. 93D-5, except those making application pursuant to G.S. 93D-6, shall appear at a time, place and before such persons as the Board may designate, to be examined by written and practical tests in order to demonstrate that the applicant is qualified to engage in the activities within the scope of a hearing aid specialist. The Board shall give one examination of the type prescribed herein each year at a duly prescribed time and place, which shall be publicized for at least 90 days in advance. Additional examinations may be given at the discretion of the Board. The examination provided in this section shall not include questions requiring a medical or surgical education but shall consist of:

(1)   Tests of knowledge in the following areas as they pertain to the fitting of hearing aids:

a.   The basic physics of sound,

b.   The human hearing mechanism, including the science of hearing and the cause and rehabilitation of abnormal hearing and hearing disorders, and

c.   The structure and function of hearing aids.

(2)   Tests of proficiency in the following techniques as they pertain to the fitting of hearing aids:

a.   Pure tone audiometry, including air conduction testing and bone conduction testing,

b.   Live voice and recorded voice speech audiometry, including speech reception threshold testing and speech discrimination testing,

c.   Effective masking,

d. Recording and evaluation of audiograms and speech audiometry to determine hearing aid candidacy,

e. Selection and adaption of hearing aids and testing of hearing aids,

f. Taking earmold impressions, and

g. Such other skills as may be required for the fitting of hearing aids in the opinion of the Board.

(b) Upon payment of a fee set by the Board, not to exceed twenty-five dollars ($25.00), the Board shall issue a license certificate to each applicant who successfully passes the examination. (1969, c. 999; 1981, c. 601, s. 9; 1991, c. 592, s. 4; 2011-311, s. 7; 2013-410, s. 32.5(g).)

§ 93D-9. Registration of apprentices.

(a) Any person age 17 or older may apply to the Board for registration as an apprentice. Each applicant must be sponsored by a Registered Sponsor.

(b) Upon receiving an application accompanied by a fee in an amount set by the Board, not to exceed one hundred dollars ($100.00), the Board may register the applicant as an apprentice, which shall entitle the applicant to fit and sell hearing aids under the supervision of Registered Sponsor.

(c) No applicant shall be registered as an apprentice by the Board under this section unless the applicant shows to the satisfaction of the Board that the applicant is or will be supervised and trained by a Registered Sponsor.

(d) If a person 18 years of age or older who is registered as an apprentice under this section does not take the next succeeding examination given after a minimum of one full year of apprenticeship, the person's apprentice registration shall not be renewed, except for good cause shown to the satisfaction of the Board.

(e) If a person who is registered as an apprentice takes and fails to pass the next succeeding examination given after one full year of apprenticeship, the Board may renew the apprenticeship license for a period of time to end 30 days after the results of the examination given next after the date of renewal of said registration. The fee for renewal of apprenticeship registration shall be set by the Board at an amount not to exceed one hundred fifty dollars ($150.00).

(f)   The Board shall adopt rules implementing initial and renewal registration of apprentices.

(g)   The Board shall adopt rules implementing initial and renewal registration of Registered Sponsors. (1969, c. 999; 1973, c. 1345, s. 4; 1981, c. 601, ss. 10-15; c. 990, s. 3; 1991, c. 592, s. 5; 2011-311, s. 8.)

§ 93D-10. Registration and notice.

The Board shall register each apprentice, Registered Sponsor, and each person to whom it grants a license. The secretary-treasurer of the Board shall keep a record of the place of business of all licensees, Registered Sponsors, and apprentices. Any notice required to be given by the Board to a person holding a license or registration may be given by mailing to him at the last address received by the Board from him. (1969, c. 999; 1981, c. 601, s. 16; 2011-311, s. 9.)

§ 93D-11. Annual fees; failure to pay; expiration of license; occupational instruction courses.

Every person licensed as a hearing aid specialist shall pay to the Board an annual license renewal fee in an amount set by the Board, not to exceed two hundred fifty dollars ($250.00). The payment shall be made prior to the first day of April in each year. In case of default in payment the license shall expire 30 days after notice by the secretary-treasurer to the last known address of the licensee by registered mail, certified mail, or in a manner provided by G.S. 1A-1, Rule 4(j)(1)d. The Board may reinstate an expired license upon the showing of good cause for late payment of fees, upon payment of said fees within 60 days after expiration of the license, and upon the further payment of a late penalty of twenty-five dollars ($25.00). After 60 days after the expiration date, the Board may reinstate the license for good cause shown upon application for reinstatement and payment of a late penalty of fifty dollars ($50.00) and the renewal fee. The Board may require all licensees to successfully attend and complete a course or courses of occupational instruction funded, conducted or approved or sponsored by the Board on an annual basis as a condition to any license renewal and evidence of satisfactory attendance and completion of any such course or courses shall be provided the Board by the licensee. (1969, c. 999; 1975, c. 550, s. 3; 1979, c. 848; 1981, c. 601, s. 17; c. 990, s. 4; 1991, c. 592, s. 6; 2007-406, s. 4; 2013-410, s. 32.5(h).)

§ 93D-12. License to be displayed at office.

Every person to whom a license, apprenticeship certificate, or sponsor registration is granted shall display the same in a conspicuous part of his office where the person conducts business as a hearing aid specialist or shall have a copy of such license certificate, or registration on his person and exhibit the same upon request when fitting or selling hearing aids outside of his office. (1969, c. 999; 1981, c. 601, s. 18; 2011-311, s. 10; 2013-410, s. 32.5(i).)

§ 93D-13. Discipline, suspension, revocation of licenses and registrations; records.

(a) The Board may in its discretion administer the punishment of private reprimand, suspension of license or registration for a fixed period or revocation of license or registration as the case may warrant in their judgment for any violation of the rules and regulations of the Board or for any of the following causes:

(1) Repealed by Session Laws 2007-406, s. 5, effective August 21, 2007.

(2) Gross incompetence.

(3) Inability to perform the functions for which the person is licensed or substantial impairment of the person's ability to perform the functions for which the person is licensed by reason of physical or mental disability.

(4) Commission of a criminal offense indicating professional unfitness.

(5) The use of a false name or alias in his or her business.

(6) Conduct involving willful deceit.

(7) Conduct involving fraud or any other business conduct involving moral turpitude.

(8) Advertising of a character or nature tending to deceive or mislead the public.

(9) Advertising declared to be unethical by the Board or prohibited by the code of ethics established by the Board.

(10) Permitting another person to use his or her license.

(10a) Failure by a Registered Sponsor to properly supervise an apprentice under his or her supervision.

(11) For violating any of the provisions of this Chapter.

(b) Board action in revoking or suspending a license or registration shall be in accordance with Chapter 150B of the General Statutes. Any person whose license or registration has been suspended for any of the grounds or reasons herein set forth, may, after the expiration of 90 days but within two years, apply to the Board to have the same reissued; upon a showing satisfactory to the Board that reissuance will not endanger the public health and welfare, the Board may reissue a license to such person for a fee set by the Board, not to exceed two hundred dollars ($200.00). If application is made subsequent to two years from date of suspension, reissuance shall be in accordance with the provisions of G.S. 93D-8.

(c) Records, papers, and other documents containing information collected or compiled by or on behalf of the Board as a result of an investigation, inquiry, or interview conducted in connection with registration, licensure, or a disciplinary matter shall not be considered public records within the meaning of Chapter 132 of the General Statutes. Any notice or statement of charges, notice of hearing, or decision rendered by the Board in connection with a hearing is a public record. However, information that identifies a consumer who has not consented to the public disclosure of services rendered to the consumer by a person registered or licensed under this Chapter shall be deleted from the public record. All other records, papers, and documents containing information collected or compiled by or on behalf of the Board shall be public records, provided that any information that identifies a consumer who has not consented to the public disclosure of services rendered to the consumer is deleted. (1969,

c. 999; 1973, c. 1331, s. 3; 1981, c. 601, s. 19; c. 990, s. 5; 1987, c. 827, s. 1; 1991, c. 592, s. 7; 2007-406, s. 5; 2011-311, s. 11.)

§ 93D-14. Persons not affected.

(a) Nothing in this Chapter shall apply to a physician licensed to practice medicine or surgery in the State of North Carolina.

(b) Any person who meets the requirements of having both a doctoral degree in Audiology and holding a valid permanent license as an audiologist under Article 22 of Chapter 90 of the General Statutes of North Carolina is exempt from licensure under this Chapter. A person who does not meet both requirements of having a doctoral degree in Audiology and holding a valid permanent license as an audiologist under Article 22 of Chapter 90 of the General Statutes of North Carolina must become a registered apprentice or be licensed by the Board before fitting or selling hearing aids in the State of North Carolina.

(c) Nothing in this Chapter shall be construed to exempt an audiology assistant or certified technician, working under the supervision of a licensee or a person exempt from licensure under this Chapter, from being subject to the provisions of this Chapter. Such a person, before engaging in fitting or selling hearing aids, as defined in this Chapter, must be registered as an apprentice under a Registered Sponsor or be licensed by the Board.

(d) The provisions of this Chapter shall not apply to the activities and services of an audiology student pursuing a course of study in an accredited college or university, if these activities and services constitute a part of such person's course of study. (1969, c. 999; 2011-311, s. 12.)

§ 93D-15. Violation of Chapter.

Any person who violates any of the provisions of this Chapter and any person who holds himself out to the public as a hearing aid specialist without having first obtained a license or apprenticeship registration as provided for herein shall be deemed guilty of a Class 2 misdemeanor. (1969, c. 999; 1981, c. 601, s. 20; 1993, c. 539, s. 660; 1994, Ex. Sess., c. 24, s. 14(c); 2013-410, s. 32.5(j).)

§ 93D-16. Severability.

If any provision of the Chapter shall be declared unconstitutional or invalid, such invalidity shall not affect other provisions or the application of the Chapter which can be given effect without the invalid provisions. To this end, the provisions of this Chapter are declared to be severable. (1969, c. 999.)

Chapter 93E.

North Carolina Appraisers Act.

Article 1.

Real Estate Appraiser.

§ 93E-1-1. Title.

This Chapter shall be known and may be cited as the "North Carolina Appraisers Act". (1993, c. 419, s. 6.)

§ 93E-1-2: Repealed by Session Laws 1995, c. 482, s. 12.

§ 93E-1-2.1. Registration, license, or certificate required of real estate appraisers.

It is unlawful for any person in this State to act as a real estate appraiser, to directly or indirectly engage or assume to engage in the business of real estate appraisal, or to advertise or hold himself or herself out as engaging in or conducting the business of real estate appraisal without first obtaining a registration, license, or certificate issued by the Appraisal Board under the provisions of this Chapter. It is also unlawful, with regard to any real property where any portion of that property is located within this State, for any person to perform any of the acts listed above without first being registered, licensed, or certified by the Appraisal Board under the provisions of this Chapter. (1995, c. 482, s. 1; 2001-399, s. 1; 2007-506, s. 1.)

§ 93E-1-3. When registration, license, or certificate not required.

(a)   No trainee registration, license, or certificate shall be issued under the provisions of this Chapter to a partnership, association, corporation, firm, or group. However, nothing herein shall preclude a registered trainee or licensed or certified real estate appraiser from rendering appraisals for or on behalf of a partnership, association, corporation, firm, or group, provided the appraisal report is prepared by a licensed or certified real estate appraiser or by a registered trainee under the immediate personal direction of the certified real estate appraiser and is reviewed and signed by that certified appraiser.

(b)   Repealed by Session Laws 2001-399, s. 1, effective October 1, 2001.

(c)   Nothing in this Chapter shall preclude a real estate broker licensed under Chapter 93A of the General Statutes from performing a broker price opinion or comparative market analysis as defined in G.S. 93E-1-4, provided the person does not represent himself or herself as being a registered trainee or a licensed or certified real estate appraiser, and provided they follow the standards set forth in Article 6 of Chapter 93A.

(d)   Nothing in this Chapter shall abridge, infringe upon, or otherwise restrict the right to use the term "certified ad valorem tax appraiser" or any similar term by persons certified by the Department of Revenue to perform ad valorem tax appraisals, provided that the term is not used in a manner that creates the impression of certification by the State to perform real estate appraisals other than ad valorem tax appraisals.

(e)   Nothing in this Chapter shall entitle a registered trainee or a licensed or certified real estate appraiser to appraise real estate for ad valorem tax purposes unless the person has first been certified by the Department of Revenue pursuant to G.S. 105-294.

(f)   A trainee registration, license, or certificate is not required under this Chapter for:

(1)   Any person, partnership, association, or corporation that performs appraisals of property owned by that person, partnership, association, or corporation for the sole use of that person, partnership, association, or corporation;

(2) Any court-appointed commissioner who conducts an appraisal pursuant to a judicially ordered evaluation of property;

(3) Any person to qualify as an expert witness for court or administrative agency testimony, if otherwise qualified;

(4) A person who appraises standing timber so long as the appraisal does not include a determination of value of any land;

(5) Any person employed by a lender in the performance of appraisals with respect to which federal regulations do not require a licensed or certified appraiser; and

(6) A person who performs ad valorem tax appraisals and is certified by the Department of Revenue under G.S. 105-294 or G.S. 105-296; however, any person who is registered, licensed, or certified under this Chapter and who performs any of the activities set forth in subdivisions (1) through (5) of this subsection must comply with all of the provisions of this Chapter. The provisions of this Chapter shall not apply to certified real estate appraisers who perform a broker price opinion or comparative market analysis pursuant to G.S. 93E-1-3(c), as long as the appraiser is licensed as a real estate broker by the North Carolina Real Estate Commission and does not refer to himself or herself as an appraiser in the broker price opinion or comparative market analysis. (1993, c. 419, s. 6; 1995, c. 482, s. 2; 2001-399, s. 1; 2007-506, s. 2; 2012-163, s. 3; 2013-403, s. 1.)

§ 93E-1-3.1. Prohibited use of title; permissible use of title.

(a) It shall be unlawful for any person to assume or use the title "registered trainee", "licensed real estate appraiser", "certified real estate appraiser", or any title, designation, or abbreviation likely to create the impression of registration, licensure, or certification as a real estate appraiser, unless the person is registered, licensed, or certified by the Appraisal Board in accordance with the provisions of this Chapter. The Board may adopt for the exclusive use of persons licensed or certified under the provisions of this Chapter, a seal, symbol, or other mark identifying the user as a licensed or certified real estate appraiser.

(b) Any person certified as a real estate appraiser by an appraisal trade organization shall retain the right to use the term "certified" or any similar term in identifying the person to the public, provided that:

(1) In each instance wherein the term is used, the name of the certifying organization or body is prominently and conspicuously displayed immediately adjacent to the term; and

(2) The use of the term does not create the impression of certification by the State.

This subsection does not entitle any person certified only by a trade organization to conduct an appraisal that requires a State registration, license, or certification.

(c) The term "registered trainee", "licensed real estate appraiser", "certified real estate appraiser", or any similar term shall not be used following or immediately in connection with the name of a partnership, association, corporation, or other firm or group, or in a manner that might create the impression of registration, licensure, or certification as a real estate appraiser under this Chapter. (1995, c. 482, s. 3; 2001-399, s. 1; 2007-506, s. 3.)

§ 93E-1-4. Definitions.

When used in this Chapter, unless the context otherwise requires, the term:

(1) "Appraisal" or "real estate appraisal" means an analysis, opinion, or conclusion as to the value of identified real estate or specified interests therein performed for compensation or other valuable consideration.

(2) "Appraisal assignment" means an engagement for which an appraiser is employed or retained to act, or would be perceived by third parties or the public as acting, as a disinterested third party in rendering an unbiased appraisal.

(3) "Appraisal Board" or "Board" means the North Carolina Appraisal Board established under G.S. 93E-1-5.

(4) "Appraisal Foundation" or "Foundation" means The Appraisal Foundation established on November 20, 1987, as a not-for-profit corporation under the laws of Illinois.

(5) "Appraisal report" means any communication, written or oral, of an appraisal.

(6) "Certificate" means that document issued by the North Carolina Appraisal Board evidencing that the person named therein has satisfied the requirements for certification as a certified real estate appraiser and bearing a certificate number assigned by the Board.

(7) "Certificate holder" means a person certified by the Board under the provisions of this Chapter.

(7a) "Certified general real estate appraiser" means a person who holds a current, valid certificate as a certified general real estate appraiser issued under the provisions of this Chapter.

(7b) "Certified residential real estate appraiser" means a person who holds a current, valid certificate as a certified residential real estate appraiser issued under the provisions of this Chapter.

(7c) "Comparative market analysis" and "broker price opinion" mean an estimate prepared by a licensed real estate broker that details the probable selling price or leasing price of a particular parcel of or interest in property and provides a varying level of detail about the property's condition, market, and neighborhood, and information on comparable properties, but does not include an automated valuation model.

(8) "License" means that document issued by the North Carolina Appraisal Board evidencing that the person named therein has satisfied the requirements for licensure as a licensed real estate appraiser and bearing a license number assigned by the Board.

(8a) "Licensed residential real estate appraiser" means a person who holds a current, valid license as a licensed residential real estate appraiser issued under the provisions of this Chapter.

(9) "Licensee" means a person licensed by the Board under the provisions of this Chapter.

(10) "Real estate" or "real property" means land, including the air above and ground below and all appurtenances and improvements thereto, as well as any interest or right inherent in the ownership of land.

(11) "Real estate appraiser" or "appraiser" means a person who for a fee or valuable consideration develops and communicates real estate appraisals or otherwise gives an opinion of the value of real estate or any interest therein.

(12) "Real estate appraising" means the practice of developing and communicating real estate appraisals.

(13) "Residential real estate" means any parcel of real estate, improved or unimproved, that is exclusively residential in nature and that includes or is intended to include a residential structure containing not more than four dwelling units and no other improvements except those which are typical residential improvements that support the residential use for the location and property type. A residential unit in a condominium, town house, or cooperative complex, or planned unit development is considered to be residential real estate.

(14) through (16) Repealed by Session Laws 2007-506, s. 4, effective October 1, 2007.

(17) "Temporary appraiser licensure or certification" means the issuance of a temporary license or certificate by the Board to a person licensed or certified in another state who enters this State for the purpose of completing a particular appraisal assignment.

(18) "Trainee", "registered trainee", or "trainee real estate appraiser" means a person who holds a current, valid registration as a trainee real estate appraiser issued under the provisions of this Chapter.

(19) "Trainee registration" or "registration as a trainee" means the document issued by the North Carolina Appraisal Board evidencing that the person named therein has satisfied the requirements of registration as a trainee real estate appraiser and bearing a registration number assigned by the Board. (1993, c. 419, s. 6; 1995, c. 482, s. 4; 2001-399, s. 1; 2007-506, s. 4; 2012-163, s. 4.)

§ 93E-1-5. Appraisal Board.

(a) There is created the North Carolina Appraisal Board for the purposes set forth in this Chapter. The Board shall consist of nine members. The Governor shall appoint five members of the Board, and the General Assembly shall appoint four members in accordance with G.S. 120-121, two upon the recommendation of the President Pro Tempore of the Senate and two upon the recommendation of the Speaker of the House of Representatives. Members appointed by the Governor shall be appointed from geographically diverse areas of the State. The appointees recommended by the Speaker of the House of Representatives and four of the appointees of the Governor shall be persons who have been engaged in the business of real estate appraising in this State for at least five years immediately preceding their appointment and are also State-licensed or State-certified real estate appraisers. One of the appointees of the Governor shall be a person representing either the real estate appraisal management industry or the banking industry. No more than three of the appointees may be members of the same appraiser trade organization at any one time. The appointees recommended by the President Pro Tempore of the Senate shall be a person not involved directly or indirectly in the real estate, real estate appraisal, or the real estate lending industry. Members of the Board shall serve three-year terms, so staggered that the terms of three members expire in one year, the terms of three members expire in the next year, and the terms of three members expire in the third year of each three-year period. The members of the Board shall elect one of their members to serve as chairman of the Board for a term of one year. The Governor may remove any member of the Board appointed by the Governor for misconduct, incompetency, or neglect of duty. The General Assembly may remove any member appointed by it for the same reasons. Successors shall be appointed by the appointing authority making the original appointment. All vacancies occurring on the Board shall be filled, for the unexpired term, by the appointing authority making the original appointment. Vacancies in appointments made by the General Assembly shall be filled in accordance with G.S. 120-122. Initial terms of office commenced July 1, 1994.

(b) The Board is an occupational licensing agency governed by Chapter 150B of the General Statutes; its decisions are final agency decisions subject to judicial review under Article 4 of Chapter 150B of the General Statutes.

(c) Members of the Board shall be paid the per diem, subsistence, and travel allowances at the rates set forth in G.S. 93B-5; provided that none of the expenses of the Board or the compensation or expenses of any officer or employee thereof shall be payable out of the treasury of the State of North Carolina; the total expenses of the administration of this Chapter shall not exceed the total income therefrom; and neither the Board nor any officer or employee thereof shall have any power or authority to make or incur any expense, debt, or other financial obligation binding upon the State of North Carolina.

(d) The Board shall adopt a seal for its use, which shall bear thereon the words "North Carolina Appraisal Board". Copies of all papers in the office of the Board duly certified and authenticated by the seal of the Board shall be received in evidence in all courts and administrative bodies and with like effect as the originals.

(e) The Board may employ an Executive Director and professional and clerical staff as may be necessary to carry out the provisions of this Chapter and to put into effect the rules that the Board may promulgate. The Board shall fix salaries. The Board shall have the authority to issue to its employees credentials or other means of identification.

(f) The Board shall be entitled to the services of the Attorney General in connection with the affairs of the Board or may, in its discretion, employ an attorney to assist or represent it in the enforcement of this Chapter.

(g) The Board may prefer a complaint for violation of this Chapter before any court of competent jurisdiction, and it may take the necessary legal steps through the proper legal offices of the State to enforce the provisions of this Chapter.

(h) The Board shall have the power to acquire, hold, rent, encumber, alienate, and otherwise deal with real property in the same manner as a private person or corporation, subject only to the approval of the Governor and the Council of State. Collateral pledged by the Board for an encumbrance is limited to the assets, income, and revenues of the Board.

(i) The Board may purchase, rent, or lease equipment and supplies and purchase liability insurance or other insurance to cover the activities of the Board, its operations, or its employees. (1993, c. 419, s. 6; 1995, c. 482, s. 5; 1996, 2nd Ex. Sess., c. 15, s. 16; 2001-399, s. 1; 2008-177, s. 6(a); 2010-141, s. 3.)

§ 93E-1-6. Qualifications for registration, licensure, and certification; applications; application fees; examinations.

(a) Any person desiring to be registered as a trainee or to obtain licensure as a licensed real estate appraiser or certification as a certified real estate appraiser shall make written application to the Board on the forms as are prescribed by the Board setting forth the applicant's qualifications for registration, licensure, or certification. Each applicant shall satisfy the following qualification requirements:

(1) Each applicant for registration as a trainee shall:

a. Have obtained a high school diploma or its equivalent; and

b. Demonstrate to the Board that the applicant possesses the knowledge and competence necessary to perform appraisals of real property, by: (i) having satisfactorily completed within the five-year period immediately preceding the date application is made, a course of instruction, approved by the Board, in real estate appraisal principles and practices consisting of at least 90 hours of classroom instruction in subjects determined by the Board; and (ii) satisfying any additional qualification the Board imposes by rule, not inconsistent with any requirements imposed by the Appraisal Foundation.

(1a) Each applicant for licensure as a licensed real estate appraiser shall:

a. Hold an associate's degree or higher from an accredited college, community college, or university;

b. Demonstrate to the Board that the applicant possesses the knowledge and competence necessary to perform appraisals of real property by having satisfactorily completed a course of instruction consisting of at least 150 hours of classroom instruction in subjects determined by the Board. All instructional courses must be completed on or after January 1, 2008;

c. Present evidence satisfactory to the Board of at least 2,500 hours, or the minimum requirement as imposed by the federal government, whichever is greater, of experience in real estate appraising within the eight-year period immediately preceding the date the application is made and over a period of at least two calendar years; and

d. Satisfy the additional qualifications criteria as may be imposed by the Board by rule, not inconsistent with any requirements imposed by the federal government, or shall possess education and experience which is found by the Board in its discretion to be equivalent to the above requirements.

(2) Each applicant for certification as a certified residential real estate appraiser shall:

a. Hold a bachelor's degree from an accredited college or university;

b. Demonstrate that the applicant possesses the knowledge and competence necessary to perform appraisals of real property as the Board may prescribe by having satisfactorily completed a course of instruction, approved by the Board, in real estate appraisal principles and practices consisting of at least 200 hours. All instructional courses shall have been completed on or after January 1, 2008;

c. Present evidence satisfactory to the Board of at least 2,500 hours or the minimum requirement as imposed by the Appraisal Foundation, whichever is greater, of experience in real estate appraising within the eight-year period immediately preceding the date application is made, and over a period of at least two calendar years; and

d. Satisfy the additional qualifications criteria as may be imposed by the Board by rule, not inconsistent with any requirements imposed by the Appraisal Foundation; or

e. Possess education and experience which is found by the Board in its discretion to be equivalent to the above requirements.

(3) Each applicant for certification as a certified general real estate appraiser shall:

a. Hold a bachelor's degree or higher from an accredited college or university;

b. Demonstrate that the applicant possesses the knowledge and competence necessary to perform appraisals of all types of real property by having satisfactorily completed a course of instruction, approved by the Board, in general real estate appraisal practices consisting of at least 300 hours. All instructional courses shall have been completed on or after January 1, 2008;

c. Present evidence satisfactory to the Board of at least 3,000 hours or the minimum requirement as imposed by the Appraisal Foundation, whichever is greater, of experience in real estate appraising within the eight-year period immediately preceding the date application is made, and over a period of at least two and one-half calendar years, fifty percent (50%) of which must be in appraising nonresidential real estate; and

d. Satisfy the additional qualifications criteria as may be imposed by the Board by rule, not inconsistent with any requirements imposed by the Appraisal Foundation; or

e. Possess education or experience which is found by the Board in its discretion to be equivalent to the above requirements.

(4) Repealed by Session Laws 2001-399, s. 1.

(b) Each application for registration as a trainee or for licensure or certification as a real estate appraiser shall be accompanied by a fee of two hundred dollars ($200.00), plus any additional fee as may be necessary to defray the cost of any competency examination administered by a private testing service.

(c) Any person who files with the Board an application for licensure or certification as a real estate appraiser shall be required to pass an examination to demonstrate the person's competence.

(c1) The Board shall also make an investigation as it deems necessary into the background of the applicant to determine the applicant's qualifications with due regard to the paramount interest of the public as to the applicant's competency, honesty, truthfulness, and integrity. All applicants shall consent to a criminal history record check. Refusal to consent to a criminal history record check may constitute grounds for the Board to deny an application. The Board shall ensure that the State and national criminal history of an applicant is checked. The Board shall be responsible for providing to the North Carolina Department of Justice the fingerprints of the applicant to be checked, a form signed by the applicant consenting to the criminal history record check, and the use of fingerprints and other identifying information required by the State or National Repositories of Criminal Histories and any additional information required by the Department of Justice in accordance with G.S. 114-19.30. The Board shall keep all information obtained pursuant to this section confidential. The Board shall collect any fees required by the Department of Justice and shall remit the fees to the Department of Justice for expenses associated with conducting the criminal history record check.

(c2)   In addition, the Board may investigate and consider whether the applicant has had any disciplinary action taken against any other professional license in North Carolina or any other state, or if the applicant has committed or done any act which, if committed or done by any real estate trainee or appraiser, would be grounds under the provisions hereinafter set forth for disciplinary action including the suspension or revocation of registration, licensure, or certification, or whether the applicant has been convicted of or pleaded guilty to any criminal act. If the results of the investigation shall be satisfactory to the Board, and the applicant is otherwise qualified, then the Board shall issue to the applicant a trainee registration or certificate authorizing the applicant to act as a registered trainee real estate appraiser or certified real estate appraiser in this State.

(d)   If the applicant has not affirmatively demonstrated that the applicant meets the requirements for registration or certification, action on the application will be deferred pending a hearing before the Board. (1993, c. 419, s. 6; 1995, c. 482, s. 6; 2001-399, s. 1; 2007-506, ss. 5, 6; 2013-403, s. 2.)

§ 93E-1-6.1. Trainee supervision.

All trainees shall perform all real estate appraisal-related activities under the immediate, active, and personal supervision of a certified real estate appraiser. All appraisal reports must be signed by the appraiser who supervised the trainee. By signing the appraisal report, the appraiser accepts shared responsibility, with the trainee, for the content of and conclusions in the report. All trainees and any appraisers desiring to supervise a trainee shall complete a course in trainee supervision as required in rules adopted by the Board. (2001-399, s. 1; 2007-506, s. 7; 2013-403, s. 3.)

§ 93E-1-7. Registration, license and certificate renewal; renewal fees; continuing education; reinstatement; replacement registrations, licenses and certificates; registration, licensure, and certification history; address changes.

(a) Trainee registrations, licenses, and certificates issued under this Chapter shall expire on the 30th day of June of every year and shall become invalid after that date unless renewed prior to the expiration date by filing an application with and paying to the Executive Director of the Board the fee of two hundred dollars ($200.00). As a prerequisite to the renewal of a trainee registration or a real estate appraiser license or certificate, the trainee registration holder, the licensee, or the certificate holder must satisfy any continuing education requirements that may be prescribed by the Board under subsection (b) of this section. The members of the General Assembly are exempt from this requirement and any education program regarding trainee supervision during their term of office. The Board may adopt rules establishing a system of trainee registration, license, and certificate renewal in which trainee registrations, licenses, and certificates expire annually with varying expiration dates.

(b) The Board may by rule require, as a prerequisite to trainee registration, license, or certificate renewal, the completion of Board-approved education courses in subject matters determined by the Board, or courses determined by the Board to be equivalent to the instruction, not inconsistent with any requirements of federal authorities.

(b1) Course sponsors shall pay to the Board a fee of five dollars ($5.00) for each licensee completing an approved continuing education course conducted by the sponsor.

(b2) The Board shall not charge a course application fee, a course renewal fee, or any other fee for a continuing education course offered by a North Carolina college, university, junior college, or community or technical college accredited by the Southern Association of Colleges and Schools or an agency of the federal, State, or local government.

(c) All trainee registrations, licenses, and certificates reinstated after the expiration dates shall be subject to a late filing fee of ten dollars ($10.00) per month for each month or part thereof that the trainee registration, license, or certificate is lapsed, not to exceed one hundred twenty dollars ($120.00). The late filing fee shall be in addition to the required renewal fee. In the event a trainee, licensee, or certificate holder fails to reinstate the trainee registration, license, or certificate within 12 months after the expiration date thereof, the Board may, in its discretion, consider the person as not having been previously registered, licensed, or certified, and thereby subject to the provisions of this Chapter relating to the issuance of an original trainee registration, license, or certificate, including the examination requirements set forth herein. Applications to reinstate trainee registrations, licenses, or certificates expired for 12 or more months shall be accompanied by the fee required for an original trainee registration, license, or certificate.

(d)   Replacement trainee registrations, licenses, and certificates may be issued by the Board upon payment of ten dollars ($10.00) by the trainee, licensee, or certificate holder. Certification by the Board of the trainee registration history or the licensure or certification history of a person registered, licensed, or certified under this Chapter shall be made only after the payment of a fee of ten dollars ($10.00) to the Board. (1993, c. 419, s. 6; 1995, c. 482, s. 7; 2001-399, s. 1; 2006-259, s. 17; 2007-506, s. 8.)

§ 93E-1-8. Education program approval and fees.

(a)   The Board may by rule prescribe minimum standards for the approval and renewal of approval of schools and other course sponsors and their instructors to conduct appraiser qualifying courses required by G.S. 93E-1-6(a). Such standards may address subject matter, program structuring, instructional materials, requirements for satisfactory course completion, instructors' qualifications, and other related matters relevant to the provision of such courses in a manner that best serves the public interest. The standards may require that schools and course sponsors obtain approval for the content of qualifying courses from the Appraiser Qualifications Board of the Appraisal Foundation as part of the application process with the Appraisal Board and pay any fees directly to the Appraiser Qualifications Board as required by the Appraiser Qualifications Board for the approval.

(b)   The Board may by rule set nonrefundable fees chargeable to private real estate appraisal schools or course sponsors, including appraisal trade organizations, for the approval and annual renewal of approval of their qualifying courses required by G.S. 93E-1-6(a), or equivalent courses. The fees shall be one hundred dollars ($100.00) per course for approval and fifty dollars ($50.00) per course for renewal of approval. No fees shall be charged for the approval or renewal of approval to conduct appraiser qualifying courses where such courses are offered by a North Carolina college, university, junior college, or community or technical college accredited by the Southern Association of Colleges and Schools, or an agency of the federal, State, or local government.

(c) The Board may by rule prescribe minimum standards for the approval and annual renewal of approval of schools and other course sponsors and their instructors to conduct appraiser continuing education courses. Such standards may address subject matter, instructional materials, requirements for satisfactory course completion, minimum course length, instructors' qualifications, and other related matters relevant to the provision of such courses in a manner that best serves the public interest.

(d) Nonrefundable fees of one hundred dollars ($100.00) per course may be charged to schools and course sponsors for the approval to conduct appraiser continuing education courses and fifty dollars ($50.00) per course for renewal of approval. However, no fees shall be charged for the approval or renewal of approval to conduct appraiser continuing education courses where such courses are offered by a North Carolina college, university, junior college, or community or technical college accredited by the Southern Association of Colleges and Schools, or by an agency of the federal, State, or local government. A nonrefundable fee of fifty dollars ($50.00) per course may be charged to current or former licensees or certificate holders requesting approval by the Board of a course for continuing education credit when approval of such course has not been previously obtained by the offering school or course sponsor. (1993, c. 419, s. 6; 2007-506, s. 9; 2013-403, s. 4.)

§ 93E-1-9. Nonresident registration, licensure, and certification.

(a) An applicant from another state which offers real estate trainee registration or the equivalent, appraiser licensing or certification privileges to residents of North Carolina may become registered, licensed, or certified in North Carolina by conforming to all of the provisions of this Chapter and, in the discretion of the Board, such other terms and conditions as are required of North Carolina residents applying for trainee registration, licensure, and certification in such other state.

(b) The Board, in its discretion, may undertake to register, license, or certify on a reciprocal basis, persons registered, licensed, or certified in other states who are deemed by the Board to possess qualifications equivalent to resident North Carolina trainees or State-licensed or State-certified real estate appraisers.

(c) The Board may by rule establish a procedure for granting temporary trainee registration, appraiser licensure or certification and may charge an application fee of one hundred fifty dollars ($150.00) for temporary trainee registration, appraiser licensure, or certification.

(d) Every applicant for trainee registration, State licensure, or certification under this Chapter who is not a resident of this State shall submit with his application an irrevocable consent that service of process in any action against the applicant arising out of the applicant's activities as a registered trainee or State-licensed or State-certified real estate appraiser may be made by delivery of the process on the Executive Director of the Board. (1993, c. 419, s. 6; 2001-399, s. 1.)

§ 93E-1-10. Rule-making authority.

The Board may adopt rules not inconsistent with the provisions of this Chapter and the General Statutes of North Carolina which may be reasonably necessary to implement, administer, and enforce the provisions of this Chapter, including, but not limited to, the authority to:

(1) Prescribe forms and procedures for submitting information to the Board;

(2) Prescribe standards of practice for persons registered as a trainee, licensed or certified under this Chapter; and

(3) Prescribe standards for the operation of real estate appraiser education programs. (1993, c. 419, s. 6; 2001-399, s. 1.)

§ 93E-1-11. Register of applicants; roster of trainees, State-licensed and State-certified appraisers; financial report to Secretary of State; administrative expenses.

(a) The Executive Director of the Board shall keep a register of all applicants for State trainee registration or for State licensure or certification as real estate appraisers, showing for each the date of application, name, business or residence address, and whether the registration, license or certificate was granted or refused. The register shall be prima facie evidence of all matters received therein.

(b) The Executive Director of the Board shall also keep a current roster showing the names and places of business of all registered trainees and State-licensed and State-certified real estate appraisers, which roster shall be kept on file in the office of the Board and be open to public inspection.

(c) On or before the first day of November of each year, the Board shall file with the Secretary of State a copy of the roster of registered trainees and real estate appraisers licensed or certified by the Board and a report containing a complete statement of income received by the Board in connection with the trainee registration and the licensure and certification of real estate trainees and appraisers for the preceding fiscal year ending June 30th, attested by the affidavit of the Executive Director of the Board.

(d) In addition to those fees prescribed in this Chapter for making application for and renewing trainee registrations, appraiser licenses, and certificates, the Board may collect from applicants and holders of the licenses and certificates and remit to the appropriate agency or instrumentality of the federal government any additional fees as may be required to render North Carolina State-licensed or State-certified appraisers eligible to perform appraisals in connection with federally related transactions as well as an additional fee of twenty dollars ($20.00) to cover the administrative costs associated therewith. (1993, c. 419, s. 6; 1995, c. 482, s. 8; 2001-399, s. 1.)

§ 93E-1-12. Disciplinary action by Board.

(a) The Board may take disciplinary action against registered trainees and State-licensed or State-certified real estate appraisers. Upon its own motion or the complaint of any person, the Board may investigate the actions of any person registered as a trainee or licensed or certified as a real estate appraiser under this Chapter, any person who performs appraisals without an appropriate registration, license, or certificate, or any person who holds himself or herself out to be registered as a trainee or licensed or certified as a real estate appraiser when the person holds no registration, license, or certificate. Under no circumstances shall the Board investigate any person registered as a trainee or licensed or certified as a real estate appraiser under this Chapter upon an anonymous complaint. If the Board finds probable cause to believe that a person registered as a trainee or licensed or certified as a real estate appraiser under this Chapter has violated any of the provisions of this Chapter, the Board may hold a hearing on the allegations of misconduct.

The Board may suspend or revoke the registration, license, or certificate granted to any person under the provisions of this Chapter or reprimand any registered trainee, licensee, or certificate holder if, following a hearing or by consent, the Board finds the registered trainee, licensee, or certificate holder to have:

(1)   Procured registration, licensure, or certification pursuant to this Chapter by making a false or fraudulent representation;

(2)   Made any willful or negligent misrepresentation or any willful or negligent omission of material fact;

(3)   Accepted an appraisal assignment when the employment is contingent upon the appraiser reporting a predetermined result, analysis, or opinion, or when the fee to be paid for the performance of the appraisal assignment is contingent upon the opinion, conclusion, or valuation reached or upon consequences resulting from the appraisal assignment;

(4)   Acted or held himself or herself out as a registered trainee or a licensed or certified real estate appraiser when not so registered, licensed, or certified;

(5)   Failed as a licensed or certified real estate appraiser to actively and personally supervise any person not licensed or certified under this Chapter who assists the licensed or certified real estate appraiser in performing real estate appraisals;

(6)   Failed to make available to the Board for its inspection without prior notice, originals or true copies of all written contracts engaging the person's services to appraise real property, and all reports and supporting data assembled and formulated by the appraiser in preparing the reports;

(7)   Paid a fee or valuable consideration to any person for acts or services performed in violation of this Chapter;

(8)   Acted as a real estate appraiser in an unworthy or incompetent manner as to endanger the interest of the public;

(9) Violated any of the standards of practice for real estate appraisers or any other rule promulgated by the Board;

(10) Performed any other act which constitutes improper, fraudulent, or other dishonest conduct; or

(11) Violated any of the provisions of this Chapter.

The Executive Director of the Board shall transmit a certified copy of all final orders of the Board suspending or revoking registrations, licenses, or certificates issued under this Chapter to the clerk of superior court of the county in which the licensee or certificate holder maintains the person's principal place of business. The clerk shall enter these orders upon the judgment docket of the county.

(b) Following a hearing, or by consent, the Appraisal Board may also suspend or revoke any registration, license, or certificate issued under the provisions of this Chapter or reprimand any registered trainee, licensee, or certificate holder when:

(1) The registered trainee, licensee, or certificate holder has been convicted of or has entered a plea of guilty or no contest upon which final judgment is entered by a court of competent jurisdiction in this State, or any other state, to an offense which involves moral turpitude, in which an essential element is dishonesty, fraud, or deceit, or which, in the discretion of the Board, would reasonably affect the performance of the registered trainee, licensee, or certificate holder in the real estate appraisal business;

(2) A final civil judgment has been entered against the registered trainee, licensee, or certificate holder on grounds of fraud, misrepresentation, or deceit in the making of any appraisal of real estate;

(3) The trainee, licensee, or certificate holder has violated any of the provisions of G.S. 93E-1-13(a) when appraising his own property;

(4) The trainee, licensee, or certificate holder has had a real estate trainee registration or its equivalent, real estate appraiser license, or real estate appraiser certification suspended, revoked, or denied by a real estate licensing board in another state;

(5) The trainee, licensee, or certificate holder has had any disciplinary action taken against any other professional license in North Carolina or any other state;

(6) The trainee, licensee, or certificate holder has been adjudged mentally incompetent by a court; or

(7) The trainee, licensee, or certificate holder performs any of the duties of a real estate appraiser, including, but not limited to, site inspection and public records checks, while impaired by alcohol or drugs.

(b1) If any of the actions taken in subdivision (1), (2), or (4) through (6) of subsection (b) of this section are taken against a trainee, licensee, or certificate holder, the trainee, licensee, or certificate holder must report such actions within 60 days of the final judgment or final order in the case.

(c) When a person registered as a trainee or licensed or certified as a real estate appraiser under this Chapter is accused of any act, omission, or misconduct which would subject the person to disciplinary action, the registered trainee, licensee, or certificate holder, with the consent and approval of the Board, may surrender his or her registration, license, or certificate and all the rights and privileges pertaining to it for a period of time established by the Board of at least five years. A person who surrenders his or her registration, license, or certificate shall not thereafter be eligible for or submit any application for registration, licensure, or certification as a real estate appraiser during the period that the registration, license, or certificate is surrendered.

(c1) During the course of an investigation of a person registered as a trainee or licensed or certified as a real estate appraiser under this Chapter, the Board may send to the trainee or licensed or certified real estate appraiser a letter of inquiry asking the trainee or licensed or certified real estate appraiser to respond to the inquiry. The letter of inquiry shall state the subject matter being investigated. Upon receipt of the letter of inquiry, the trainee or licensed or certified real estate appraiser shall respond to the Board within 30 calendar days. A trainee or licensed or certified real estate appraiser shall include in the written response copies of all documents requested by the Board in the letter of inquiry.

(d) The Board shall have the power to issue subpoenas requiring the attendance of persons and the production of papers and records before the Board in any hearing, investigation, inquiry, or other proceeding conducted by it.

Upon the production of any papers, records, or documents, the Board shall have the power to authorize true copies thereof to be substituted in the permanent record of the matter in which the books, records, or documents shall have been introduced in evidence.

(e) No appraiser shall be disciplined for completing an appraisal that includes a reduced scope of work or reporting level as long as it is appropriate for the intended use and is performed in accordance with the Uniform Standards of Professional Appraisal Practice. (1993, c. 419, s. 6; 1995, c. 482, s. 9; 2001-399, s. 1; 2007-447, ss. 1, 2; 2007-506, ss. 10, 11; 2012-163, s. 5.)

§ 93E-1-12.1. Investigations and complaints.

(a) The Board may dismiss a complaint, accept a consent order, or hold a hearing, or may accept a voluntary surrender of a registration, license, or certificate or of approval as a course sponsor.

(b) Records, papers, and other documents containing information received, collected, or compiled by the Board, its members, or its employees, as a result of a complaint or investigation, shall not be considered public records within the meaning of Chapter 132 of the General Statutes. Any statement of charges contained within a notice of a hearing to be held by the Board is a public record, even though it may contain information collected and compiled as a result of a complaint or investigation against a trainee, licensee, or certificate holder or an applicant. Any record, paper, or other document admitted into evidence in a hearing held by the Board, and any final decisions and orders by the Board, including consent orders, shall be public records within the meaning of Chapter 132 of the General Statutes.

(c) The Board may inspect records maintained pursuant to this Chapter periodically, without prior notice, and may also inspect these records whenever the Board determines that they are pertinent to an investigation of any specific complaint against a person registered, licensed, or certified by the Board. (2001-399, s. 1.)

§ 93E-1-13. Penalty for violation of this Chapter.

(a) Any person who acts as, or holds himself or herself out to be, a registered trainee or a State-licensed or State-certified real estate appraiser without first obtaining a registration, license, or certificate as provided in this Chapter, or who willfully performs the acts specified in G.S. 93E-1-12(a) shall be guilty of a Class 1 misdemeanor.

(b) The Board may appear in its own name in superior court in actions for injunctive relief to prevent any person from violating the provisions of this Chapter or the rules promulgated by the Board. The superior court shall have the power to grant these injunctions whether or not criminal prosecution has been or may be instituted as a result of the violations, and whether or not the person is the holder of a registration, license, or certificate issued by the Board under this Chapter. (1993, c. 419, s. 6; 1994, Ex. Sess., c. 14, s. 49; 1995, c. 482, s. 10; 2001-399, s. 1.)

§ 93E-1-14. Referral of cases by courts.

Whenever any registered trainee, licensee, or certificate holder is adjudged by a civil or criminal court to have injured or damaged any person, partnership, association, or corporation through gross negligence, incompetency, fraud, dishonesty, or other civil or criminal misconduct, the court may, as part of its judgment or decree, order a written copy of the transcript of the record in said case to be forwarded by the clerk of court to the Board with a recommendation that the registration, license, or certificate of the registered trainee, licensee, or certificate holder be revoked or otherwise subject to disciplinary action. (1993, c. 419, s. 6; 1995, c. 482, s. 11.)

Article 2.

Real Estate Appraisal Management Companies.

§ 93E-2-1. Registration required of real estate appraisal management companies; exceptions.

Beginning January 1, 2011, it shall be unlawful for any person, corporation, partnership, sole proprietorship, subsidiary, unit, or any other business entity in this State to do any of the following without first registering with the Board under the provisions of this Article:

(1)   Directly or indirectly engage or attempt to engage in business as an appraisal management company.

(2)   Advertise or make a representation that the person or entity is engaging in or conducting business as an appraisal management company.

(3)   In any way act as or provide the services of an appraisal management company. (2010-141, s. 1.)

§ 93E-2-2. Definitions.

(a)   The following definitions apply in this Article:

(1)   Appraisal management company. - A corporation, partnership, sole proprietorship, subsidiary, unit, or other business entity that utilizes an appraisal panel or fee panel and performs, directly or indirectly, appraisal management services.

An appraisal management company does not include any of the following:

a.   Any agency of the federal government or any State or municipal government.

b.   An appraiser who enters into an agreement, whether written or otherwise, with another appraiser for the performance of an appraisal, and upon completion of the appraisal, the appraisal report is signed both by the appraiser who completed the appraisal and the appraiser who requested the completion of the appraisal, except that an appraisal management company may not avoid the requirements of this Article by requiring that an employee of the appraisal management company who is an appraiser sign an appraisal report that is completed by an appraiser who is a member of the appraisal panel of the appraisal management company.

c. Any state or federally chartered bank, farm credit system, savings institution, or credit union.

d. Any licensed real estate broker performing only activities in accordance with Article 1 of this Chapter.

e. Any officer or employee of an exempt entity described in this subdivision when acting in the scope of employment for the exempt entity.

f. Any person licensed to practice law in this State, a court-appointed personal representative or trustee who orders an appraisal in connection with a bona fide client relationship in which the person directly contracts with an independent appraiser.

(2) Appraisal management services. - Direct or indirect performance of any of the following functions on behalf of a lender, financial institution, client, or any other person:

a. Administer an appraiser panel.

b. Recruit, qualify, and/or verify licensing or certification of appraisers who are or may become part of an appraiser panel.

c. Negotiate fees and service level expectations with appraisers who are part of an appraiser panel.

d. Receive an order for an appraisal from one person and deliver the order for the appraisal to an appraiser that is part of an appraiser panel for completion.

e. Take and determine the status of orders for appraisals.

f. Conduct quality control of a completed appraisal performed by an appraiser who is part of an appraiser panel prior to the delivery of the appraisal to the person that ordered the appraisal.

g. Provide a completed appraisal performed by an appraiser who is part of an appraiser panel to one or more persons who have ordered an appraisal.

(3) Appraisal review. - The act or process of developing and communicating an opinion about the quality of another appraiser's work that was performed as

part of an appraisal assignment, except that an examination of an appraisal for grammatical, typographical, or other similar errors shall not be an appraisal review.

(4) Appraiser panel or fee panel. - A network of licensed or certified appraisers who are independent contractors to the appraisal management company that have:

a. Responded to an invitation, request, or solicitation from an appraisal management company, in any form, to perform appraisals for persons that have ordered appraisals through the appraisal management company or to perform appraisals for the appraisal management company directly, on a periodic basis, as requested and assigned by the appraisal management company; and

b. Been selected and approved by an appraisal management company to perform appraisals for any client or the appraisal management company that has ordered an appraisal through the appraisal management company or to perform appraisals for the appraisal management company directly, on a periodic basis, as assigned by the appraisal management company.

(5) Board. - The North Carolina Appraisal Board under Article 1 of this Chapter.

(6) Employee. - An individual who has an employment relationship acknowledged by both the individual and the company and is treated as an employee for purposes of compliance with federal income tax laws.

(7) Registrant. - A real estate appraisal management company registered pursuant to this Article.

(b) The definitions contained in G.S. 93E-1-4 also apply in this Article. (2010-141, s. 1.)

§ 93E-2-3. Rule-making authority.

The Board shall have the authority to adopt rules that are reasonably necessary to implement, administer, and enforce the provisions of this Article. (2010-141, s. 1.)

§ 93E-2-4. Qualifications for registration; duties of registrants.

(a) Any person or entity desiring to be registered as an appraisal management company in this State shall make written application to the Board on forms prescribed by the Board setting forth the applicant's qualifications for registration. The application shall be accompanied by the applicable fee under G.S. 93E-2-6 and any other information the Board deems necessary pursuant to rules adopted by the Board. Upon receipt of a properly completed application and fee and upon a determination by the Board that the applicant is of good moral character, the Board shall issue to the applicant a certificate of registration authorizing the applicant to act as a real estate appraisal management company in this State.

(b) The registration required by subsection (a) of this section shall include the following information:

(1) Legal name of the entity seeking registration.

(2) Business address of the entity seeking registration.

(3) Phone contact information of the entity seeking registration.

(4) If the entity is not a corporation that is domiciled in this State, the name and contact information for the company's agent for service of process in this State.

(5) The name, address, and contact information for any individual or any corporation, partnership, or other business entity that owns ten percent (10%) or more of the appraisal management company.

(6) The name, address, and contact information for the compliance manager.

(7) A certification that the entity has a system and process in place to verify that a person being added to the appraiser panel of the appraisal management company holds a license in good standing in this State pursuant to the North Carolina Appraisers Act if a license or certification is required to perform appraisals.

(8) A certification that the entity has a system in place to require that appraisers inform the appraisal management company of their areas of geographic competency, the types of properties the appraiser is competent to appraise, and the methodologies the appraiser is competent to perform.

(9) A certification that the entity has a system in place to review the work of all independent appraisers that are performing real estate appraisal services for the appraisal management company on a periodic basis to validate that the real estate appraisal services are being conducted in accordance with the Uniform Standards of Professional Appraisal Practice.

(10) A certification that the entity maintains a detailed record of each service request that it receives and the independent appraiser that performs the residential real estate appraisal services for the appraisal management company.

(10a) A certification that the entity has obtained a surety bond as required by this Article.

(11) An irrevocable Uniform Consent to Service of Process.

(12) Any other information required by the Board pursuant to G.S. 93E-2-3.

(c) Any registrant having a good faith belief that a real estate appraiser licensed or certified in this State has violated applicable law or the Uniform Standards of Professional Appraisal Practice or engaged in unethical conduct shall promptly file a complaint with the Board.

(d) Registered appraisal management companies shall pay fees to an appraiser within 30 days of the date the appraisal is transmitted by the real estate appraiser to the registrant, except in cases of noncompliance with the conditions of the engagement. In such cases, the registrant shall notify the real estate appraiser in writing that the fees will not be paid.

(e) To qualify to be registered as an appraisal management company, each individual who owns, directly or indirectly, more than ten percent (10%) of the appraisal management company shall be of good moral character, as determined by the Board, and shall submit all information the Board deems necessary pursuant to the rules adopted by the Board. Additionally, each owner shall certify that he or she has never had a license to act as an appraiser refused, denied, cancelled, or revoked by the State of North Carolina or any other state.

(f) A registered appraisal management company shall not enter into any contracts or agreements with an independent appraiser for the performance of residential real estate appraisal services for properties located in this State unless the independent appraiser is licensed or certified in good standing pursuant to the North Carolina Appraisers Act.

(g) Each applicant for registration or for a renewal of a registration shall post with the Board and maintain a surety bond in the amount of twenty-five thousand dollars ($25,000):

(1) The bond shall be in a form satisfactory to the Board.

(2) The bond will accrue to the Board for the benefit of a claimant against the registrant to secure the faithful performance of the registrant's obligations under this Article and to a real estate appraiser who has performed an appraisal for the registrant for which the appraiser has not been paid.

(3) The aggregate liability of the surety shall not exceed the principal sum of the bond.

(4) A party having a claim against the registrant may bring suit directly on the surety bond, or the Board may bring suit on behalf of the party having a claim against the registrant, either in one action or in successive actions.

(5) A claim reducing the face amount of the bond shall be annually restored upon renewal of the registrant's registration.

(6) The bond shall remain in effect until cancellation, which may occur only after 90 days written notice to the Board. Cancellation shall not affect any liability incurred or accrued during that period.

(7) The surety bond shall remain in place for no less than two years after the registrant ceases operations in this State. However, notwithstanding this provision, the Board may permit the surety bond to be reduced or eliminated prior to that time to the extent that the amount of the registrant's outstanding obligations to appraisers is reduced. (2010-141, s. 1; 2013-403, s. 5.)

§ 93E-2-5. Compliance manager.

Each appraisal management company registered under this Article shall designate a compliance manager who is responsible for ensuring the company operates in compliance with this Article. The compliance manager shall be a certified real estate appraiser on active status and in good standing, certified under Article 1 of this Chapter or under the comparable laws of another state. The appraisal management company shall file a form with the Board indicating the appraisal management company's designation of compliance manager and the individual's acceptance of the responsibility. An appraisal management company shall notify the Board of any change in the appraisal management company's compliance manager. Any appraisal management company that does not comply with this section shall have the appraisal management company's registration suspended pursuant to G.S. 93E-2-8 until the appraisal management company complies with this section. An individual operating an appraisal management company as a sole proprietorship shall be considered the compliance manager for purposes of this Article. (2010-141, s. 1.)

§ 93E-2-6. Fees and renewals.

(a) Each application for registration as an appraisal management company under this Article shall be accompanied by a registration fee in an amount set by the Board not to exceed three thousand five hundred dollars ($3,500). Registration issued under this Article shall expire on June 30, 2012, and on June 30 of each year thereafter. The registration shall become invalid after that date unless renewed before the expiration date by filing an application with and paying to the Board a fee in an amount set by the Board not to exceed two thousand dollars ($2,000).

(b) All registrations reinstated after the expiration date are subject to a late filing fee of twenty dollars ($20.00) for each month or part thereof that the registration is lapsed, not to exceed one hundred twenty dollars ($120.00). The late filing fee shall be in addition to the required renewal fee. In the event a registrant fails to reinstate the registration within six months after the expiration date, the registration shall expire and the registrant shall be required to file a new application for registration. Reinstatement of a registration shall not be retroactive.

(c) The Board may issue a replacement registration to the registrant upon payment of fifty dollars ($50.00) to the Board. The Board may certify the registration history of an appraisal management company registered under this Article upon payment of a fee of one hundred dollars ($100.00) to the Board. (2010-141, s. 1.)

§ 93E-2-7. Prohibited acts.

(a) No employee, director, officer, or agent of a registered appraisal management company or any other third party acting as joint venture partner or independent contractor shall influence or attempt to influence the development, reporting, result, or review of a real estate appraisal through coercion, extortion, collusion, compensation, inducement, intimidation, bribery, or in any other manner, including:

(1) Withholding or threatening to withhold timely payment for a real estate appraisal report.

(2) Withholding or threatening to withhold future business from a real estate appraiser or demoting or terminating or threatening to demote or terminate a real estate appraiser.

(3) Expressly or impliedly promising future business, promotions, or increased compensation for a real estate appraiser.

(4) Conditioning the ordering of a real estate appraisal report or the payment of a real estate appraisal fee, salary, or bonus on the opinion, conclusion, or valuation to be reached or on a preliminary estimate requested from a real estate appraiser.

(5) Requesting that a real estate appraiser provide an estimated, predetermined, or desired valuation in a real estate appraisal report or provide estimated values or comparable sales at any time before the appraiser's completion of the appraisal report.

(6) Providing to a real estate appraiser an anticipated, estimated, encouraged, or desired value for a subject property or a proposed or targeted amount to be loaned to the borrower. However, a real estate appraiser may be provided with a copy of the sales contract for purchase transactions.

(7) Providing to a real estate appraiser, or any entity or person related to the appraiser, stock or other financial or nonfinancial benefits.

(8) Allowing the removal of a real estate appraiser from a list of qualified appraisers used by any entity without prior written notice to the appraiser. The notice shall include written evidence of the appraiser's illegal conduct, substandard performance, or otherwise improper or unprofessional behavior or any violation of the Uniform Standards of Professional Appraisal Practice or State licensing standards.

(9) Any other act or practice that impairs or attempts to impair a real estate appraiser's independence, objectivity, or impartiality.

(10) Requesting or requiring a real estate appraiser to collect a fee from the borrower, homeowner, or any other person in the provision of real estate appraisal services.

(11) Altering, modifying, or otherwise changing a completed appraisal report submitted by an independent appraiser without the appraiser's written knowledge and consent.

(12) Using an appraisal report submitted by an independent appraiser for any other transaction.

(13) Requiring an appraiser to indemnify an appraisal management company or hold an appraisal management company harmless for any liability, damage, losses, or claims arising out of the services performed by the appraisal management company, and not the services performed by the appraiser.

(14) Requiring an appraiser to provide the company with the appraiser's digital signature or seal.

(15) Requiring or attempting to require an appraiser to prepare an appraisal if the appraiser, in the appraiser's own independent professional judgment, believes the appraiser does not have the necessary expertise for the assignment or for the specific geographic area and has notified the appraisal management company and declined the assignment.

(16) Requiring or attempting to require an appraiser to prepare an appraisal under a time frame that the appraiser, in the appraiser's own professional judgment, believes does not afford the appraiser the ability to meet all the

relevant legal and professional obligations if the appraiser has notified the appraisal management company and declined the assignment.

(b) Nothing in this section shall be construed as prohibiting an appraisal management company from requesting that a real estate appraiser:

(1) Consider additional appropriate property information.

(2) Provide further detail, substantiation, or explanation for the real estate appraiser's value conclusion, through the registrant's established dispute process.

(3) Correct errors in the real estate appraisal report. (2010-141, s. 1.)

§ 93E-2-8. Disciplinary authority.

(a) The Board may, by order, deny, suspend, revoke, or refuse to issue or renew a registration of an appraisal management company under this Article or may restrict or limit activities of a person who owns an interest in or participates in the business of an appraisal management company if the Board determines that an applicant, registrant, or any partner, member, manager, officer, director, compliance manager, or person occupying a similar status, performing similar functions, or directly or indirectly controlling the applicant or registrant has done any of the following:

(1) Filed an application for registration that, as of its effective date or as of any date after filing, contained any statement that, in light of the circumstances under which it was made, is false or misleading with respect to any material fact.

(2) Violated or failed to comply with any provision of this Article or any rules adopted by the Board.

(3) Been convicted of any felony or, within the past 10 years, been convicted of any misdemeanor involving mortgage lending or real estate appraisal or any offense involving breach of trust, moral turpitude, or fraudulent or dishonest dealing.

(4) Been permanently or temporarily enjoined by any court of competent jurisdiction from engaging in or continuing any conduct or practice involving any aspect of the real estate appraisal management business.

(5) Been the subject of an order of the Board or any other state appraiser regulatory agency denying, suspending, or revoking the person's license as a real estate appraiser.

(6) Acted as an appraisal management company while not properly licensed by the Board.

(7) Failed to pay the proper filing or renewal fee under this Article.

(8) Failed to maintain the bond required by G.S. 93E-2-4.

(b) The Board may, by order, summarily postpone or suspend the registration of an appraisal management company pending final determination of any proceeding under this section. Upon entering the order, the Board shall promptly notify the registrant that the order has been entered and the reasons for the order. The Board shall calendar a hearing within 15 days after the Board receives a written request for a hearing. If a registrant does not request a hearing, the order shall remain in effect until the order is modified or vacated by the Board. If a hearing is requested, after notice of and opportunity for hearing, the Board may modify or vacate the order or extend the order until the Board makes its final determination.

(c) The Board may, by order, impose a civil penalty upon a registrant or any partner, officer, director, compliance manager, or other person occupying a similar status or performing similar functions on behalf of a registrant for any violation of this Article. The civil penalty shall not exceed ten thousand dollars ($10,000) for each violation of this Article.

(d) In addition to other powers under this Article, upon finding that any action of a person is in violation of this Article, the Board may order the person to cease from the prohibited action. If the person subject to the order fails to appeal the order of the Board or the person appeals the order and the appeal is denied or dismissed and the person continues to engage in the prohibited action in violation of the Board's order, the person shall be subject to a civil penalty of up to twenty-five thousand dollars ($25,000) for each violation of the order. The penalty provision of this section shall be in addition to and not in lieu of any other provision of law applicable to a registrant for the registrant's failure to comply with an order of the Board.

(e)   Unless otherwise provided, all actions and hearings under this Article shall be governed by Article 3A of Chapter 150B of the General Statutes.

(f)   When a registrant is accused of any act, omission, or misconduct that would subject the registrant to disciplinary action, the registrant, with the consent and approval of the Board, may surrender the registrant's registration and all the rights and privileges pertaining to the registrant for a minimum period of five years. A person who surrenders a registration shall not be eligible for or submit any application for registration during the period the registration is surrendered.

(g)   If the Board has reasonable grounds to believe that an appraisal management company has violated the provisions of this Article or that facts exist that would be the basis for an order against an appraisal management company, the Board may at any time, either personally or by a person duly designated by the Board, investigate or examine the books, accounts, records, and files of any registrant or other person relating to the complaint or matter under investigation.

(g1)   The Board may require any registrant or other person to submit a criminal history record check and a set of that person's fingerprints in connection with any examination or investigation. Refusal to submit the requested criminal history record check or a set of fingerprints shall be grounds for disciplinary action. The reasonable cost of the investigation or examination shall be charged against the registrant.

(h)   The Board shall have the power to issue subpoenas requiring the attendance of persons and the production of papers and records before the Board in any hearing, investigation, inquiry, or other proceeding conducted by the Board. Upon the production of any papers, records, or documents, the Board shall have the power to authorize true copies of the papers, records, or documents to be substituted in the permanent record of the matter in which the books, records, or documents shall have been introduced in evidence.

(i)   Upon a request by the Board and with reasonable notice, an appraisal management company shall produce within this State all books and records related to real estate appraisal management services provided for properties located in North Carolina. (2010-141, s. 1; 2013-403, ss. 6, 7.)

§ 93E-2-9. Records.

(a)   The Board shall maintain a list of all applicants for registration under this Article that includes for each applicant the date of application, the name and primary business location of the applicant, and whether the registration was granted or refused.

(b)   The Board shall maintain a current roster showing the names and places of business of all registered appraisal management companies that lists the appraisal management companies' respective officers and directors. The rosters shall: (i) be kept on file in the office of the Board; (ii) contain information regarding all orders or other action taken against the company, its officers, and other persons; and (iii) be open to public inspection.

(b1)   The Board shall report annually by December 31 to the Department of Revenue the following information about registered appraisal management companies:

(1)   Name and name used to do business in the State.

(2)   Main address of company.

(3)   Name and address of agent for service of process in the State if not domiciled in the State.

(4)   Legal structure, such as domestic corporation, foreign corporation, domestic partnership, or foreign partnership.

(5)   Employer identification number or social security number.

(6)   Secretary of State identification number if required.

(c)   Every registered appraisal management company shall maintain the accounts, correspondence, memoranda, papers, books, and other records related to services provided by the appraisal management company as prescribed in rules adopted by the Board, including in electronic form. All records shall be preserved for five years unless the Board, by rule, prescribes otherwise for particular types of records.

(d)   If the information contained in any document filed with the Board is or becomes inaccurate or incomplete in any material respect, the appraisal management company shall promptly file a correcting amendment to the information contained in the document. (2010-141, s. 1; 2012-65, s. 1.)

§ 93E-2-10. Penalty; injunctive relief.

(a)   Any person violating the provisions of this Article shall be guilty of a Class 1 misdemeanor.

(b)   The Board may appear in its own name in superior court in actions for injunctive relief to prevent any person from violating the provisions of this Article or rules adopted by the Board. The superior court shall have the power to grant these injunctions whether criminal prosecution has been or may be instituted as a result of the violations or whether the person is the holder of a registration issued by the Board under this Article. (2010-141, s. 1.)

§ 93E-2-11. Criminal history record checks of applicants or registrants for registration as appraisal management companies.

(a)   Definitions. - The following definitions shall apply in this section:

(1)   Applicant. - A person applying for registration as an appraisal management company pursuant to G.S. 93E-2-4.

(2)   Criminal history. - A history of conviction of a state or federal crime, whether a misdemeanor or felony, that bears on an applicant's fitness for registration to act as a real estate appraisal management company. The crimes include the criminal offenses set forth in any of the following Articles of Chapter 14 of the General Statutes: Article 5, Counterfeiting and Issuing Monetary Substitutes; Article 5A, Endangering Executive and Legislative Officers; Article 6, Homicide; Article 7A, Rape and Other Sex Offenses; Article 8, Assaults; Article 10, Kidnapping and Abduction; Article 13, Malicious Injury or Damage by Use of Explosive or Incendiary Device or Material; Article 14, Burglary and Other Housebreakings; Article 15, Arson and Other Burnings; Article 16, Larceny; Article 17, Robbery; Article 18, Embezzlement; Article 19, False Pretenses and Cheats; Article 19A, Obtaining Property or Services by False or Fraudulent Use of Credit Device or Other Means; Article 19B, Financial Transaction Card Crime Act; Article 20, Frauds; Article 21, Forgery; Article 26,

Offenses Against Public Morality and Decency; Article 26A, Adult Establishments; Article 27, Prostitution; Article 28, Perjury; Article 29, Bribery; Article 31, Misconduct in Public Office; Article 35, Offenses Against the Public Peace; Article 36A, Riots, Civil Disorders, and Emergencies; Article 39, Protection of Minors; Article 40, Protection of the Family; Article 59, Public Intoxication; and Article 60, Computer-Related Crime. The crimes also include possession or sale of drugs in violation of the North Carolina Controlled Substances Act in Article 5 of Chapter 90 of the General Statutes and alcohol-related offenses, including sale to underage persons in violation of G.S. 18B-302 or driving while impaired in violation of G.S. 20-138.1 through G.S. 20-138.5. In addition to the North Carolina crimes listed in this subdivision, such crimes also include similar crimes under federal law or under the laws of other states.

(b) The Board may require that an applicant for registration as an appraisal management company or a registrant consent to a criminal history record check. Refusal to consent to a criminal history record check may constitute grounds for the Board to deny registration to an applicant or registrant. The Board shall ensure that the State and national criminal history of an applicant or registrant is checked. The Board shall be responsible for providing to the North Carolina Department of Justice the fingerprints of the applicant or registrant to be checked, a form signed by the applicant or registrant consenting to the criminal record check and the use of fingerprints and other identifying information required by the State or National Repositories of Criminal Histories, and any additional information required by the Department of Justice in accordance with G.S. 114-19.30. The Board shall keep all information obtained pursuant to this section confidential. The Board shall collect any fees required by the Department of Justice and shall remit the fees to the Department of Justice for expenses associated with conducting the criminal history record check.

(c) If an applicant's or registrant's criminal history record check reveals one or more convictions listed under subdivision (a)(2) of this section, the conviction shall not automatically bar registration. The Board shall consider all of the following factors regarding the conviction:

(1) The level of seriousness of the crime.

(2) The date of the crime.

(3) The age of the person at the time of the conviction.

(4) The circumstances surrounding the commission of the crime, if known.

(5) The nexus between the criminal conduct of the person and the job duties of the position to be filled.

(6) The person's prison, jail, probation, parole, rehabilitation, and employment records since the date the crime was committed.

(7) The subsequent commission by the person of a crime listed in subdivision (a)(2) of this section.

If, after reviewing these factors, the Board determines that the applicant's or registrant's criminal history disqualifies the applicant or registrant for registration, the Board may deny registration of the applicant or registrant. The Board may disclose to the applicant or registrant information contained in the criminal history record check that is relevant to the denial. The Board shall not provide a copy of the criminal history record check to the applicant or registrant. The applicant or registrant shall have the right to appear before the Board to appeal the Board's decision. However, an appearance before the full Board shall constitute an exhaustion of administrative remedies in accordance with Chapter 150B of the General Statutes.

(d) Limited Immunity. - The Board, its officers, and employees, acting in good faith and in compliance with this section, shall be immune from civil liability for denying registration to an applicant or registrant based on information provided in the applicant's or registrant's criminal history record check. (2010-141, s. 1; 2012-12, s. 2(mm).)

Chapter 94.

Apprenticeship.

§ 94-1. Purpose.

The purposes of this Chapter are: to open to young people the opportunity to obtain training that will equip them for profitable employment and citizenship; to set up, as a means to this end, a program of voluntary apprenticeship under approved apprentice agreements providing facilities for their training and guidance in the arts and crafts of industry and trade, with parallel instruction in related and supplementary education; to promote employment opportunities for young people under conditions providing adequate training and reasonable earnings; to relate the supply of skilled workers to employment demands; to establish standards for apprentice training; to establish an Apprenticeship Council and apprenticeship committees and sponsors to assist in effectuating the purposes of this Chapter; to provide for a Director of Apprenticeship within the Department of Commerce; to provide for reports to the legislature and to the public regarding the status of apprentice training in the State; to establish a procedure for the determination of apprentice agreement controversies; and to accomplish related ends. (1939, c. 229, s. 1; 1979, c. 673, s. 1; 2013-330, s. 2(c).)

§ 94-2. Apprenticeship Council.

The Secretary of Commerce shall appoint an Apprenticeship Council composed of four representatives each from employer and employee organizations respectively and three representatives from the public at large. One State official designated by the Department of Public Instruction and one State official designated by the Department of Community Colleges shall be a member ex officio of said council, without vote. The terms of office of the members of the Apprenticeship Council first appointed by the Secretary of Commerce shall expire as designated by the Secretary at the time of making the appointment: two representatives each of employers and employees, being appointed for one year and one representative of the public at large being appointed for two years; and one representative each of employers, employees, and the public at large being appointed for a term of three years. Any member appointed to fill a vacancy occurring prior to the expiration of the term of his predecessor shall be appointed for the remainder of said term. Each member of the Council not otherwise compensated by public moneys, shall be reimbursed for transportation and shall receive such per diem compensation as is provided generally for boards and commissions under the biennial maintenance appropriation acts for each day spent in attendance at meetings of the Apprenticeship Council. The Secretary of Commerce shall annually appoint one member of the Council to act as its chairman.

The Apprenticeship Council shall meet at the call of the Secretary of Commerce and shall aid him in formulating policies for the effective administration of this Chapter. Subject to the approval of the Secretary, the Apprenticeship Council shall establish standards for apprentice agreement which in no case shall be lower than those prescribed by this Chapter, shall issue such rules and regulations as may be necessary to carry out the intent and purposes of said Chapter, and shall perform such other functions as the Secretary may direct. Not less than once a year the Apprenticeship Council shall make a report through the Secretary of its activities and findings to the legislature and to the public. (1939, c. 229, s. 2; 1973, c. 476, s. 138; 1977, c. 896; 2013-330, s. 2(c).)

§ 94-3. Director of Apprenticeship.

The Secretary of Commerce is hereby directed to appoint a Director of Apprenticeship which appointment shall be subject to the confirmation of the State Apprenticeship Council by a majority vote. The Secretary of Commerce is further authorized to appoint and employ such clerical, technical, and professional help as shall be necessary to effectuate the purposes of this Chapter. (1939, c. 229, s. 3; 2013-330, s. 2(c).)

§ 94-4. Powers and duties of Director of Apprenticeship.

The Director, under the supervision of the Secretary of Commerce and with the advice and guidance of the Apprenticeship Council is authorized to administer the provisions of this Chapter; in cooperation with the Apprenticeship Council and apprenticeship committees and sponsors, to set up conditions and training standards for apprentice agreements, which conditions or standards shall in no case be lower than those prescribed by this Chapter; to act as secretary of the Apprenticeship Council; to approve for the Council if in his opinion approval is for the best interest of the apprenticeship any apprentice agreement which meets the standards established under this Chapter; to terminate or cancel any apprentice agreement in accordance with the provisions of such agreement; to keep a record of apprentice agreements and their disposition; to issue certificates of completion of apprenticeship; and to perform such other duties as are necessary to carry out the intent of this Chapter, including other on-job training necessary for emergency and critical civilian production: Provided, that the administration and supervision of related and supplemental instruction for apprentices, coordination of instruction with job experiences, and the selection and training of teachers and coordinators for such instruction shall be the responsibility of State and local boards responsible for vocational education. (1939, c. 229, s. 4; 1951, c. 1031, s. 1; 1979, c. 673, s. 2; 2013-330, s. 2(c).)

§ 94-5. Apprenticeship committees and program sponsors.

(a) As used in this Chapter:

(1) "Apprenticeship program" means a plan containing all terms and conditions for the qualification, recruitment, selection, employment, and training of apprentices, including such matters as the requirement for a written apprenticeship agreement.

(2) "Apprenticeship agreement" means a written agreement between an apprentice and either his employer or an apprenticeship committee or sponsor acting as agent for employer(s), which agreement satisfies the requirements of G.S. 94-7.

(3) "Sponsor" means any person, firm, corporation, organization, association or committee operating an apprenticeship program and in whose name the apprenticeship program is approved.

(4) "Employer" means any person, firm, corporation or organization employing an apprentice whether or not such person, firm, corporation or organization is a party to an apprenticeship agreement with the apprentice.

(5) "Apprenticeship committee" means those persons designated by the sponsor, and approved by the Apprenticeship Council, to act for it in the administration of the apprenticeship program. A committee may be "joint," i.e., it is composed of an equal number of representatives of the employer(s) and of the employees represented by a bona fide collective bargaining agent(s) and has been established to conduct, operate or administer an apprenticeship program and enter into apprenticeship agreements with apprentices. A committee may be "unilateral" or "nonjoint" which shall mean a program sponsor in which employees or a bona fide collective bargaining agent is not a party.

(b) An apprenticeship committee may be appointed by the Apprenticeship Council in any trade or group of trades in a city or trade area, whenever the apprentice training needs of such trade or group of trades justifies such establishment.

(c) The function of the apprenticeship committee, or sponsor when there is no apprenticeship committee, shall be: to cooperate with school authorities in regard to the education of apprentices; in accordance with the standards set up by the apprenticeship committee for the same trade or group of trades, where such committee has been appointed, to work in an advisory capacity with employers and employees in matters regarding schedule of operations, application of wage rates, and working conditions for apprentices and to specify the number of apprentices which shall be employed locally in the trade under the apprenticeship agreements under this Chapter; and to adjust apprenticeship disputes, subject to the approval of the director; to ascertain the prevailing rate for journeymen in the city or trade area and specify the graduated scale of wages applicable to apprentices in such trade in such area; to ascertain employment needs in such trade or group of trades and specify the appropriate current ratio of apprentices to journeymen; and to make recommendations for the general good of apprentices engaged in the trade or trades represented by the committee. An apprenticeship committee may appoint a representative and delegate to such representative the authority for implementation and performance of any standards adopted by the committee pursuant to any of the aforementioned functions. (1939, c. 229, s. 5; 1979, c. 673, s. 3.)

§ 94-6. Definition of an apprentice.

The term "apprentice," as used herein, shall mean a person at least 16 years of age who is covered by a written apprenticeship agreement approved by the Apprenticeship Council, which apprenticeship agreement provides for not less than 2,000 hours of reasonably continuous employment for such person for his participation in an approved schedule of work experience and for organized, related supplemental instruction in technical subjects related to the trade. A minimum of 144 hours of related supplemental instruction for each year of apprenticeship is recommended. The required hours for apprenticeship agreements and the recommended hours for related supplemental instruction may be decreased or increased in accordance with standards adopted by the apprenticeship committee or sponsor, subject to approval of the Secretary of Commerce. (1939, c. 229, s. 6; 1979, c. 479, ss. 1, 2; c. 673, s. 4; 2013-330, s. 2(c).)

§ 94-7. Contents of agreement.

Every apprentice agreement entered into under this Chapter shall contain:

(1)   The names of the contracting parties.

(2) The date of birth of the apprentice.

(3) A statement of the trade, craft, or business which the apprentice is to be taught, and the time at which the apprenticeship will begin and end.

(4) A statement showing (i) the number of hours to be spent by the apprentice in work on the job, and (ii) the number of hours to be spent in related and supplemental instruction, which is recommended to be not less than 144 hours per year: Provided, that in no case shall the combined weekly hours of work and of required related and supplemental instruction of the apprentice exceed the maximum number of hours of work prescribed by law for a person of the age of the apprentice.

(5) A statement setting forth a schedule of the processes in the trade or industry division in which the apprentice is to be taught and the approximate time to be spent at each process.

(6) A statement of the graduated scale of wages to be paid the apprentice and whether the required school time shall be compensated.

(7) A statement providing for a period of probation of not more than 500 hours of employment and instruction extending over not more than four months, during which time the apprentice agreement shall be terminated by the Director at the request in writing of either party, and providing that after such probationary period the apprentice agreement may be terminated by the Director by mutual agreement of all parties thereto, or canceled by the Director for good and sufficient reason. The Council at the request of a joint apprentice committee may lengthen the period of probation.

(8) A provision that all controversies or differences concerning the apprentice agreement which cannot be adjusted locally in accordance with G.S. 94-5 shall be submitted to the Director for determination.

(9) A provision that an employer who is unable to fulfill his obligation under the apprentice agreement may with the approval of the Director transfer such contract to any other employer: Provided, that the apprentice consents and that such other employer agrees to assume the obligations of said apprentice agreement.

(10) Such additional terms and conditions as may be prescribed or approved by the Director not inconsistent with the provisions of this Chapter. (1939, c. 229, s. 7; 1945, c. 729, s. 1; 1977, c. 550, s. 1; 1979, c. 673, s. 5.)

§ 94-8. Approval of apprentice agreements; signatures.

No apprentice agreement under this Chapter shall be effective until approved by the Director. Every apprentice agreement shall be signed by the employer, or by an association of employers or an organization of employees as provided in G.S. 94-9, and by the apprentice, and if the apprentice is a minor, by either of the minor's lawful parents, or by any person, agency, organization or institution standing in loco parentis. Where a minor enters into an apprentice agreement under this Chapter for a period of training extending into his majority, the apprentice agreement shall likewise be binding for such a period as may be covered during the apprentice's majority. (1939, c. 229, s. 8; 1977, c. 550, s. 2.)

§ 94-9. Rotation of employment.

For the purpose of providing greater diversity of training or continuity of employment, any apprentice agreement made under this Chapter may in the discretion of the Director of Apprenticeship be signed by an association of employers or an organization of employees instead of by an individual employer. In such a case, the apprentice agreement shall expressly provide that the association of employers or organization of employees does not assume the obligation of an employer but agrees to use its best endeavors to procure employment and training for such apprentice with one or more employers who will accept full responsibility, as herein provided, for all the terms and conditions of employment and training set forth in said agreement between the apprentice and employer association or employee organization during the period of each such employment. The apprentice agreement in such a case shall also expressly provide for the transfer of the apprentice, subject to the approval of the Director, to such employer or employers who shall sign in written agreement with the apprentice, and if the apprentice is a minor with his parent or guardian, as specified in G.S. 94-8, contracting to employ said apprentice for the whole or a definite part of the total period of apprenticeship under the terms and conditions of employment and training set forth in the said agreement entered into between the apprentice and employer association or employee organization. (1939, c. 229, s. 9.)

§ 94-10. Repealed by Session Laws 1945, c. 729, s. 2.

§ 94-11. Limitation.

Nothing in this Chapter or in any apprentice agreement approved under this Chapter shall operate to invalidate any apprenticeship provision in any collective agreement between employers and employees, setting up higher apprenticeship standards; provided, that none of the terms or provisions of this Chapter shall apply to any person, firm, corporation or crafts unless, until, and only so long as such person, firm, corporation or crafts voluntarily elects that the terms and provisions of this Chapter shall apply. Any person, firm, corporation or crafts terminating an apprenticeship agreement shall notify the Director of Apprenticeship. (1939, c. 229, s. 11; 1945, c. 729, s. 3.)

§ 94-12. Fees.

The following fees are imposed on each apprentice who is covered by a written apprenticeship agreement entered into under this Chapter: (i) a new registration fee of fifty dollars ($50.00); and (ii) an annual fee of fifty dollars ($50.00). The fees are departmental receipts and must be applied to the costs of administering the apprenticeship program. The Secretary of Commerce may adopt rules pursuant to Chapter 150B of the General Statutes to implement this section. (2009-451, s. 12.1; 2010-31, s. 12.1; 2013-330, s. 2(c).)

Chapter 95.

Department of Labor and Labor Regulations.

Article 1.

Department of Labor.

§ 95-1. Department of Labor established.

A Department of Labor is hereby created and established. The duties of said Department shall be exercised and discharged under the supervision and direction of a commissioner, to be known as the Commissioner of Labor. (Rev., s. 3909; 1919, c. 314, s. 4; C.S., s. 7309; 1931, c. 312, s. 1.)

§ 95-2. Election of Commissioner; term; salary; vacancy.

The Commissioner of Labor shall be elected by the people in the same manner as is provided for the election of the Secretary of State. The term of office of the Commissioner of Labor shall be four years, and the salary of the Commissioner of Labor shall be set by the General Assembly in the Current Operations Appropriations Act. Any vacancy in the office shall be filled by the Governor, until the next general election. The office of the Department of Labor shall be kept in the City of Raleigh and shall be provided for as are other public offices of the State. In addition to the salary set by the General Assembly in the Current Operations Appropriations Act, longevity pay shall be paid on the same basis as is provided to employees of the State who are subject to the North Carolina Human Resources Act. (Rev., ss. 3909, 3910; 1919, c. 314, s. 4; C.S., s. 7310; 1931, c. 312, s. 2; 1933, c. 282, s. 5; 1935, c. 293; 1937, c. 415; 1939, c. 349; 1943, c. 499, s. 2; 1947, c. 1041; 1949, c. 1278; 1953, c. 1, s. 2; 1957, c. 1; 1963, c. 1178, s. 5; 1967, c. 1130; c. 1237, s. 5; 1969, c. 1214, s. 5; 1971, c. 912, s. 5; 1973, c. 778, s. 5; 1975, 2nd Sess., c. 983, s. 20; 1977, c. 802, s. 42.11; 1983, c. 761, s. 207; 1983 (Reg. Sess., 1984), c. 1034, s. 164; 1987, c. 738, s. 32(b); 2013-382, s. 9.1(c).)

§ 95-3. Divisions of Department; Commissioner; administrative officers.

The Department of Labor shall consist of the following officers, divisions and sections:

A Commissioner of Labor.

A Division of Standards and Inspections.

A Division of Statistics.

Each division shall be in the charge of a chief administrative officer and shall be organized under such rules and regulations as the Commissioner of Labor and the head of the division concerned, with the approval of the Governor, shall prescribe and promulgate. The Commissioner of Labor, with the approval of the Governor, may make provision for one person to act as chief administrative officer of two or more divisions, when such is deemed advisable. The chief administrative officers of the several divisions shall be appointed by the Commissioner of Labor with the approval of the Governor. The Commissioner of Labor, with the approval of the Governor may combine or consolidate the activities of two or more of the divisions of the Department, or provide for the setting up of other divisions when such action shall be deemed advisable for the more efficient and economical administration of the work and duties of the Department. (1931, c. 277; c. 312, s. 4; 1933, c. 46; 1963, c. 313, s. 2.)

§ 95-4. Authority, powers and duties of Commissioner.

The Commissioner of Labor shall be the executive and administrative head of the Department of Labor. In addition to the other powers and duties conferred upon the Commissioner of Labor by this Article, the said Commissioner shall have authority and be charged with the duty:

(1) To appoint and assign to duty such clerks, stenographers, and other employees in the various divisions of the Department, with approval of said director of division, as may be necessary to perform the work of the Department, and fix their compensation, subject to the approval of the Department of Administration. The Commissioner of Labor may assign or transfer stenographers, or clerks, from one division to another, or inspectors from one division to another, or combine the clerical force of two or more divisions, or require from one division assistance in the work of another division, as he may consider necessary and advisable: Provided, however, the provisions of this subdivision shall not apply to the Industrial Commission, or the Division of Workers' Compensation.

(2) To make such rules and regulations with reference to the work of the Department and of the several divisions thereof as shall be necessary to properly carry out the duties imposed upon the said Commissioner and the work of the Department; such rules and regulations to be made subject to the approval of the Governor.

(3) To take and preserve testimony, examine witnesses, administer oaths, and under proper restriction enter any public institution of the State, any factory, store, workshop, laundry, public eating house or mine, and interrogate any person employed therein or connected therewith, or the proper officer of a corporation, or file a written or printed list of interrogatories and require full and complete answers to the same, to be returned under oath within 30 days of the receipt of said list of questions.

(4) To secure the enforcement of all laws relating to the inspection of factories, mercantile establishments, mills, workshops, public eating places, and commercial institutions in the State. To aid him in the work, he shall have power to appoint factory inspectors and other assistants. The duties of such inspectors and other assistants shall be prescribed by the Commissioner of Labor.

(5) To visit and inspect, personally or through his assistants and factory inspectors, at reasonable hours, as often as practicable, the factories, mercantile establishments, mills, workshops, public eating places, and commercial institutions in the State, where goods, wares, or merchandise are manufactured, purchased, or sold, at wholesale or retail.

(6) To enforce the provisions of this section and to prosecute all violations of laws relating to the inspection of factories, mercantile establishments, mills, workshops, public eating houses, and commercial institutions in this State before any court of competent jurisdiction. It shall be the duty of the district attorney of the proper district upon the request of the Commissioner of Labor, or any of his assistants or deputies, to prosecute any violation of a law, which it is made the duty of the said Commissioner of Labor to enforce. (1925, c. 288; 1931, c. 277; c. 312, ss. 5, 6; 1933, cc. 46, 244; 1945, c. 723, s. 2; 1957, c. 269, s. 1; 1973, c. 47, s. 2; c. 108, s. 41; 1991, c. 636, s. 3.)

§ 95-5. Annual report to Governor; recommendation as to legislation needed.

The Commissioner of Labor shall annually, on or before the first day of January, file with the Governor a report covering the activities of the Department, and the report so made on or before January 1 of the years in which the General Assembly shall be in session shall be accompanied by recommendations of the Commissioner with reference to such changes in the law applying to or affecting industrial and labor conditions as the Commissioner may deem advisable. The report of the Commissioner of Labor shall be printed and distributed in such manner and form as the Director of the Budget shall authorize. (1931, c. 312, s. 7.)

§ 95-6. Statistical report to Governor; publication of information given by employers.

It shall be the duty of the Commissioner of Labor to collect in the manner herein provided for, and to assort, systematize, and present to the Governor as a part of the report provided for in G.S. 95-5, statistical details relating to all divisions of labor in the State, and particularly concerning the following: the extent of unemployment, the hours of labor, the number of employees and sex thereof, and the daily wages earned; the conditions with respect to labor in all manufacturing establishments, hotels, stores, and workshops; and the industrial, social, educational, moral, and sanitary conditions of the labor classes, in the productive industries of the State. Such statistical details shall include the names of firms, companies, or corporations, where the same are located, the kind of goods produced or manufactured, the period of operation of each year, the number of employees, male or female, the number engaged in clerical work and the number engaged in manual labor, with the classification of the number of each sex engaged in such occupation and the average daily wage paid each: Provided, that the Commissioner shall not, nor shall anyone connected with his office, publish or give or permit to be published or given to any person the individual statistics obtained from any employer, and all such statistics, when published, shall be published in connection with other similar statistics and be set forth in aggregates and averages. (1931, c. 312, s. 8.)

§ 95-7. Power of Commissioner to compel the giving of such information; refusal as contempt.

The Commissioner of Labor, or his authorized representative, for the purpose of securing the statistical details referred to in G.S. 95-6, shall have power to examine witnesses on oath, to compel the attendance of witnesses and the giving of such testimony and production of such papers as shall be necessary to enable him to gain the necessary information. Upon the refusal of any witness to comply with the requirements of the Commissioner of Labor or his representative in this respect, it shall be the duty of any judge of the superior court, upon the application of the Commissioner of Labor, or his representative, to order the witness to show cause why he should not comply with the requirements of the said Commissioner, or his representative, if in the discretion of the judge such requirement is reasonable and proper. Refusal to comply with the order of the judge of the superior court shall be dealt with as for contempt of court. (1931, c. 312, s. 9.)

§ 95-8. Employers required to make statistical report to Commissioner; refusal as contempt.

It shall be the duty of every owner, operator, or manager of every factory, workshop, mill, mine, or other establishment, where labor is employed, to make to the Department, upon blanks furnished by said Department, such reports and returns as the said Department may require, for the purpose of compiling such labor statistics as are authorized by this Article, and the owner or business manager shall make such reports and returns within the time prescribed therefor by said Commissioner, and shall certify to the correctness of the same. Upon the refusal of any person, firm, or corporation to comply with the provisions of this section, it shall be the duty of any judge of the superior court, upon application by the Commissioner or by any representative of the Department authorized by him, to order the person, firm, or corporation to show cause why he or it should not comply with the provisions of this section. Refusal to comply with the order of the judge of the superior court shall be dealt with as for contempt of court. (1931, c. 312, s. 10.)

§ 95-9. Employers to post notice of laws.

It shall be the duty of every employer to keep posted in a conspicuous place in every room where five or more persons are employed a printed notice stating the provisions of the law relative to the employment of adult persons and children and the regulation of hours and working conditions. The Commissioner of Labor shall furnish the printed form of such notice upon request. (1933, c. 244, s. 6.)

§ 95-9.1. Notice of employer's rights during farm inspections.

The Department of Labor shall, in consultation with farm organizations and the Department of Agriculture and Consumer Services, prepare a notice to be delivered to the employer, at the beginning of an inspection of any premises engaged in agricultural employment in this State. The notice shall advise the employer of any rights or recourse to which the employer and employees are entitled under State or federal law in connection with any inspection of the employer's premises or operation conducted by the Department of Labor. The Department shall deliver the notice to the employer at the beginning of an inspection of premises used for agricultural employment. For purposes of this section, the term "agricultural employment" shall have the same meaning as defined in G.S. 95-223(1). (2012-187, s. 10.1(b).)

§ 95-10. Repealed by Session Laws 1963, c. 313, s. 1.

§ 95-11. Division of Standards and Inspection.

(a) The chief administrative officer of the Division of Standards and Inspection shall be known as the Director of the Division. It shall be his duty, under the direction and supervision of the Commissioner of Labor, and under rules and regulations to be adopted by the Department as herein provided, to make or cause to be made all necessary inspections to see that all laws, rules and regulations concerning the safety and well-being of labor are promptly and effectively carried out.

(b) The Division shall make studies and investigations of special problems connected with the labor of women and children, and create the necessary organization, and appoint an adequate number of investigators, with the consent of the Commissioner of Labor and the approval of the Governor; and the Director of said Division, under the supervision and direction of the Commissioner of Labor and under such rules and regulations as shall be prescribed by said Commissioner, with the approval of the Governor, shall perform all duties devolving upon the Department of Labor, or the Commissioner of Labor with relation to the enforcement of laws, rules, and regulations governing the employment of women and children.

(c) The Director shall report annually to the Commissioner of Labor the activities of the Division, with such recommendations as may be considered advisable for the improvement of the working conditions for women and children.

(d)   The Division shall collect and collate information and statistics concerning the location, estimated and actual horsepower and condition of valuable water powers, developed and undeveloped, in this State; also concerning farmlands and farming, the kinds, character, and quantity of the annual farm products in this State; also of timber lands and timbers, truck gardening, dairying, and such other information and statistics concerning the agricultural and industrial welfare of the citizens of this State as may be deemed to be of interest and benefit to the public. The Director shall also perform the duties of mine inspector as prescribed in the Chapter on Mines and Quarries.

(e)   The Division shall conduct such research and carry out such studies as will contribute to the health, safety, and general well-being of the working classes of the State. The finding of such investigations, with the approval of the Commissioner of Labor and the Governor and the cooperation of the chief administrative officer of the Division or Divisions directly concerned, shall be promulgated as rules and regulations governing work places and working conditions. All recommendations and suggestions pertaining to health, safety, and well-being of employees shall be transmitted to the Commissioner of Labor in an annual report which shall cover the work of the Division of Standards and Inspection.

(f)   The Division shall make, promulgate and enforce rules and regulations for the protection of employees from accident and from occupational disease; and shall upon request, and after such investigation as it deems proper, issue certificates of compliance to such employers as are found by it to be in compliance with the rules and regulations made and promulgated in accordance with the provisions of this paragraph. (1931, c. 312, s. 12; c. 426; 1935, c. 131.)

§ 95-12. Division of Statistics.

The Division of Statistics shall be in charge of a Chief Statistician. It shall be his duty, under the direction and supervision of the Commissioner of Labor, to collect, assort, systematize, and print all statistical details relating to all divisions of labor in this State as is provided in G.S. 95-6. (1931, c. 312, s. 13.)

§ 95-13. Enforcement of rules and regulations.

In the event any person, firm or corporation shall, after notice by the Commissioner of Labor, violate any of the rules or regulations promulgated under the authority of this Article or any laws amendatory hereof relating to safety devices, or measures, the Attorney General of the State, upon the request of the Commissioner of Labor, may take appropriate action in the civil courts of the State to enforce such rules and regulations. Upon request of the Attorney General, any district attorney of the State of North Carolina in whose district such rule or regulation is violated may perform the duties hereinabove required of the Attorney General. (1939, c. 398; 1973, c. 47, s. 2.)

§ 95-14. Agreements with certain federal agencies for enforcement of Fair Labor Standards Act.

The North Carolina State Department of Labor may and it is hereby authorized to enter into agreements with the Wage and Hour Division, and the Children's Bureau, United States Department of Labor, for assistance and cooperation in the enforcement within this State of the act of Congress known as the Fair Labor Standards Act of 1938, approved June 25, 1938, and is further authorized to accept payment and/or reimbursement for its services as provided by said act of Congress. Any such agreement may be subject to the regulations of the administrator of the Wage and Hour Division, or the chief of the Children's Bureau of the United States Department of Labor, as the case may be, and shall be subject to the approval of the Director of the State Budget. Nothing in this section shall be construed as authorizing the State Department of Labor to spend in excess of its appropriation from State funds, except to the extent that such excess may be paid and/or reimbursed to it by the United States Department of Labor. All payments received by the State Department of Labor under this section shall be deposited in the State treasury and are hereby appropriated to the State Department of Labor to enable it to carry out the agreements entered into under this section. (1939, c. 245.)

§ 95-14.1: Repealed by Session Laws 2011-145, s. 12.1, effective July 1, 2011.

Article 2.

Maximum Working Hours.

§§ 95-15 through 95-25. Recodified as §§ 95-25.1 to 95-25.25.

Article 2A.

Wage and Hour Act.

§ 95-25.1. Short title and legislative purpose.

(a) This Article shall be known and may be cited as the "Wage and Hour Act."

(b) The public policy of this State is declared as follows: The wage levels of employees, hours of labor, payment of earned wages, and the well-being of minors are subjects of concern requiring legislation to promote the general welfare of the people of the State without jeopardizing the competitive position of North Carolina business and industry. The General Assembly declares that the general welfare of the State requires the enactment of this law under the police power of the State. (1937, c. 409, s. 2; 1979, c. 839, s. 1.)

§ 95-25.2. Definitions.

In this Article, unless the context otherwise requires:

(1)   "Agriculture" includes farming in all its branches performed by a farmer or on a farm as an incident to or in conjunction with farming operations.

(2)   "Commissioner" means the Commissioner of Labor.

(3)   "Employ" means to suffer or permit to work.

(4)   "Employee" includes any individual employed by an employer.

(5)   "Employer" includes any person acting directly or indirectly in the interest of an employer in relation to an employee.

(6) "Establishment" means a physical location where business is conducted.

(7) "The Fair Labor Standards Act" means the Fair Labor Standards Act of 1938, as amended and as the same may be amended from time to time by the United States Congress.

(8) "Hours worked" includes all time an employee is employed.

(9) "Payday" means that day designated for payment of wages due by virtue of the employment relationship.

(10) "Pay periods" may be daily, weekly, biweekly, semimonthly, or monthly.

(11) "Person" means an individual, partnership, association, corporation, business trust, legal representative, or any organized group of persons. For the purposes of G.S. 95-25.2, G.S. 95-25.3, G.S. 95-25.14, and G.S. 95-25.20, it also means the State of North Carolina, any city, town, county, or municipality, or any State or local agency or instrumentality of government. The Government of the United States and any agency of the United States (including the United States Postal Service and Postal Rate Commission) are not included as persons for any purpose under this Article.

(12) "Seasonal food service establishment" means a restaurant, food and drink stand or other establishment generally recognized as a commercial food service establishment, preparing and serving food to the public but operating 180 days or less per year.

(13) "Seasonal religious or nonprofit educational conference center or a seasonal amusement or recreational establishment" means an establishment which does not operate for more than seven months in any calendar year, or during the preceding calendar year had average receipts for any six months of such year of not more than thirty-three and one-third percent (33 1/3%) of its average receipts for the other six months of that year.

(14) "Tipped employee" means any employee who customarily receives more than twenty dollars ($20.00) a month in tips.

(15) "Tip" shall mean any money or part thereof over and above the actual amount due a business for goods, food, drink, services or articles sold which is

paid in cash or by credit card, or is given to or left for an employee by a patron or patrons of the business where the employee is employed.

(16) "Wage" paid to an employee means compensation for labor or services rendered by an employee whether determined on a time, task, piece, job, day, commission, or other basis of calculation, and the reasonable cost as determined by the Commissioner of furnishing employees with board, lodging, or other facilities. For the purposes of G.S. 95-25.6 through G.S. 95-25.13 "wage" includes sick pay, vacation pay, severance pay, commissions, bonuses, and other amounts promised when the employer has a policy or a practice of making such payments.

(17) "Workweek" means any period of 168 consecutive hours.

(18) "Enterprise" means the related activities performed either through unified operations or common control by any person or persons for a common business purpose and includes all such activities whether performed in one or more establishments or by one or more corporate units but shall not include the related activities performed for such enterprise by an independent contractor or franchisee. (1959, c. 475; 1961, c. 652; 1969, c. 34, s. 2; c. 218; 1971, c. 1231, s. 1; 1975, c. 413, s. 1; c. 605; 1977, c. 653; c. 672, s. 1; c. 826, s. 1; 1979, c. 839, s. 1; 1981, c. 663, ss. 10, 11; 1983, c. 708, s. 3; 1991, c. 330, s. 1.)

§ 95-25.3. Minimum wage.

(a) Every employer shall pay to each employee who in any workweek performs any work, wages of at least six dollars and fifteen cents ($6.15) per hour or the minimum wage set forth in paragraph 1 of section 6(a) of the Fair Labor Standards Act, 29 U.S.C. 206(a)(1), as that wage may change from time to time, whichever is higher, except as otherwise provided in this section.

(b) In order to prevent curtailment of opportunities for employment, the wage rate for full-time students, learners, apprentices, and messengers, as defined under the Fair Labor Standards Act, shall be ninety percent (90%) of the rate in effect under subsection (a) above, rounded to the lowest nickel.

(c) The Commissioner, in order to prevent curtailment of opportunities for employment, may, by regulation, establish a wage rate less than the wage rate in effect under section (a) which may apply to persons whose earning or productive capacity is impaired by age or physical or mental deficiency or injury, as such persons are defined under the Fair Labor Standards Act.

(d) The Commissioner, in order to prevent curtailment of opportunities for employment of the economically disadvantaged and the unemployed, may, by regulation, establish a wage rate not less than eighty-five percent (85%) of the otherwise applicable wage rate in effect under subsection (a) which shall apply to all persons (i) who have been unemployed for at least 15 weeks and who are economically disadvantaged, or (ii) who are, or whose families are, receiving Work First Family Assistance or who are receiving supplemental security benefits under Title XVI of the Social Security Act.

Pursuant to regulations issued by the Commissioner, certificates establishing eligibility for such subminimum wage shall be issued by the Division of Employment Security.

The regulation issued by the Commissioner shall not permit employment at the subminimum rate for a period in excess of 52 weeks.

(e) The Commissioner, in order to prevent curtailment of opportunities for employment, and to not adversely affect the viability of seasonal establishments, may, by regulation, establish a wage rate not less than eighty-five percent (85%) of the otherwise applicable wage rate in effect under subsection (a) which shall apply to any employee employed by an establishment which is a seasonal amusement or recreational establishment, or a seasonal food service establishment.

(f) Tips earned by a tipped employee may be counted as wages only up to the amount permitted in section 3(m) of the Fair Labor Standards Act, 29 U.S.C. 203(m), if the tipped employee is notified in advance, is permitted to retain all tips and the employer maintains accurate and complete records of tips received by each employee as such tips are certified by the employee monthly or for each pay period. Even if the employee refuses to certify tips accurately, tips may still be counted as wages when the employer complies with the other requirements of this section and can demonstrate by monitoring tips that the employee regularly receives tips in the amount for which the credit is taken. Tip pooling shall also be permissible among employees who customarily and regularly receive tips; however, no employee's tips may be reduced by more than fifteen percent (15%) under a tip pooling arrangement.

(g) Repealed by Session Laws 2006-259, s. 18, effective August 23, 2006. (1959, c. 475; 1963, c. 816; 1965, c. 229; 1969, c. 34, s. 1; 1971, c. 138; 1973, c. 802; 1975, c. 256, s. 1; 1977, c. 519; 1979, c. 839, s. 1; 1981, c. 493, s. 1; c. 663, s. 13; 1983, c. 708, s. 1; 1985, c. 97; 1987, c. 79; 1991, c. 270, ss. 1, 2; c. 330, s. 5; 1997-146, s. 1; 1997-443, s. 12.25; 2006-114, s. 1; 2006-259, s. 18; 2011-401, s. 3.6.)

§ 95-25.3A: Repealed by Session Laws 2003-308, s. 8, effective July 1, 2003.

§ 95-25.4. Overtime.

(a) Every employer shall pay each employee who works longer than 40 hours in any workweek at a rate of not less than time and one half of the regular rate of pay of the employee for those hours in excess of 40 per week; provided that employers of seasonal amusement or recreational establishment employees are required to pay those employees the overtime rate only for hours in excess of 45 per workweek.

(b) Repealed by Session Laws 1991, c. 330, s. 2. (1973, c. 685, s. 1; 1979, c. 839, s. 1; 1991, c. 330, s. 2, c. 492, s. 1.)

§ 95-25.5. Youth employment.

(a) No youth under 18 years of age shall be employed by any employer in any occupation without a youth employment certificate unless specifically exempted. The Commissioner of Labor shall prescribe regulations for youths and employers concerning the issuance, maintenance and revocation of certificates. Certificates will be issued, subject to review by the Department of Labor, by county directors of social services and such of their designees as are approved by the Commissioner; provided, the Commissioner may also issue certificates, both directly and electronically.

(a1) During the regular school term, no youth under 18 years of age who is enrolled in school in grade 12 or lower may be employed between 11 P.M. and 5 A.M. when there is school for the youth the next day. This restriction does not apply to youths 16 and 17 years of age if the employer receives written approval for the youth to work beyond the stated hours from the youth's parent or guardian and from the youth's principal or the principal's designee.

(b)   No youth under 18 years of age may be employed by an employer in any occupation which the United States Department of Labor shall find and by order declare to be hazardous and without exemption under the Fair Labor Standards Act, or in any occupation which the Commissioner of Labor after public hearing shall find and declare to be detrimental to the health and well-being of youths.

(c)   No youth 14 or 15 years of age may be employed by an employer in any occupation except those determined by the United States Department of Labor to be permitted occupations under the Fair Labor Standards Act; provided, such youths may be employed by employers:

(1)   No more than three hours on a day when school is in session for the youth;

(2)   No more than eight hours on a day when school is not in session for the youth;

(3)   Only between 7 A.M. and 7 P.M., except to 9 P.M. during the summer (when school is not in session);

(4)   No more than 40 hours in any one week when school is not in session for the youth;

(5)   No more than 18 hours in any one week when school is in session for the youth; and

(6)   Only outside school hours.

Notwithstanding the above, enrollees in high school apprenticeships or in work experience and career exploration programs as defined under the Fair Labor Standards Act may work up to 23 hours in any one week when school is in session, any portion of which may be during school hours.

(d)   No youth 13 years of age or less may be employed by an employer, except youths 12 and 13 years of age may be employed outside school hours in the distribution of newspapers to the consumer but not more than three hours per day. An employment certificate shall not be required for any youth under 18 years of age engaged in the distribution of newspapers to the consumer outside of school hours.

(e) No youth under 16 years of age shall be employed for more than five consecutive hours without an interval of at least 30 minutes for rest. No period of less than 30 minutes shall be deemed to interrupt a continuous period of work.

(f) For any youth 13 years of age or older, the Commissioner may waive any provision of this section and authorize the issuance of an employment certificate when:

(1) He receives a letter from a social worker, court, probation officer, county department of social services, a letter from the North Carolina Alcohol Beverage Control Commission or school official stating those factors which create a hardship situation and how the best interest of the youth is served by allowing a waiver; and

(2) He determines that the health or safety of the youth would not be adversely affected; and

(3) The parent, guardian, or other person standing in loco parentis consents in writing to the proposed employment.

(g) Youths employed as models, or as actors or performers in motion pictures or theatrical productions, or in radio or television productions are exempt from all provisions of this section except the certificate requirements of subsection (a).

(h) Youths employed by an outdoor drama directly in production-related positions such as stagehands, lighting, costumes, properties and special effects are exempt from all provisions of this section except the certificate requirements of subsection (a). Positions such as office workers, ticket takers, ushers and parking lot attendants have no exemption and are subject to all provisions of this section.

(i) Youth under 18 years of age employed by their parent, guardian, or other person standing in loco parentis are exempt from all provisions of this section, except for all of the following:

(1) The certificate requirements of subsection (a) of this section.

(2) The prohibition from hazardous or detrimental occupations of subsection (b) of this section.

(3) The prohibitions of subsection (j)(2) of this section if the youths only work at the establishment when another employee at least 21 years of age is in charge of and present at the licensed premises.

(j) No person who holds any ABC permit issued pursuant to the provisions of Chapter 18B of the General Statutes for the on-premises sale or consumption of alcoholic beverages, including any mixed beverages, shall employ a youth:

(1) Under 16 years of age on the premises for any purpose, unless the youth is at least 14 years of age and each of the following conditions is met:

a. The person obtains the written consent of a parent or guardian of the youth.

b. The youth is employed to work on the outside grounds of the premises for a purpose that does not involve the preparation, serving, dispensing, or sale of alcoholic beverages.

(2) Under 18 years of age to prepare, serve, dispense or sell any alcoholic beverages, including mixed beverages.

(k) Persons and establishments required to comply with or subject to regulation of child labor under the Fair Labor Standards Act are exempt from all provisions of this section, except the certificate requirements of subsection (a), the provisions of subsection (a1), the prohibition from occupations found and declared to be detrimental by the Commissioner of Labor pursuant to subsection (b), and the prohibitions of subsection (j). In addition, employment certificates will not be issued if such person's employment will be in violation of the applicable child labor provisions of the Fair Labor Standards Act. Such employers may also be assessed civil penalties pursuant to G.S. 95-25.23 for each violation of the provisions of this section or any regulation issued hereunder from which there is no exemption.

(l) Notwithstanding any other provision of this section, any youth who holds a North Carolina driver's license valid for the type of driving involved may be assigned as part of his employment to drive an automobile or truck not exceeding 6,000 pounds gross vehicle weight within a 25-mile radius of the principal place of employment, provided that the youth has completed a State-approved driver-education course, and provided that the assignment does not involve the towing of vehicles. "Gross vehicle weight" includes the truck chassis with lubricants, water and full tank or tanks of fuel, plus the weight of the cab or driver's compartment, body and special chassis and body equipment, and payload.

(m) Notwithstanding any other provision of this section, youths who are enrolled at an institution of higher education may be employed by the institution provided the employment is not hazardous. As used in this subsection, "institution of higher education" means any constituent institution of The University of North Carolina, any North Carolina community college, or any college or university that awards postsecondary degrees.

(n) Nothing in this section prohibits qualified youths under 18 years of age from participating in training through their fire department, the Office of State Fire Marshal, or the North Carolina Community College System. As used in this subsection, the term "qualified youth under 18 years of age" means an uncompensated fire department or rescue squad member who is at least the age of 15 and under the age of 18 and who is a member of a bona fide fire department, as that term is defined in G.S. 58-86-25, or of a rescue squad described in G.S. 58-86-30. (1937, c. 317, ss. 1-3, 6, 9, 18; 1943, c. 670; 1951, c. 1187, s. 1; 1967, cc. 173, 764; 1969, c. 962; 1973, c. 649, s. 1; c. 758, s. 1; 1977, c. 551, ss. 1-4; 1979, c. 839, s. 1; 1981, c. 412, ss. 3, 4; c. 489, ss. 1-7; c. 747, s. 66; 1985, c. 97, s. 1; 1987, c. 154; 1991, c. 492, s. 2; 1991 (Reg. Sess., 1992), c. 991, s. 1; 1993, c. 239, s. 1; 1995, c. 214, s. 1; 1999-237, s. 14.1; 2001-312, s. 3; 2001-515, s. 5; 2005-453, s. 15; 2009-21, s. 2; 2010-97, s. 9.)

§ 95-25.6. Wage payment.

Every employer shall pay every employee all wages and tips accruing to the employee on the regular payday. Pay periods may be daily, weekly, bi-weekly, semi-monthly, or monthly. Wages based upon bonuses, commissions, or other forms of calculation may be paid as infrequently as annually if prescribed in advance. (1975, c. 413, s. 3; 1977, c. 826, s. 3; 1979, c. 839, s. 1.)

§ 95-25.7. Payment to separated employees.

Employees whose employment is discontinued for any reason shall be paid all wages due on or before the next regular payday either through the regular pay channels or by mail if requested by the employee. Wages based on bonuses, commissions or other forms of calculation shall be paid on the first regular payday after the amount becomes calculable when a separation occurs. Such wages may not be forfeited unless the employee has been notified in accordance with G.S. 95-25.13 of the employer's policy or practice which results in forfeiture. Employees not so notified are not subject to such loss or forfeiture. (1975, c. 413, s. 4; 1979, c. 839, s. 1; 1981, c. 663, s. 1; 1993, c. 214, s. 1.)

§ 95-25.7A. Wages in dispute.

(a) If the amount of wages is in dispute, the employer shall pay the wages, or that part of the wages, which the employer concedes to be due without condition, within the time set by this Article. The employee retains all remedies that the employee might otherwise be entitled to regarding any balance of wages claimed by the employee, including those remedies provided under this Article.

(b) Acceptance of a partial payment of wages under this section by an employee does not constitute a release of the balance of the claim. Further, any release of the claim required by an employer as a condition of partial payment is void. (1989, c. 687, s. 1.)

§ 95-25.8. Withholding of wages.

(a) An employer may withhold or divert any portion of an employee's wages when:

(1) The employer is required or empowered to do so by State or federal law;

(2) When the amount or rate of the proposed deduction is known and agreed upon in advance, the employer must have written authorization from the employee which (i) is signed on or before the payday(s) for the pay period(s) from which the deduction is to be made; (ii) indicates the reason for the

deduction; and (iii) states the actual dollar amount or percentage of wages which shall be deducted from one or more paychecks. Provided, that if the deduction is for the convenience of the employee, the employee shall be given a reasonable opportunity to withdraw the authorization; or

(3) When the amount of the proposed deduction is not known and agreed upon in advance, the employer must have written authorization from the employee which (i) is signed on or before the payday(s) for the pay period(s) from which the deduction is to be made; and (ii) indicates the reason for the deduction. Prior to any deductions being made under this section, the employee must (i) receive advance written notice of the actual amount to be deducted; (ii) receive written notice of their right to withdraw the authorization; and (iii) be given a reasonable opportunity to withdraw the authorization in writing.

(b) The withholding or diversion of wages owed for the employer's benefit must comply with the following requirements:

(1) In nonovertime workweeks, an employer may reduce wages to the minimum wage level.

(2) In overtime workweeks, employers may reduce wages to the minimum wage level for nonovertime hours.

(3) No reductions may be made to overtime wages owed.

(c) In addition to complying with the requirements in subsections (a) and (b) of this section, an employer may withhold or divert a portion of an employee's wages for cash shortages, inventory shortages, or loss or damage to an employer's property after giving the employee written notice of the amount to be deducted seven days prior to the payday on which the deduction is to be made, except that when a separation occurs the seven-day notice is not required.

(d) Notwithstanding subsections (a) and (b), above, an overpayment of wages to an employee as a result of a miscalculation or other bona fide error, advances of wages to an employee or to a third party at the employee's request, and the principal amount of loans made by an employer to an employee are considered prepayment of wages and may be withheld or deducted from an employee's wages. Deductions for interest and other charges related to loans by an employer to an employee shall require written authorization in accordance with subsection (a), above.

(e) Notwithstanding subsections (a) and (c), above, if criminal process has issued against an employee, an employee has been indicted, or an employee has been arrested pursuant to Articles 17, 20, and 32 of Chapter 15A of the General Statutes for a charge incident to a cash shortage, inventory shortage, or damage to an employer's property, an employer may withhold or divert a portion of the employee's wages in order to recoup the amount of the cash shortage, inventory shortage, or damage to the employer's property, without the written authorization required by this section, but the amount of such withholdings shall comply with the provisions of subsection (b) of this section. If the employee is not found guilty, then the amount deducted shall be reimbursed to the employee by the employer.

(f) For purposes of this section, a written authorization or written notice may be in the form of an electronic record in compliance with Article 40 of Chapter 66 (the Uniform Electronic Transactions Act).

(g) Nothing in this Article shall preclude an employer from bringing a civil action in the General Court of Justice to collect any amounts due the employer from the employee. (1975, c. 413, s. 6; 1979, c. 839, s. 1; 1981, c. 663, s. 2; 2005-453, s. 16.)

§§ 95-25.9, 95-25.10: Repealed by Session Laws 2005-453, ss. 17 and 18, effective October 1, 2005.

§ 95-25.11. Employers' remedies preserved.

(a) Repealed by Session Laws 2005-453, s. 19.

(b) Nothing in this Article shall preclude an employer from bringing a civil action in the General Court of Justice to collect any amounts due the employer from the employee. (1979, c. 839, s. 1; 1981, c. 663, s. 5; 2005-453, s. 19.)

§ 95-25.12. Vacation pay plans.

No employer is required to provide vacation pay plans for employees. However, if an employer provides these promised benefits for employees, the employer shall give all vacation time off or payment in lieu of time off in accordance with the company policy or practice. Employees shall be notified in accordance with G.S. 95-25.13 of any policy or practice which requires or results in loss or forfeiture of vacation time or pay. Employees not so notified are not subject to such loss or forfeiture. (1979, c. 839, s. 1; 1981, c. 663, s. 6; 2005-453, s. 20.)

§ 95-25.13. Notification, posting, and records.

Every employer shall:

(1) Notify its employees, orally or in writing at the time of hiring, of the promised wages and the day and place for payment;

(2) Make available to its employees, in writing or through a posted notice maintained in a place accessible to its employees, employment practices and policies with regard to promised wages;

(3) Notify employees, in writing or through a posted notice maintained in a place accessible to its employees, at least 24 hours prior to any changes in promised wages. Wages may be retroactively increased without the prior notice required by this subsection; and

(4) Furnish each employee with an itemized statement of deductions made from that employee's wages under G.S. 95-25.8 for each pay period such deductions are made. (1975, c. 413, s. 7; 1979, c. 839, s. 1; 1981, c. 663, s. 12; 1993, c. 203, s. 1; 2005-453, s. 21.)

§ 95-25.14. Exemptions.

(a) The provisions of G.S. 95-25.3 (Minimum Wage), G.S. 95-25.4 (Overtime), and G.S. 95-25.5 (Youth Employment), and the provisions of G.S. 95-25.15(b) (Record Keeping) as they relate to these exemptions, do not apply to:

(1) Any person employed in an enterprise engaged in commerce or in the production of goods for commerce as defined in the Fair Labor Standards Act:

a. Except as otherwise specifically provided in G.S. 95-25.5;

b. Notwithstanding the above, any employee other than a learner, apprentice, student, or handicapped worker as defined in the Fair Labor Standards Act who is not otherwise exempt under the other provisions of this section, and for whom the applicable minimum wage under the Fair Labor Standards Act is less than the minimum wage provided in G.S. 95-25.3, is not exempt from the provisions of G.S. 95-25.3 or G.S. 95-25.4;

c. Notwithstanding the above, any employer or employee exempt from the minimum wage, overtime, or child labor requirements of the Fair Labor Standards Act for whom there is no comparable exemption under this Article shall not be exempt under this subsection except that where an exemption in the Fair Labor Standards Act provides a method of computing overtime which is an alternative to the method required in 29 U.S.C.S. § 207(a), the employer or employee subject to that alternate method shall be exempt from the provisions of G.S. 95-25.4(a); provided that, persons not employed at an enterprise described in subdivision (1) of this subsection shall also be subject to the same alternative methods of overtime calculation in the circumstances described in the Fair Labor Standards Act exemptions providing those alternative methods;

(2) Any person employed in agriculture, as defined under the Fair Labor Standards Act;

(3) Any person employed as a domestic, including baby sitters and companions, as defined under the Fair Labor Standards Act;

(4) Any person employed as a page in the North Carolina General Assembly or in the Governor's Office;

(5) Bona fide volunteers in medical, educational, religious, or nonprofit organizations where an employer-employee relationship does not exist;

(6) Persons confined in and working for any penal, correctional or mental institution of the State or local government;

(7) Any person employed as a model, or as an actor or performer in motion pictures or theatrical, radio or television productions, as defined under the Fair Labor Standards Act, except as otherwise specifically provided in G.S. 95-25.5;

(8) Any person employed by an outdoor drama in a production role, including lighting, costumes, properties and special effects, except as otherwise specifically provided in G.S. 95-25.5; but this exemption does not include such positions as office workers, ticket takers, ushers and parking lot attendants.

(b) The provisions of G.S. 95-25.3 (Minimum Wage) and G.S. 95-25.4 (Overtime), and the provisions of G.S. 95-25.15(b) (Record Keeping) as they relate to these exemptions, do not apply to:

(1) Any employee of a boys' or girls' summer camp or of a seasonal religious or nonprofit educational conference center;

(2) Any person employed in the catching, processing or first sale of seafood, as defined under the Fair Labor Standards Act;

(3) The spouse, child, or parent of the employer or any person qualifying as a dependent of the employer under the income tax laws of North Carolina;

(4) Any person employed in a bona fide executive, administrative, professional or outside sales capacity, as defined under the Fair Labor Standards Act;

(5) Repealed by Session Laws 1989, c. 687, s. 2.

(6) Any person while participating in a ridesharing arrangement as defined in G.S. 136-44.21;

(7) Any person who is employed as a computer systems analyst, computer programmer, software engineer, or other similarly skilled worker, as defined in the Fair Labor Standards Act.

(b1) The provisions of G.S. 95-25.3 (Minimum Wage) and G.S. 95-25.4 (Overtime), and the provisions of G.S. 95-25.15(b) (Record Keeping) as they relate to the exemptions provided for in this subsection, do not apply to any of the following:

(1) Hours worked as a bona fide volunteer firefighter in an incorporated, nonprofit volunteer or community fire department.

(2) Hours worked as a bona fide volunteer rescue and emergency medical services personnel in an incorporated, nonprofit volunteer or community fire department, or an incorporated, nonprofit rescue squad.

Hours worked in accordance with this subsection shall not be considered hours worked for purposes of G.S. 95-25.3 or G.S. 95-25.4.

(c) The provisions of G.S. 95-25.4 (Overtime), and the provisions of G.S. 95-25.15(b) (Record Keeping) as they relate to this exemption, do not apply to:

(1) Drivers, drivers' helpers, loaders and mechanics, as defined under the Fair Labor Standards Act;

(2) Taxicab drivers;

(3) Seamen, employees of railroads, and employees of air carriers, as defined under the Fair Labor Standards Act;

(4) Salespersons, mechanics and partsmen employed by automotive, truck, and farm implement dealers, as defined under the Fair Labor Standards Act;

(5) Salespersons employed by trailer, boat, and aircraft dealers, as defined under the Fair Labor Standards Act;

(6) Live-in child care workers or other live-in employees in homes for dependent children;

(7) Radio and television announcers, news editors, and chief engineers, as defined under the Fair Labor Standards Act.

(d) The provisions of this Article do not apply to the State of North Carolina, any city, town, county, or municipality, or any State or local agency or instrumentality of government, except for the following provisions, which do apply:

(1) The minimum wage provisions of G.S. 95-25.3;

(2) The definition provisions of G.S. 95-25.2 necessary to interpret the applicable provisions;

(3) The exemptions of subsections (a) and (b) of this section;

(4) The complainant protection provisions of G.S. 95-25.20.

(e) Employment in a seasonal recreation program by the State of North Carolina, any city, town, county, or municipality, or any State or local agency or instrumentality of government, is exempt from all provisions of this Article, including G.S. 95-25.3 (Minimum Wage). (1937, c. 406; c. 409, s. 3; 1939, c. 312, s. 1; 1943, c. 59; 1947, c. 825; 1949, c. 1057; 1959, cc. 475, 629; 1961, cc. 602, 1070; 1963, c. 1123; 1965, c. 724; 1967, c. 998; 1973, c. 600, s. 1; 1975, c. 19, s. 26; c. 413, s. 2; 1977, c. 146; 1979, c. 839, s. 1; 1981, c. 493, s. 2; c. 606, s. 2; c. 663, s. 7; 1983, c. 708, s. 2; 1989, c. 687, s. 2; 1991, c. 330, s. 3; 1993, c. 214, s. 2; 1995, c. 509, s. 47; 1997-146, s. 2; 2002-113, s. 2.)

§ 95-25.15. Investigations and inspection of records; notice of law.

(a) The Commissioner or his designated representative shall have the power and authority to enter any place of employment and gather such facts as are essential to determine whether or not the employer is covered by any provision of this Article.

With respect to any provision of this Article under which the employer is covered, the Commissioner or the Commissioner's designated representative may inspect such places and such records, make transcriptions of any and all such records, question employees and investigate such facts, conditions, practices, or matters as are necessary to determine whether the employer has violated said provision of this Article.

With respect to the provisions of G.S. 95-25.6 through 95-25.12 (Wage Payment) as those provisions apply to persons covered by the Fair Labor Standards Act, the Commissioner or his designated representative shall have no authority under this subsection unless the Commissioner or his designated representative has received a complaint from an employee of the covered establishment.

(b)   Except as otherwise provided in this Article, every employer subject to any provision of this Article shall make, keep, and preserve such records of the persons employed by the employer, including the ages of employees, and of the wages, hours, and other conditions and practices of employment which are essential to the enforcement of this Article and are prescribed by regulation of the Commissioner, except that the Commissioner shall have no authority to prescribe records for the State of North Carolina, a city, town, county or other municipality or agency or instrumentality of government.

(c)   A poster summarizing the major provisions of this Article shall be displayed in every establishment subject to this Article. (1937, c. 317, ss. 5, 19; 1959, c. 475; 1971, c. 1231, s. 2; 1973, c. 649, s. 4; 1975, c. 413, ss. 7, 9; 1979, c. 839, s. 1; 2005-453, s. 22; 2009-351, s. 2.)

§ 95-25.16. Enforcement.

(a)   The Commissioner shall enforce and administer the provisions of this Article, and the Commissioner or his authorized representative is empowered to hold hearings and to institute criminal and civil proceedings hereunder.

(b)   The Commissioner or his authorized representative shall have power to administer oaths and examine witnesses, issue subpoenas, compel the attendance of witnesses and the production of papers, books, accounts, records, payrolls, documents, and take depositions and affidavits in any proceeding hereunder.

(c)   The Commissioner is empowered to enter into reciprocal agreements with the labor department or corresponding agency of any other state or with the person, board, officer, or commission authorized to act on behalf of the department or agency, for the collection in the other state of claims and judgments for wages based upon investigations and findings made by the Commissioner or his authorized representative.

The Commissioner may, to the extent provided for by any reciprocal agreement entered into by law or with an agency of another state, as provided in this section, maintain actions in the courts of any other state for the collection of claims or judgments for wages and may assign the claims and judgments to the labor department or agency of the other state for collection to the extent that such an assignment may be permitted or provided for by the law of that state or by reciprocal agreement.

Except as provided in subsection (d) of this section, the Commissioner may, upon the written consent of the labor department or corresponding agency of any other state or of any person, board, officer, or commission authorized to act on behalf of the department or agency, maintain actions in the courts of this State upon assigned claims and judgments for wages arising in the other state in the same manner and to the same extent that these actions by the Commissioner are authorized when arising in this State.

(d) Subsection (c) of this section applies only to those states that extend comity to this State. (1937, c. 317, s. 19; c. 409, s. 7; 1971, c. 1231, s. 2; 1973, c. 649, s. 4; 1975, c. 473, s. 9; c. 475; 1979, c. 839, s. 1; 1989, c. 687, s. 3.)

§ 95-25.17. Wage and Hour Division established.

The Commissioner of Labor is charged with enforcement of this Article. The Commissioner shall appoint a Wage and Hour Director and any other employees the Commissioner deems necessary for enforcement of this Article. The Commissioner shall continue to prescribe the powers, duties, and responsibilities of the Director and employees engaged in the administration of this Article. (1979, c. 839, s. 1; 2005-453, s. 23.)

§ 95-25.18. Legal representation.

It shall be the duty of the Attorney General of North Carolina, when requested, to represent the Department of Labor in actions or proceedings in connection with this Article. (1979, c. 839, s. 1.)

§ 95-25.19. Rules.

The Commissioner may adopt rules needed to implement this Article. (1937, c. 317, s. 18; 1975, c. 413, s. 12; 1979, c. 839, s. 1; 1987, c. 827, s. 262.)

§ 95-25.20. Records.

Files and other records relating to investigations and enforcement proceedings pursuant to this Article, or pursuant to Article 21 of this Chapter with respect to Wage and Hour Act violations, shall not be subject to inspection and examination as authorized by G.S. 132-6 while such investigations and proceedings are pending. Nothing under this section shall impede the right to discovery under G.S. 1A-1, Rules of Civil Procedure. (1979, c. 839, s. 1; 1981, c. 663, s. 8; 1991 (Reg. Sess., 1992), c. 1021, s. 3.)

§ 95-25.21. Illegal acts.

(a)   It shall be unlawful for any person to interfere unduly with, hinder, or delay the Commissioner or any authorized representative in the performance of official duties or refuse to give the Commissioner or his authorized representative any information required for the enforcement of this Article.

(b)   It shall be unlawful for any person to make any statement or report, or keep or file any record pursuant to this Article or regulations issued thereunder, knowing such statement, report, or record to be false in a material respect.

(c)   Any person who violates this section shall be guilty of a Class 2 misdemeanor. (1937, c. 409, ss. 6, 8; 1979, c. 839, s. 1; 1993, c. 539, s. 661; 1994, Ex. Sess., c. 24, s. 14(c).)

§ 95-25.22. Recovery of unpaid wages.

(a)   Any employer who violates the provisions of G.S. 95-25.3 (Minimum Wage), G.S. 95-25.4 (Overtime), or G.S. 95-25.6 through 95-25.12 (Wage Payment) shall be liable to the employee or employees affected in the amount of their unpaid minimum wages, their unpaid overtime compensation, or their unpaid amounts due under G.S. 95-25.6 through 95-25.12, as the case may be, plus interest at the legal rate set forth in G.S. 24-1, from the date each amount first came due.

(a1)   In addition to the amounts awarded pursuant to subsection (a) of this section, the court shall award liquidated damages in an amount equal to the amount found to be due as provided in subsection (a) of this section, provided that if the employer shows to the satisfaction of the court that the act or omission constituting the violation was in good faith and that the employer had reasonable grounds for believing that the act or omission was not a violation of this Article, the court may, in its discretion, award no liquidated damages or may award any amount of liquidated damages not exceeding the amount found due as provided in subsection (a) of this section.

(b) Action to recover such liability may be maintained in the General Court of Justice by any one or more employees.

(c) Action to recover such liability may also be maintained in the General Court of Justice by the Commissioner at the request of the employees affected. Any sums thus recovered by the Commissioner on behalf of an employee shall be held in a special deposit account and shall be paid directly to the employee or employees affected.

(d) The court, in any action brought under this Article may, in addition to any judgment awarded plaintiff, order costs and fees of the action and reasonable attorneys' fees to be paid by the defendant. In an action brought by the Commissioner in which a default judgment is entered, the clerk shall order attorneys' fees of three hundred dollars ($300.00) to be paid by the defendant.

The court may order costs and fees of the action and reasonable attorneys' fees to be paid by the plaintiff if the court determines that the action was frivolous.

(e) The Commissioner is authorized to determine and supervise the payment of the amounts due under this section, including interest at the legal rate set forth in G.S. 24-1, from the date each amount first came due, and the agreement to accept such amounts by the employee shall constitute a waiver of the employee's right to bring an action under subsection (b) of this section.

(f) Actions under this section must be brought within two years pursuant to G.S. 1-53.

(g) Prior to initiating any action under this section, the Commissioner shall exhaust all administrative remedies, including giving the employer the opportunity to be heard on the matters at issue and giving the employer notice of the pending action. (1959, c. 475; 1975, c. 413, s. 11; 1979, c. 839, s. 1; 1989, c. 687, s. 4; 1991, c. 298.)

§ 95-25.23. Violation of youth employment; civil penalty.

(a) Any employer who violates the provisions of G.S. 95-25.5 (Youth Employment) or any regulation issued thereunder, shall be subject to a civil penalty not to exceed five hundred dollars ($500.00) for the first violation and not to exceed one thousand dollars ($1,000) for each subsequent violation. In determining the amount of such penalty, the appropriateness of such penalty to the size of the business of the person charged and the gravity of the violation shall be considered. The determination by the Commissioner shall be final, unless within 15 days after receipt of notice thereof by certified mail with return receipt, by signature confirmation as provided by the U.S. Postal Service, by a designated delivery service authorized pursuant to 26 U.S.C. § 7502(f)(2) with delivery receipt, or via hand delivery, the person charged with the violation takes exception to the determination, in which event final determination of the penalty shall be made in an administrative proceeding pursuant to Article 3 of Chapter 150B and in a judicial proceeding pursuant to Article 4 of Chapter 150B.

(b) The amount of such penalty when finally determined may be recovered in the manner set forth in G.S. 95-25.23B.

(c) The clear proceeds of civil penalties provided for in this section shall be remitted to the Civil Penalty and Forfeiture Fund in accordance with G.S. 115C-457.2.

(d) Assessment of penalties under this section shall be subject to a two-year statute of limitations commencing at the time of the occurrence of the violation. (1979, c. 839, s. 1; 1981, c. 663, s. 9; 1989, c. 687, s. 6; 1993, c. 225, s. 1; 1998-215, s. 107; 2003-308, s. 1; 2007-231, s. 4; 2009-351, s. 1.)

§ 95-25.23A. Violation of record-keeping requirement; civil penalty.

(a) Any employer who violates the provisions of G.S. 95-25.15(b) or any regulation issued pursuant to G.S. 95-25.15(b), shall be subject to a civil penalty of up to two hundred fifty dollars ($250.00) per employee with the maximum not to exceed two thousand dollars ($2,000) per investigation by the Commissioner or the Commissioner's authorized representative. In determining the amount of the penalty, the Commissioner shall consider each of the following:

(1) The appropriateness of the penalty for the size of the business of the employer charged.

(2) The gravity of the violation.

(3) Whether the violation involves an employee under 18 years of age.

The determination by the Commissioner shall be final, unless within 15 days after receipt of notice thereof by certified mail with return receipt, by signature confirmation as provided by the U.S. Postal Service, by a designated delivery service authorized pursuant to 26 U.S.C. § 7502(f)(2) with delivery receipt, or via hand delivery, the person charged with the violation takes exception to the determination, in which event final determination of the penalty shall be made in an administrative proceeding pursuant to Article 3 of Chapter 150B and in a judicial proceeding pursuant to Article 4 of Chapter 150B.

(b) The amount of the penalty when finally determined may be recovered in the manner set forth in G.S. 95-25.23B.

(c) The clear proceeds of civil penalties provided for in this section shall be remitted to the Civil Penalty and Forfeiture Fund in accordance with G.S. 115C-457.2.

(d) Assessment of penalties under this section shall be subject to a two-year statute of limitations commencing at the time of the occurrence of the violation. (1989, c. 687, s. 5; 1993, c. 225, s. 2; 1998-215, s. 108; 2003-308, s. 2; 2007-231, s. 5; 2009-351, s. 3.)

§ 95-25.23B. Civil penalty collection.

The Commissioner may file in the office of the clerk of the superior court of any county a certified copy of an assessment, either unappealed from or affirmed in whole or in part upon appeal, of a civil money penalty under G.S. 95-25.23 or G.S. 95-25.23A. Upon such filing, the clerk shall enter judgment in accordance with the unappealed or affirmed portion of the assessment and shall notify the parties. Such judgment shall have the same effect, and all proceedings in relation to the judgment shall thereafter be the same, as though the judgment had been rendered in a suit duly heard and determined by the superior court of the General Court of Justice. (1993, c. 225, s. 3.)

§ 95-25.23C. Report on youth employment enforcement activities.

(a) Findings. - The General Assembly finds that:

(1) There is an increasing need to protect the educational opportunities of youths under age 18 and to prohibit their employment in jobs and under conditions that are detrimental to their health and well-being.

(2) Although the statutory protections available for youths under age 18 who are employed in this State are comprehensive, those protections are rendered meaningless without effective enforcement.

(3) It is in the best interest of the State and its youngest workers to ensure that North Carolina employers are in full compliance with the youth employment laws and regulations enacted under the Wage and Hour Act.

(b) Intent. - Recognizing that the Department of Labor is the State agency charged with enforcing the Wage and Hour Act as it pertains to youth employment, the General Assembly intends to review the Department's education and enforcement activities on a regular basis in order to identify effective measures for enhancing youth employment protections in this State.

(c) Report. - No later than February 1 of each year, the Commissioner shall submit a written report to the General Assembly, the Joint Legislative Education Oversight Committee, and the Fiscal Research Division of the General Assembly on the Department of Labor's investigative, inspection, and enforcement activities under the Wage and Hour Act pertaining to youth employment. Each report submitted pursuant to this subsection shall contain data and information about the calendar year preceding the date on which the last written report was submitted. The report shall include at least all of the following:

(1) All activities the Department of Labor has sponsored or participated in for the purpose of educating employers about their responsibilities under the Wage and Hour Act.

(2) The total number of complaints received by the Department of Labor alleging youth employment violations under the Wage and Hour Act, or any regulations issued under the Wage and Hour Act, or both.

(3) The specific types of youth employment violations alleged and the ages of the youths referenced in the complaints received by the Department of Labor.

(4) The total number of investigations conducted by the Department of Labor concerning alleged youth employment violations, the length of the investigations, and the number of investigators assigned to conduct the investigations. For purposes of this subdivision, the Commissioner shall provide a separate analysis of (i) investigations initiated by the Department in response to a complaint, (ii) investigations initiated by the Department in the absence of a complaint, and (iii) alleged record-keeping violations pertaining to youth employment.

(5) The total number of administrative proceedings involving youth employment violations.

(6) The total number and identity of employers cited for youth employment violations and the industries or occupations that received the greatest and the least number of complaints alleging youth employment violations.

(7) The total number and dollar amount of civil penalties assessed pursuant to G.S. 95-25.23 and the total number and dollar amount of civil penalties actually collected pursuant to that section. For purposes of this subdivision, the Commissioner shall provide a detailed, itemized list of each civil penalty represented in the total number and dollar amounts reported pursuant to this subdivision and indicate whether each civil penalty is the result of a complaint.

(8) The total number and dollar amount of civil penalties assessed pursuant to G.S. 95-25.23A and the total number and dollar amount of civil penalties actually collected pursuant to that section. For purposes of this subdivision, the Commissioner shall provide a detailed, itemized list of each civil penalty represented in the total number and dollar amounts reported pursuant to this subdivision and indicate whether each civil penalty is the result of a complaint.

(9) An explanation of any obstacles that prevented the Department of Labor from enforcing any provision of the Wage and Hour Act as it pertains to youth employment, any recommended changes to the Wage and Hour Act to strengthen the Department of Labor's oversight and enforcement of youth employment laws and regulations in this State, and any other information related to the Department of Labor's enhanced enforcement of the State's youth employment laws and regulations.

(10) Recommendations about the funding needed by the Department to (i) eliminate any identified obstacles to enforcement of youth employment laws and regulations and (ii) effectively implement any recommended changes. (2009-139, s. 1; 2011-291, s. 2.21.)

§ 95-25.24. Restraint of violations.

The General Court of Justice has jurisdiction and authority upon application of the Commissioner to enjoin or restrain violations of this Article, including the restraint of any withholding of payment of unpaid wages, minimum wages, or overtime compensation found by the court to be due to employees under this Article (except sums which employees are barred from recovering, at the time of the commencement of the action to restrain the violations, by virtue of the applicable statute of limitations). (1979, c. 839, s. 1; 1991, c. 330, s. 4.)

§ 95-25.25. Construction of Article and severability.

This Article shall receive a liberal construction to the end that the welfare of adult and minor workers may be protected. If any provisions of this Article or the application thereof to any person or circumstance is held to be invalid, such invalidity shall not affect the provisions or application of the Article which can be given effect without the invalid provision or application, and to this end the provisions of this Article are severable. (1979, c. 839, s. 1.)

Article 3.

Various Regulations.

§ 95-26. Repealed by Session Laws 1971, c. 56.

§ 95-27. Repealed by Session Laws 1973, c. 660, s. 3.

§ 95-28: Repealed by Session Laws 1997-443, s. 19.14.

§ 95-28.1. Discrimination against any person possessing sickle cell trait or hemoglobin C trait prohibited.

No person, firm, corporation, unincorporated association, State agency, unit of local government or any public or private entity shall deny or refuse employment to any person or discharge any person from employment on account of the fact such person possesses sickle cell trait or hemoglobin C trait. The term "sickle cell trait" is defined as the condition wherein the major natural hemoglobin components present in the blood of the individual are hemoglobin A (normal) and hemoglobin S (sickle hemoglobin) as defined by standard chemical and physical analytic techniques, including electrophoresis; and the proportion of hemoglobin A is greater than the proportion of hemoglobin S or one natural parent of the individual is shown to have only normal hemoglobin components (hemoglobin A, hemoglobin A2, hemoglobin F) in the normal proportions by standard chemical and physical analytic tests. The term "hemoglobin C trait" is defined as the condition wherein the major natural hemoglobin components present in the blood of the individual are hemoglobin A (normal) and hemoglobin C as defined by standard chemical and physical analytic techniques, including electrophoresis; and the proportion of hemoglobin A is greater than the proportion of hemoglobin C or one natural parent of the individual is shown to have only normal hemoglobin components (hemoglobin A, hemoglobin A2, hemoglobin F) in the normal proportions by standard chemical and physical analytic tests, provided, however, that this section shall not be construed to give employment, promotion, or layoff preference to persons who possess the above traits, or to prevent such persons being discharged for cause. (1975, c. 463, s. 1.)

§ 95-28.1A. Discrimination against persons based on genetic testing or genetic information prohibited.

(a) No person, firm, corporation, unincorporated association, State agency, unit of local government, or any public or private entity shall deny or refuse employment to any person or discharge any person from employment on account of the person's having requested genetic testing or counseling services, or on the basis of genetic information obtained concerning the person or a member of the person's family. This section shall not be construed to prevent the person from being discharged for cause.

(b) As used in this section, the term "genetic test" means a test for determining the presence or absence of genetic characteristics in an individual or a member of the individual's family in order to diagnose a genetic condition or characteristic or ascertain susceptibility to a genetic condition. The term "genetic characteristic" means any scientifically or medically identifiable genes or chromosomes, or alterations or products thereof, which are known individually or in combination with other characteristics to be a cause of a disease or disorder, or determined to be associated with a statistically increased risk of development of a disease or disorder, and which are asymptomatic of any disease or disorder. The term "genetic information" means information about genes, gene products, or inherited characteristics that may derive from an individual or a family member. (1997-350, s. 2.)

§ 95-28.2. Discrimination against persons for lawful use of lawful products during nonworking hours prohibited.

(a) As used in this section, "employer" means the State and all political subdivisions of the State, public and quasi-public corporations, boards, bureaus, commissions, councils, and private employers with three or more regularly employed employees.

(b) It is an unlawful employment practice for an employer to fail or refuse to hire a prospective employee, or discharge or otherwise discriminate against any employee with respect to compensation, terms, conditions, or privileges of employment because the prospective employee or the employee engages in or has engaged in the lawful use of lawful products if the activity occurs off the premises of the employer during nonworking hours and does not adversely affect the employee's job performance or the person's ability to properly fulfill the responsibilities of the position in question or the safety of other employees.

(c) It is not a violation of this section for an employer to do any of the following:

(1) Restrict the lawful use of lawful products by employees during nonworking hours if the restriction relates to a bona fide occupational requirement and is reasonably related to the employment activities. If the

restriction reasonably relates to only a particular employee or group of employees, then the restriction may only lawfully apply to them.

(2) Restrict the lawful use of lawful products by employees during nonworking hours if the restriction relates to the fundamental objectives of the organization.

(3) Discharge, discipline, or take any action against an employee because of the employee's failure to comply with the requirements of the employer's substance abuse prevention program or the recommendations of substance abuse prevention counselors employed or retained by the employer.

(d) This section shall not prohibit an employer from offering, imposing, or having in effect a health, disability, or life insurance policy distinguishing between employees for the type or price of coverage based on the use or nonuse of lawful products if each of the following is met:

(1) Differential rates assessed employees reflect actuarially justified differences in the provision of employee benefits.

(2) The employer provides written notice to employees setting forth the differential rates imposed by insurance carriers.

(3) The employer contributes an equal amount to the insurance carrier on behalf of each employee of the employer.

(e) An employee who is discharged or otherwise discriminated against, or a prospective employee who is denied employment in violation of this section, may bring a civil action within one year from the date of the alleged violation against the employer who violates the provisions of subsection (b) of this section and obtain any of the following:

(1) Any wages or benefits lost as a result of the violation;

(2) An order of reinstatement without loss of position, seniority, or benefits; or

(3) An order directing the employer to offer employment to the prospective employee.

(f) The court may award reasonable costs, including court costs and attorneys' fees, to the prevailing party in an action brought pursuant to this section. (1991 (Reg. Sess., 1992), c. 1023, s. 1.)

§ 95-28.3. Leave for parent involvement in schools.

(a) It is the belief of the General Assembly that parent involvement is an essential component of school success and positive student outcomes. Therefore, employers shall grant four hours per year leave to any employee who is a parent, guardian, or person standing in loco parentis of a school-aged child so that the employee may attend or otherwise be involved at that child's school. However, any leave under this section is subject to the following conditions:

(1) The leave shall be at a mutually agreed upon time between the employer and the employee.

(2) The employer may require an employee to provide the employer with a written request for the leave at least 48 hours before the time desired for the leave.

(3) The employer may require that the employee furnish written verification from the child's school that the employee attended or was otherwise involved at that school during the time of the leave.

For the purpose of this section, "school" means any (i) public school, (ii) private church school, church of religious charter, or nonpublic school described in Parts 1 and 2 of Article 39 of Chapter 115C of the General Statutes that regularly provides a course of grade school instruction, (iii) preschool, and (iv) child care facility as defined in G.S. 110-86(3).

(b) Employers shall not discharge, demote, or otherwise take an adverse employment action against an employee who requests or takes leave under this section. Nothing in this section shall require an employer to pay an employee for leave taken under this section.

(c) An employee who is demoted or discharged or who has had an adverse employment action taken against him or her in violation of this section may bring a civil action within one year from the date of the alleged violation against the employer who violates this section and obtain either of the following:

(1) Any wages or benefits lost as a result of the violation; or

(2) An order of reinstatement without loss of position, seniority, wages, or benefits.

The burden of proof shall be upon the employee. (1993, c. 509, s. 1; 1997-506, s. 34.)

§ 95-28.4. Veterans preference.

A private, nonpublic employer in the State may provide a preference to a veteran for employment. Spouses of honorably discharged veterans who have a service-connected permanent and total disability also may be preferred for employment. Granting of this preference is not a violation of any State or local equal employment opportunity law. (2013-413, s. 14.)

§ 95-29. Repealed by Session Laws 1973, c. 660, s. 4.

§ 95-30. Repealed by Session Laws 1971, c. 240.

§ 95-31. Acceptance by employer of assignment of wages.

No employer of labor shall be responsible for any assignment of wages to be earned in the future, executed by an employee, unless and until such assignment of wages is accepted by the employer in a written agreement to pay same. (1935, c. 410; 1937, c. 90.)

Article 4.

Conciliation Service and Mediation of Labor Disputes.

§ 95-32. Declaration of policy.

It is hereby declared as the public policy of this State that the best interests of the people of the State are served by the prevention or prompt settlement of labor disputes; that strikes and lockouts and other forms of industrial strife, regardless of where the merits of the controversy lie, are forces productive ultimately of economic waste; that the interests and rights of the consumers and the people of the State, while not direct parties thereto, should always be considered, respected and protected; and that the conciliation and voluntary mediation of such disputes under the guidance and supervision of a governmental agency will tend to promote permanent industrial peace and the health, welfare, comfort and safety of the people of the State. To carry out such policy, the necessity for the enactment of the provisions of this Article is hereby declared as a matter of legislative determination. (1941, c. 362, s. 1.)

§ 95-33. Scope of Article.

The provisions of this Article shall apply to all labor disputes in North Carolina. (1941, c. 362, s. 2.)

§ 95-34. Administration of Article.

The administration of this Article shall be under the general supervision of the Commissioner of Labor of North Carolina. (1941, c. 362, s. 3.)

§ 95-35. Conciliation service established; personnel; removal; compensation.

There is hereby established in the Department of Labor a conciliation service. The Commissioner of Labor may appoint such employees as may be required for the consummation of the work under this Article, prescribe their duties and fix their compensation, subject to existing laws applicable to the appointment and compensation of employees of the State of North Carolina. Any member of or employee in the conciliation service may be removed from office by the Commissioner of Labor, acting in his discretion. (1941, c. 362, s. 4.)

§ 95-36. Powers and duties of Commissioner and conciliator.

Upon his own motion in an existent or imminent labor dispute, the Commissioner of Labor may, and, upon the direction of the Governor, must order a conciliator to take such steps as seem expedient to effect a voluntary, amicable and expeditious adjustment and settlement of the differences and issues between employer and employees which have precipitated or culminated in or threaten to precipitate or culminate in such labor dispute.

The conciliator shall promptly put himself in communication with the parties to such controversy, and shall use his best efforts, by mediation, to bring them to agreement.

The Commissioner of Labor, any conciliator or conciliators and all other employees of the Commissioner of Labor engaged in the enforcement and duties prescribed by this Article, shall not be compelled to disclose to any administrative or judicial tribunal any information relating to, or acquired in the course of their official activities under the provisions of this Article, nor shall any reports, minutes, written communications, or other documents or copies of documents of the Commissioner of Labor and the above employees pertaining to such information be subject to subpoena: Provided, that the Commissioner of Labor, any conciliator or conciliators and all other employees of the Commissioner of Labor engaged in the enforcement of this Article, may be required to testify fully in any examination, trial, or other proceeding in which the commission of a crime is the subject of inquiry. (1941, c. 362, s. 5; 1949, c. 673.)

Article 4A.

Voluntary Arbitration of Labor Disputes.

§ 95-36.1. Declaration of policy.

It is hereby declared as the public policy of this State that the best interests of the people of the State are served by the prompt settlement of labor disputes; that strikes and lockouts and other forms of industrial strife, regardless of where the merits of the controversy lie, are forces productive ultimately of economic waste; that the interests and rights of the consumers and the people of the State, while not direct parties to such disputes, should always be considered, respected and protected; and, where efforts at amicable settlement have been unsuccessful, that the voluntary arbitration of such disputes will tend to promote permanent industrial peace and the health, welfare, comfort and safety of the people of the State. To carry out such policies, the necessity for the enactment of the provisions of this Article is hereby declared as a matter of legislative determination. (1945, c. 1045, s. 1; 1951, c. 1103, s. 1.)

§ 95-36.2. Scope of Article.

The provisions of this Article shall apply only to voluntary agreements to arbitrate labor disputes including, but not restricted to, all controversies between employers, employees and their respective bargaining representatives, or any of them, relating to wages, hours, and other conditions of employment. (1945, c. 1045, s. 2; 1951, c. 1103, s. 1.)

§ 95-36.3. Administration of Article.

(a) The administration of this Article shall be under the general supervision of the Commissioner of Labor of North Carolina.

(b) There is hereby established in the Department of Labor an arbitration service. The Commissioner of Labor may appoint such employees as may be required for the consummation of the work under this Article, prescribe their duties and fix their compensation, subject to existing laws applicable to the appointment and compensation of employees of the State of North Carolina. Any member of or employee in the arbitration service may be removed from office by the Commissioner of Labor, acting in his discretion.

(c) The Commissioner of Labor, with the written approval of the Attorney General as to legality, shall have power to adopt, alter, amend or repeal appropriate rules of procedure for selection of the arbitrator or panel and for conduct of the arbitration proceedings in accordance with this Article: Provided, however, that such rules shall be inapplicable to the extent that they are inconsistent with the arbitration agreement of the parties. (1945, c. 1045, s. 3; 1951, c. 1103, s. 1.)

§ 95-36.4. Voluntary arbitrators.

(a) It shall be the duty of the Commissioner of Labor to maintain a list of qualified and public-spirited citizens who will serve as arbitrators. All appointments of a single arbitrator or member of an arbitration panel by the Commissioner of Labor shall be made from the list of qualified arbitrators maintained by him.

(b) No person named by the Commissioner of Labor to act as an arbitrator in a dispute shall be qualified to serve as such arbitrator if such person has any financial or other interest in the company or labor organization involved in the dispute. (1945, c. 1045, s. 4; 1951, c. 1103, s. 1.)

§ 95-36.5. Fees and expenses.

(a) All the costs of any arbitration proceeding under this Article, including the fees and expenses of the arbitrator or arbitration panel, shall be paid by the parties to the proceeding in accordance with any agreement between them. In the absence of such an agreement, the award in the proceeding shall normally require the payment of such fees, expenses and other proper costs by one or more of the parties: Provided, that if the Commissioner of Labor deems that the public interest so requires, he may provide for the payment to any arbitrator appointed by him of per diem compensation at the rate established by the Commissioner, and actual travel and other necessary expenses incurred while performing duties arising under this Article.

(b) In cases where an arbitrator has been appointed by the Commissioner, the Department of Labor may furnish necessary stenographic, clerical and technical service and assistance to the arbitrator or arbitration panel.

(c) Expenditures of public funds authorized under this section shall be paid from funds appropriated for the administration of this Article. (1945, c. 1045, s. 5; 1947, c. 379, ss. 1-3; 1951, c. 1103, s. 1.)

§ 95-36.6. Appointment of arbitrators.

The parties may by agreement determine the method of appointment of the arbitrator or arbitration panel. If the parties have agreed upon arbitration under this Article and have not otherwise agreed upon the number of arbitrators or the method for their appointment, the controversy shall be heard and decided by a single arbitrator designated in such manner as the Commissioner of Labor shall determine. Any person or agency selected by agreement or otherwise to appoint an arbitrator or arbitrators shall send by registered mail to each of the parties to the proposed proceeding notice of the demand for arbitration. The arbitrator or arbitration panel, as the case may be, shall have such powers and duties as are conferred by the voluntary agreement of the parties, and, if there is no agreement to the contrary, shall have power to decide the arbitrability as well as the merits of the dispute. (1945, c. 1045, s. 5; 1947, c. 379, ss. 1-3; 1951, c. 1103, s. 1.)

§ 95-36.7. Arbitration procedure.

Upon the selection or appointment of an arbitrator or arbitration panel in any labor dispute, a statement of the issues or questions in dispute shall be submitted to said arbitrator or panel in writing, signed by one or more of the parties or their authorized agents. The arbitrator or panel shall appoint a time and place for the hearing, and notify the parties thereof, and may postpone or adjourn the hearing from time to time as may be necessary, subject to any time limits which are agreed upon by the parties. If any party neglects to appear before the arbitrator or panel after reasonable notice, the arbitrator or panel may nevertheless proceed to hear and determine the controversy. Unless the parties have otherwise agreed, the findings and decision of a majority of an arbitration panel shall constitute the award of the panel and, if a majority vote of the panel cannot be obtained, then the findings and decision of the impartial chairman of the panel shall constitute such award. To be enforceable, the award shall be handed down within 60 days after the written statement of the issues or questions in dispute has been received by the arbitrator or panel, or within such further time as may be agreed to by the parties. (1945, c. 1045, s. 5; 1947, c. 379, ss. 1-3; 1951, c. 1103, s. 1.)

§ 95-36.8. Enforcement of arbitration agreement and award.

(a) Written agreements to arbitrate labor disputes, including but not restricted to controversies relating to wages, hours and other conditions of employment, shall be valid, enforceable and irrevocable, except upon such grounds as exist in law or equity for the rescission or revocation of any contract, in either of the following cases:

(1)   Where there is a provision in a collective bargaining agreement or any other contract, hereafter made or extended, for the settlement by arbitration of a controversy or controversies thereafter arising between the parties;

(2)   Where there is an agreement to submit to arbitration a controversy or controversies already existing between the parties.

(b) Any arbitration award, made pursuant to an agreement of the parties described in subsection (a) of this section and in accordance with this Article, shall be final and binding upon the parties to the arbitration proceedings. (1945, c. 1045, s. 5; 1947, c. 379, ss. 1-3; 1951, c. 1103, s. 1.)

§ 95-36.9. Stay of proceedings.

(a) If any action or proceeding be brought in any court upon any issue referable to arbitration under an agreement described in subsection (a) of G.S. 95-36.8, the court where the action or proceeding is pending or a judge of the superior court having jurisdiction in any county where the dispute arose shall stay the action or proceeding, except for any temporary relief which may be appropriate pending the arbitration award, until such arbitration has been had in accordance with the terms of the agreement. The application for stay may be made by motion in writing of a party to the agreement, but such motion must be made before answer or demurrer to the pleading by which the action or proceeding was begun.

(b) Any party against whom arbitration proceedings have been initiated may, within 10 days after receiving written notice of the issue or questions to be passed upon at the arbitration hearing, apply to any judge of the superior court having jurisdiction in any county where the dispute arose for a stay of the arbitration upon the ground that he has not agreed to the arbitration of the controversy involved. Any such application shall be made in writing and heard in a summary way in the manner and upon the notice provided by law or rules of court for the making and hearing of motions generally, except that it shall be entitled to priority in the interest of prompt disposition. If no such application is made within said 10-day period, a party against whom arbitration proceedings have been initiated cannot raise the issue of arbitrability except before the arbitrator and in proceedings subsequent to the award.

(c) Any party against whom an arbitration award has been issued may, within 10 days after receiving written notice of such award, apply to any judge of the superior court having jurisdiction in any county where the dispute arose for a stay of the award upon the ground that it exceeds the authority conferred by the arbitration agreement. Any such application shall be made in writing and heard in a summary way in the manner and upon the notice provided by law or rules of court for the making and hearing of motions generally, except that it shall be entitled to priority in the interest of prompt disposition. If no such application is made within said 10-day period, a party against whom arbitration proceedings have been initiated cannot raise the issue of arbitrability except before the arbitrator or arbitrators, or in proceedings to enforce the award. Any failure to abide by an award shall not constitute a breach of the contract to arbitrate, pending disposition of a timely application for stay of the award pursuant to this paragraph. (1951, c. 1103, s. 1.)

Article 5.

Regulation of Employment Agencies.

§§ 95-37 through 95-47. Recodified as §§ 95-47.1 to 95-47.13.

Article 5A.

Regulation of Private Personnel Services.

§ 95-47.1. Definitions.

As used in this Article, unless the context clearly requires otherwise:

(1) "Accept" employment means to accept an employer's offer of employment or to begin work for an employer.

(2) "Applicant," except where it refers to an applicant for a private personnel services license, means any person who uses or attempts to use the services of a private personnel service in seeking employment.

(3) "Commissioner" means the North Carolina Commissioner of Labor or any person designated by the Commissioner as the representative of the Commissioner.

(4) "Complaint" means a communication to the Commissioner or department alleging facts that could support issuance of a warning or citation under G.S. 95-47.9.

(5) "Contract" means any agreement between a private personnel service and an applicant obligating the applicant to pay a fee or any agreement subsequent to such contract reducing the obligations of the private personnel service to the applicant under the contract.

(6) "Employee" means a person performing work or services of any kind or character for compensation.

(7) "Employer" means a person employing or seeking to employ a person for compensation, or any representative or employee of such employer.

(8) "Employment" means any service or engagement rendered or undertaken for wages, salary, commission, or other form of compensation.

(9) "Fee" means anything of value, including money or other valuable consideration or services or the promise of any of the foregoing, required or received by a private personnel service, in payment for any of its services, or act rendered or to be rendered by any private personnel service.

(10) "Interview" means a meeting between an employer and an applicant to discuss potential employment.

(11) "Job order" means an oral or written communication from an employer authorizing a private personnel service to refer applicants for a position the employer has available.

(12) "Licensee" means any person licensed by the Commissioner to operate a private personnel service.

(13) "Manager" of a private personnel service means the person who is responsible for the operation of an office of a private personnel service.

(14) "Owner" of a private personnel service means the sole proprietor of a private personnel service operated as a sole proprietorship; any partner in a partnership that owns or operates a private personnel service; any stockholder with a financial interest greater than 10 percent (10%) in a corporation that owns or operates a private personnel service.

(15) "Person" means any individual, association, partnership or corporation.

(16) "Private personnel service" means any business operated in the State of North Carolina by any person for profit which secures employment or by any form of advertising holds itself out to applicants as able to secure employment or to provide information or service of any kind purporting to promote, lead to or result in employment for the applicant with any employer other than itself, where any applicant may become liable for the payment of a fee to the private personnel service, either directly or indirectly. "Private personnel service" does not include:

a. Any educational, religious, charitable, fraternal or benevolent organization which charges no fee for services rendered in securing employment or providing information about employment;

b. Any employment service operated by the State of North Carolina, the Government of the United States, or any city, county, or town, or any agency thereof;

c. Any temporary help service that at no time advertises or represents that its employee may, with the approval of the temporary help service, be employed by one of its client companies on a permanent basis and which does not act as a private personnel service or an employer fee paid personnel service;

d. Any newspaper of general circulation or other business engaged primarily in communicating information other than information about specific positions of employment and that does not purport to adapt the information provided to the needs or desires of an individual subscriber;

e. Employment offices that charge no fee to the applicant other than union dues or to the employer and which are used solely for the hiring of employees under a valid union contract by the employer subscribing to this contract;

f. Any employer fee paid personnel consulting service or temporary help service that offers temporary to permanent placement when the service operates on a one hundred percent (100%) employer fee paid service basis, requires no applicant placement contract, and has no recourse against an applicant for a fee under any circumstances.

(17) "Refer" an applicant means to submit resumes to an employer, arrange interviews between an applicant and an employer, or to provide an employer with the name of an applicant. (1929, c. 178, ss. 1, 10; 1979, c. 780, s. 1; 1989, c. 414, s. 1.)

§ 95-47.2. Licensing procedures.

(a) No person shall open, keep, maintain, own, operate or carry on a private personnel service unless the person has first procured a license therefor as provided in this Article.

(b) An application for license shall be made to the Commissioner. If the private personnel service is owned by an individual, the application shall be made by that individual; if the service is owned by a partnership, the application shall be made by all partners; if the service is owned by a corporation, the application shall be made by all stockholders who own at least twenty percent (20%) of the issued and outstanding voting stock of the corporation, or if the service is owned by an association, society, or corporation in which no one individual owns at least twenty percent (20%) of the issued and outstanding voting stock, the application shall be made by the president, vice-president, secretary and treasurer of the owner, by whatever title designated. The application shall state the name and address of the individual who is responsible for the direction and operation of the placement activities of the private personnel service whether that individual be one of the applicants or another person; whether or not that individual has ever been employed in a private personnel service; the name and address of each of the license applicant's prior employers during the five years immediately preceding the license application; and such other information relating to the good moral character of that individual as the Commissioner may require. No change in such persons shall take place without prior notification to the Commissioner.

(c) Each application for license shall be in writing and in the form prescribed by the Commissioner, and shall state truthfully the name under which the business is to be conducted; the street and number of the building or place where the business is to be conducted.

(d) Upon the receipt of an application for a license the Commissioner:

(1) Shall publish a notice of the pending application in a newspaper of general circulation in the area of the proposed location of the employment agency and may publish the notice in a newspaper of general circulation in each area in which the applicant (or if a corporation, the president and majority shareholder) has resided during the five years preceding the time of the application. The applicant shall incur the cost associated with the publication of this legal advertisement. The notice shall include a statement informing individuals of their right to protest the issuance of a license by filing within 10 days written comments with the Commissioner. The protest shall be in writing and signed by the person filing the protest or by his authorized agent or attorney, and shall state reasons why the license should not be granted. Upon the filing of a protest, the Commissioner, if he determines the protest to be of such a nature that a hearing should be conducted and that the protest is for a cause on which denial of a license may properly be based, shall appoint a time and place for a hearing on the application and shall give at least seven days' notice of that time and place to the license applicant and to the person filing the protest. The hearing shall be conducted in accordance with the provisions of the rules of the Administrative Procedure Act.

(2) Shall investigate the character, criminal record and business integrity of each applicant for agency license and shall investigate the criminal records of all persons listed as agency owners, officers, directors or managers. The applicant and all agency owners, officers, directors and managers shall assist the department in obtaining necessary information by authorizing the release of all relevant information. The applicant shall incur the cost associated with this background investigation.

(2a) The Department of Justice may provide a criminal record check to the Commissioner for a person or agency who has applied for a license through the Commissioner. The Commissioner shall provide to the Department of Justice, along with the request, the fingerprints of all applicants, any additional information required by the Department of Justice, and a form signed by the applicants consenting to the check of the criminal record and to the use of the fingerprints and other identifying information required by the State or national repositories. The applicants' fingerprints shall be forwarded to the State Bureau of Investigation for a search of the State's criminal history record file, and the State Bureau of Investigation shall forward a set of the fingerprints to the Federal Bureau of Investigation for a national criminal history check. The Commissioner shall keep all information pursuant to this subdivision privileged, in accordance with applicable State law and federal guidelines, and the information shall be confidential and shall not be a public record under Chapter 132 of the General Statutes.

The Department of Justice may charge each applicant a fee for conducting the checks of criminal history records authorized by this subdivision.

(3) Upon completion of the investigation, or 60 days after the application was received, whichever is later, but in no case more than 75 days after the application was received, shall determine whether or not a license should be issued. The license shall be denied for any of the following reasons:

a. If the applicant for agency license, or the president or majority shareholder of a corporate applicant, omits or falsifies any material information asked for in the application and required by the Commissioner.

b. If any owner, officer, director or manager of the employment agency:

1. Has been convicted in any state of the criminal offense of embezzlement, obtaining money under false pretenses, forgery, conspiracy to defraud or any similar offense involving fraud or moral turpitude;

2. Was an owner, officer, director or manager of an employment agency or other business whose license was revoked or that was otherwise caused to cease operation by action of any State or federal agency or court because of violations of law or regulation relating to deceptive or unfair practices in the conduct of business;

3. As an owner or manager of an employment agency or other business or as an employment counselor was found by any State or federal agency or court to have violated any law or regulation relating to deceptive or unfair practices in the conduct of business; or

4. In any other demonstrable way engaged in deceptive or unfair practices in the conduct of business.

c. If the employment agency will be operated on the same premises as a loan agency (as defined in G.S. 105-88) or collection agency (as defined in G.S. 58-70-15).

(e) If it appears upon the hearing or from the inspection, examination or investigation made by the Commissioner that the owners, partners, corporation officers or the agency manager are not persons of good moral character or that the license applicant has not complied with the provisions of this Article, the application shall be denied and a license shall not be granted. The Commissioner shall find facts to substantiate his denial of the issuance of a license. Each application shall be granted or refused within 60 days from the date of its filing, or if a hearing is held, within 75 days. Any license heretofore or hereafter issued shall expire 12 months from the date of its issuance, and shall be renewed as hereinafter provided unless sooner revoked by the Commissioner.

(f) No license shall be granted to a person to operate as a private personnel service where the name of the business is similar or identical to that of any existing licensed business (except where a franchiser has licensed two or more persons to use the same name within the State) or directly or indirectly expresses or connotes any limitation, specification or discrimination contrary to current State or federal laws against discrimination in employment.

(g) Every license shall contain the name of the person licensed and shall designate the city in which the license is issued, the name of the manager and date of the license. The license shall be displayed in a conspicuous place in the area where job applicants are received by the agency.

(h) A license granted as provided in this Article shall not be valid for any person other than the person to whom it is issued or for any place other than that designated in the license and shall not be assigned or transferred without the consent of the Commissioner, whose consent must be based on the standards contained in this Article. Applications for consent to assign or transfer shall be made in the same manner as an application for a license, and all the provisions of this Article shall apply to applications for consent. The location of a private personnel service shall not be changed without notice to the Commissioner, and any change of location shall be endorsed upon the license. A person who has obtained a license in accordance with the provisions of this Article may apply for additional licenses to conduct additional private personnel services in accordance with the provisions of this Article. The manner of application, and the conditions and terms applicable to the issuance of the additional licenses shall be the same as for an original license. The same agency manager may be designated in all such licenses.

(i) Temporary license. - If ownership of a licensed private personnel service is transferred, the department shall issue a temporary license to any new owner or successor if it appears to the department that issuance of such a license would serve the public interest. A temporary license shall be effective for a period of 90 days and shall not be renewed.

(j) Each licensee shall, before the license is issued or renewed, deposit with the department a bond payable to the State of North Carolina and executed by a surety company duly authorized to transact business in the State of North Carolina in the amount of ten thousand dollars ($10,000) and upon condition that the private personnel service will pay to applicants all refunds due under this Article and regulations adopted hereunder if the private personnel service terminates its business. (1929, c. 178, ss. 2, 3; 1931, c. 312, s. 3; 1979, c. 780, s. 1; 1987, c. 282, s. 12; 1989, c. 414, s. 2; 2002-147, s. 12; 2003-308, s. 9.)

§ 95-47.3. Fees and contracts; filing with Commissioner.

(a) Every license applicant shall file with the Commissioner a schedule of fees or charges made by the private personnel service to applicants for employment for any services rendered, stating clearly the conditions under which the private personnel service refunds or does not refund a fee, together with all rules or regulations that may in any manner affect the fees charged or to be charged for any service. Every license applicant and licensee shall include in its schedule of fees or charges a clear description of how it determines fees for placement of employment, the compensation of which is based, in whole or in part, on commission. Changes in the schedule may be made, but no change shall become effective until seven calendar days after the filing thereof with the Commissioner. It is unlawful for a private personnel service to charge, demand, collect or receive a greater compensation from an applicant for employment for any service performed than as specified in the schedule filed with the Commissioner.

(b)   Every license applicant shall file with the Commissioner a copy of the contract which the private personnel service will require applicants for employment to execute. (1979, c. 780, s. 1; 1991 (Reg. Sess., 1992), c. 970, s. 1.)

§ 95-47.3A. Fee reimbursement from employers due to overstated earnings expectations.

(a)   An applicant who accepts employment that is compensated in whole or in part on a commission basis, and who pays a fee to the licensee calculated on the commission-based compensation amount stated by the employer in the written job order, may file a written complaint with the Commissioner if the applicant did not earn at least eighty percent (80%) of the compensation amount stated by the employer in the written job order. If the applicant files the written complaint before the period upon which the anticipated earnings is based has ended, the Commissioner shall prorate the amount earned over the period of time the applicant worked prior to the filing of the complaint in order to determine whether or not the applicant earned at least eighty percent (80%) of the compensation amount stated by the employer in the written job order.

(b)   The Commissioner shall investigate all complaints filed pursuant to subsection (a) of this section. After completion of the investigation and a hearing, the Commissioner shall order the employer to reimburse the applicant for part or all of the fee paid by the applicant to the licensee if the Commissioner finds the applicant is entitled to the refund based on all of the following:

(1)   The applicant did not earn at least eighty percent (80%) of the compensation amount stated by the employer in the written job order;

(2)   The licensee reasonably relied on the compensation information provided by the employer in calculating the fee paid by the applicant;

(3)   It is unrealistic to expect that an employee could earn substantially the amount of commission-based compensation stated by the employer in the written job order filed with the licensee; and

(4) The fee paid by the applicant to the licensee was calculated based on the commission-based compensation stated by the employer in the written job order.

(c) The reimbursement due the applicant under subsection (b) shall be the difference between the fee actually paid by the applicant to the licensee, and the fee that the applicant would have paid if the compensation stated by the employer in the written job order had been what the applicant actually earned or reasonably could have earned during the applicable employment period.

(d) The Commissioner shall adopt rules setting forth procedures for complaints and investigations, and standards for determining whether a statement by the employer in the licensee's written job order of potential or anticipated commission-based earnings is realistic under the circumstances. The Commissioner or his authorized representative shall have power to administer oaths and examine witnesses, issue subpoenas, compel the attendance of witnesses and the production of papers, books, accounts, records, payrolls, documents, and take depositions and affidavits in any proceeding hereunder. Additionally, the Commissioner shall adopt rules setting forth procedures for enforcement of any order made under subsections (b) and (c) of this section. Rules adopted by the Commissioner pursuant to this section shall be in accordance with Chapter 150B of the General Statutes.

(e) The Commissioner shall enforce and administer the provisions of this section, and the Commissioner or his authorized representative is empowered to hold hearings and to institute civil proceedings to collect on behalf of the applicant any amounts determined to be owed by the employer. (1991 (Reg. Sess., 1992), c. 970, s. 3.)

§ 95-47.4. Contracts; contents; approval; tying contracts forbidden.

(a) A contract between a private personnel service and an applicant shall be in writing, labeled as a contract, physically separate from any application and made in duplicate. One copy shall be given to the applicant and the other shall be kept by the private personnel service as required by G.S. 95-47.5(2).

(b) Any contract that obligates an applicant to pay a fee to the private personnel service shall include:

(1) The name, address and telephone number of the private personnel service;

(2) The name of the applicant;

(3) The date the contract was signed;

(4) A clear schedule of the fees to be charged to the applicant at various salary levels;

(5) A clear explanation of when the applicant becomes obligated to pay a fee;

(6) A clear refund policy (or no refund policy) that conforms to the requirements of G.S. 95-47.4(f) and (g);

(7) If the applicant is obligated whether or not the applicant accepts employment, a clear explanation of the services provided and a statement that the private personnel service does not guarantee that the applicant will obtain employment as a result of its services;

(8) A statement, in a type size no smaller than nine point, directly above the place for the applicant's signature, that reads as follows: "I have read and received a copy of this CONTRACT, which I understand makes me legally obligated to pay a fee under conditions outlined above." In the preceding statement the word "CONTRACT" and no others shall be in all capitals; and

(9) A statement that the private personnel service is licensed and regulated by the Commissioner and the address at which a copy of laws and regulations governing private personnel services may be obtained.

(c) A copy of each contract form to be used with applicants shall be filed with the Commissioner. Until the private personnel service receives written notification from the Commissioner that the form conforms to the requirements of this Article and regulations adopted hereunder, it shall not be used with applicants.

(d) A private personnel service shall not require an applicant to sign a contract with the private personnel service before the applicant has had an opportunity to read the contract and discuss the contract with an employee of the personnel agency who regularly arranges contacts and assists in negotiations between employers and applicants. A private personnel service shall not coerce an applicant into signing a contract by applying or using duress, undue influence, fraud or misrepresentation sufficient to invalidate the contract under North Carolina law.

(e) Any contract that obligates an applicant to pay a fee to the private personnel service when the applicant accepts employment shall be physically separate from any contract that obligates an applicant to pay a fee whether or not the applicant accepts employment. A private personnel service shall not require an applicant to sign one contract as a prerequisite to signing another contract or to pay a fee as a prerequisite to signing a contract. Express violations of this subsection are the following:

(1) Refusal to allow an applicant to contract for counseling, job information or resume writing services, if the applicant does not agree to pay an additional fee upon acceptance of employment; and

(2) Refusal to allow an applicant to contract for services which obligate the applicant only upon acceptance of employment, if the applicant does not agree to pay a registration fee or to contract for counseling, resume writing or other services.

(f) If a private personnel service has a refund policy, included on each contract that obligates an applicant upon acceptance of employment will be a statement defining:

(1) The length of the period of time covered by the refund policy;

(2) The exact manner of computing the refund so that the amount of refund due the applicant will be clear;

(3) The conditions under which a refund becomes due to the applicant. The conditions of the refund, if other than unconditional policy is used, shall contain a definition of the reasons for which a refund will not be made. A refund will not be denied except for a reason so stated in the definition of the contract;

(4) A personnel service shall abide by the refund policy stated on its contract by promptly paying to applicants any refund due under the terms of the contract.

(g) If a private personnel service has no refund policy, the private personnel service shall include on each contract that obligates an applicant upon acceptance of employment, in a type size no smaller than nine point, a statement that reads as follows:

"_____ (name of private personnel service) will make NO REFUND under any circumstances of fees paid by the applicant." In the preceding statement the words NO REFUND and no others shall be in all capitals.

(h) If a private personnel service places an applicant in a position of employment, the compensation of which is based, in whole or in part, on commission, the private personnel service shall:

(1) Have a written job order from the employer that includes the anticipated earnings upon which the private personnel service may base its fee, or

(2) In lieu of the written job order required by subdivision (1) of this subsection, have a policy of providing the same fee reimbursement as may be available to applicants from employers under the provisions of G.S. 95-47.3A.

In no case may the applicant collect the same reimbursement from both the employer and the private personnel service. When the private personnel service elects to obtain the written job order from the employer and not have its own reimbursement policy as described in subdivision (2) of this subsection, the private personnel service shall explain to the applicant and the employer how the fee for the placement is calculated, and shall inform in writing both the applicant and the employer of the provisions of G.S. 95-47.3A governing fee refunds from employers. (1979, c. 780, s. 1; 1991 (Reg. Sess., 1992), c. 970, s. 2; 1993, c. 202, s. 1; 1993 (Reg. Sess., 1994), c. 769, s. 29(a).)

§ 95-47.5. Records.

Every private personnel service shall maintain for a period of two years, the following records:

(1) Job orders or job specifications.

(2) Executed applicant contracts.

(3) Information on all placements made, including the employer's name and address; name and address of applicant placed; salary of the position; amount of fee charged; and refunds, where applicable. (1929, c. 178, s. 4; 1931, c. 312, s. 3; 1979, c. 780, s. 1.)

§ 95-47.6. Prohibited acts.

A private personnel service shall not engage in any of the following activities or conduct:

(1) Induce or attempt to induce any employee placed by that private personnel service to terminate his employment in order to obtain other employment through the private personnel service; or procure or attempt to procure the discharge of any person from his employment.

(2) Publish or cause to be published any false or fraudulent information, representation, promise, notice or advertisement.

(3) Advertise in newspapers or otherwise, unless the advertising contains the name of the private personnel service and the word "personnel service."

(4) Direct an applicant to visit or call upon an employer for the purpose of obtaining employment without having first obtained a job order or authorization from the employer for the interview. A private personnel service may attempt to sell the services of an applicant to an employer from whom no job order has been received and may charge a fee if the efforts result in the applicant's being employed.

(5) Send or cause to be sent any person to any employer where the private personnel service knows that the prospective employment is or would be in violation of State or federal laws governing minimum wages or child labor, or has been notified that a labor dispute is in progress, without notifying the applicant of that fact, or knowingly arrange an interview for an employment or occupation prohibited by law.

(6) Send or cause to be sent any person to any place which the private personnel service knows is maintained for immoral or illicit purposes.

(7) Divide or share, either directly or indirectly, the fees collected by the private personnel service, with contractors, sub-contractors, employers or their agents, foremen or anyone in their employ, or if the contractors, sub-contractors or employers be a corporation, any of the officers, directors or employees of the corporation to whom applicants for employment are sent.

(8) Make, cause to be made, or use any name, sign or advertising device bearing a name which is similar to or may reasonably be confused with the name of a federal, State, city, county or other governmental unit or agency.

(9) Knowingly make any false or misleading promise or representation or give any false or misleading information to any applicant or employer in regard to any employment, work or position, its nature, location, duration, compensation or the circumstances surrounding any employment, work or position including the availability thereof.

(10) Accept a registration fee from an applicant.

(11) Impose or attempt to collect any fee from any applicant unless that applicant accepts employment with an employer to which the applicant was directly or indirectly introduced by the private personnel service.

(12) A fee may be charged for resume writing provided the private personnel service does not require the applicant to become obligated for any other services. (1979, c. 780, s. 1.)

§ 95-47.7: Repealed by Session Laws 2003-308, s. 10, effective July 1, 2003.

§ 95-47.8: Repealed by Session Laws 2003-308, s. 11, effective July 1, 2003.

§ 95-47.9. Enforcement of Article; rules; hearing; penalty; criminal penalties.

(a) This Article shall be enforced by the Commissioner. The Commissioner or any duly authorized agent, deputies or assistants designated by the Commissioner, may upon receipt of a complaint that a private personnel service has violated a specific section of this Article, inspect those records relevant to the complaint which this Article requires the private personnel service to retain. The Commissioner may also subpoena those records and witnesses and may conduct investigations of any employer or other person where the Commissioner has reasonable grounds for believing that the employer or person has conspired or is conspiring with a private personnel service to violate this Article.

(b)   The Commissioner shall adopt rules necessary to carry out and administer the provisions of this Article.

(c)   Complaints against any licensed person shall be made in writing to the Commissioner.

(1)   If the complaint alleges a violation of this Article, the Commissioner shall cause an investigation to be made. If, as a result of the investigation, the Commissioner has reason to believe that a material violation of this Article has been committed by a private personnel service, the Commissioner may, after compliance with Chapter 150B of the General Statutes, deny, suspend, or revoke a license issued under this Article if it is determined that the licensee or any employee of the licensee is guilty of violating the provisions of this Article. In addition, the Commissioner may issue warnings or levy a fine against the private personnel service that shall not exceed two hundred fifty dollars ($250.00).

(2)   The denial, revocation, or suspension of a license or the issuance of a warning or fine by the Commissioner shall be in writing, shall be signed by the Commissioner or the Commissioner's designee, and shall state the grounds upon which the decision is based. The aggrieved person shall have the right to appeal from the decision as provided by Chapter 150B of the General Statutes.

(d)   Whenever a license is revoked pursuant to subsection (c) of this section, another license shall not be issued to the same person within three years from the date of the revocation.

(e)   Any person who operates as a private personnel service without first obtaining the appropriate license (i) shall be guilty of a Class 1 misdemeanor; and (ii) be subject to a civil penalty of not less than fifty dollars ($50.00) nor more than one hundred dollars ($100.00) for each day the private personnel service operates without a license, the penalty not to exceed a total of two thousand dollars ($2,000). Actions to recover civil penalties shall be initiated by the Attorney General. The clear proceeds of civil penalties provided for in this section shall be remitted to the Civil Penalty and Forfeiture Fund in accordance with G.S. 115C-457.2. (1929, c. 178, ss. 3-5, 7, 9; 1931, c. 312, s. 3; 1979, c. 780, s. 1; 1993, c. 539, s. 663; 1994, Ex. Sess., c. 24, s. 14(c); 1998-215, s. 109; 2003-308, s. 12.)

§ 95-47.10. Power of Commissioner to seek injunction.

The Commissioner may apply to courts having jurisdiction for injunctions to prevent violations of this Chapter or of rules issued pursuant thereto, and such courts are empowered to grant such injunctions regardless of whether criminal prosecution or other action has been or may be instituted as a result of such violation. A single act of unauthorized or illegal practice shall be sufficient, if shown, to invoke the injunctive relief of this section or criminal or civil penalties under G.S. 95-47.9(e). (1979, c. 780, s. 1.)

§ 95-47.11. Government employment agencies unaffected.

This Article shall not in any manner affect or apply to the State of North Carolina, the government of the United States, or to any city, county or town, or any agency of any of those governments. (1929, c. 178, s. 10; 1979, c. 780, s. 1.)

§ 95-47.12. License taxes placed upon agencies not affected.

This Article is not intended to conflict with or affect any license tax placed upon private personnel services by the revenue laws of North Carolina, but instead shall be construed as supplementary thereto in exercising the police powers of the State. (1929, c. 178, s. 11; 1979, c. 780, s. 1.)

§ 95-47.13. Severability.

If any provision of this Article or the application thereof to any person or circumstance is held invalid, such invalidity shall not affect other provisions or applications, and to this end the provisions of this Article are severable. (1929, c. 178, s. 9; 1979, c. 780, s. 1.)

§ 95-47.14. Notification requirement.

Any temporary help service as described in G.S. 95-47.1(16)c. that operates in North Carolina shall notify the Department of Labor in writing that the temporary help service:

(1)   Operates only as a temporary help service;

(2)   Establishes an employer-employee relationship with its temporaries;

(3)   Does not operate as a private personnel service or an employer fee paid personnel consulting service. (1989, c. 414, s. 3.)

§ 95-47.15. Certification requirement.

Any employer fee paid personnel consulting service or temporary help service, as the two terms are described in G.S. 95-47.1(16)f., that operates in North Carolina shall certify annually to the Department of Labor on a form prescribed by the Commissioner that the service:

(1)   Operates on a one hundred percent (100%) employer fee paid basis;

(2)   Requires no applicant placement contract; and

(3)   Has no recourse against an applicant for a fee under any circumstances. (1989, c. 414, s. 3.)

§§ 95-47.16 through 95-47.18. Reserved for future codification purposes.

Article 5B.

Regulation of Job Listing Services.

§ 95-47.19. Definitions.

Definitions of terms used in this Article shall be the same as in Chapter 95, Article 5A (Regulation of Private Personnel Services), with the words "job listing service" substituted, where appropriate, for the words "private personnel service." "Job listing service" means any business operated in the State of North Carolina by any person for profit which publishes, either orally or in writing, lists of specific positions of employment available with any employer other than itself or which holds itself out to applicants as able to provide information about specific positions of employment available with any employer other than itself, which charges a fee to any applicant for its services or purported services and which performs none of the activities of a private personnel service other than the publishing of job listings. "Job listing service" does not include:

(1) Any educational, religious, charitable, fraternal or benevolent organization which charges no fee for services rendered in providing information about employment;

(2) Any employment service operated by the State of North Carolina, the Government of the United States, or any city, county or town, or any agency thereof;

(3) Any temporary help service that charges no fee for services rendered in providing information about employment;

(4) Any newspaper of general circulation or other business engaged primarily in communicating information other than information about specific positions of employment and that does not purport to adapt the information provided to the needs or desires of an individual subscriber;

(5) Employment offices that charge no fee to the applicant other than union dues and which are used solely for the hiring of employees under a valid union contract by the employers subscribing to this contract. (1979, c. 780, s. 2.)

§ 95-47.20. License required.

No person shall operate a job listing service in North Carolina without first obtaining a license from the Commissioner. A job listing service shall have a separate license for each location at which it maintains an office. (1979, c. 780, s. 2.)

§ 95-47.21. Violation of this Article; criminal and civil penalty.

Any person who violates the provisions of this Article by operating a job listing service without a valid license from the Commissioner shall be subject, under current regulations adopted pursuant to this Article, to criminal and civil penalties in the same amount and under substantially the same procedure as that provided under G.S. 95-47.9(e) for a person operating a private personnel service. (1979, c. 780, s. 2.)

§ 95-47.22. Licensing procedure.

(a) In addition to the requirements of subsection (b) of this section, the procedure, under rules adopted pursuant to this Article, for the issuance, denial and renewal of job listing service licenses and other aspects of the licensing of job listing services by the Commissioner shall be substantially the same as that provided under Article 5A of this Chapter for the licensing of private personnel services.

(b) Before the Department may issue or renew a license under this Article, each licensee shall deposit with the Department a bond payable to the State of North Carolina and executed by a surety company duly authorized to transact business in this State. The bond shall be in the amount of twenty-five thousand dollars ($25,000) and, if the job listing service terminates its business, shall be held by the Department until all refunds due applicants under this Article have been paid by the job listing service. (1979, c. 780, s. 2; 1993, c. 172, s. 1.)

§ 95-47.23. Enforcement.

Under regulations adopted pursuant to this Article, a job listing service may be issued a warning, citation or notice of violation, or may have its license revoked or suspended, or its licensee reprimanded, censured or placed on probation in substantially the same manner and under substantially the same procedure as that provided for a private personnel service under Article 5A of this Chapter. (1979, c. 780, s. 2.)

§ 95-47.24. Certain practices prohibited.

Under regulations adopted pursuant to this Article, a job listing service shall abide by provisions substantially the same as those provided under G.S. 95-47.6(7) (kickbacks), G.S. 95-47.6(9) (misrepresentation), and G.S. 95-47.2(d)(3)c. (loan or collection agencies) for a private personnel service. (1979, c. 780, s. 2; 1993, c. 172, s. 2.)

§ 95-47.25. Contracts; contents; approval.

A contract between a job listing service and an applicant shall be in writing, labeled as a contract, physically separate from any application form and made in duplicate, and shall include:

(1) A clear explanation of the services provided and the amount of the fee;

(2) In a type size no smaller than nine point, a statement that reads "I understand that _____ (name of job listing service) does not guarantee that I will obtain employment through its services. I understand that _____ (name of job listing service) does not refund fees for any reason," unless the job listing service agrees in the contract to refund to the applicant any fee the applicant paid to the job listing service if within three months of paying such a fee the applicant has not accepted an employment position listed in a publication of the job listing service;

(3) A statement that the job listing service is not a private personnel service or employment agency, that no additional fee will be charged to the applicant upon acceptance of employment and that the job listing service will not set up interviews or otherwise arrange direct contacts between an employer and the applicant; and

(4) A statement that the job listing service is licensed and regulated by the Commissioner and the address at which a copy of regulations governing job listing services may be obtained.

A copy of each contract form to be used with applicants shall be filed with the Commissioner. Until the job listing service receives written notification from the Commissioner that the form conforms to the requirements of this Article and regulations adopted hereunder, it shall not be used with applicants. A job listing service shall not accept a fee from any applicant before the applicant has read and received a copy of the contract. (1979, c. 780, s. 2.)

§ 95-47.26. Advertising and publication.

(a) In conducting any form of advertising, a job listing service shall identify itself by its business name and identify itself as a job listing service by using in the name or elsewhere in the advertising the term "job listing service."

(b) Prior to advertising or publishing information about an available job, a job listing service shall receive a job order and shall record the job order, the date it was received and the name of the employer representative or other business who gave the job order to the job listing service. No description or representation of an employment position shall be stated in any advertising or other publication, unless the information is included on the recorded job order for the position. Information about a single employment position shall not be used in more than one advertisement or listing in a single issue of any publication.

(c) A job listing service shall not publish or cause to be published any information which it knows or reasonably ought to know is false or deceptive or which it has no reasonable basis for believing to be true.

(d) In conducting any form of advertising, a job listing service shall not use the term "no fee" or any other term indicating that applicants will not be financially obligated to the job listing service. (1979, c. 780, s. 2.)

§ 95-47.27. Fee receipts.

A job listing service shall give every applicant from whom payment is received a receipt stating the name and address of the job listing service, the name of the applicant, the date and the amount of the payment. (1979, c. 780, s. 2.)

§ 95-47.28. Prohibited job listings.

A job listing service shall not publish information about a position of employment with an employer that the job listing service knows or has reason to know:

(1)   Has included false information in the job order; or

(2)   Has a strike or lockout at its business, unless the applicant is so informed in the publication; or

(3)   Is engaging in unlawful or immoral activity; or

(4)   Is in financial or other difficulty likely to lead to imminent cessation of operation, unless the applicant is so informed in the publication; or

(5)   Is an employer in which the job listing service or any owner of the job listing service has a financial interest greater than ten percent (10%), unless the applicant is so informed in the publication. (1979, c. 780, s. 2.)

§ 95-47.29. Records of the job listing service.

Each job listing service shall maintain and make available for inspection by the Commissioner the following records of the operation of the job listing service for the 18 months immediately preceding:

(1)   The job listing service's copies of all contracts executed with applicants;

(2)   Copies of all fee receipts;

(3)   Copies of all advertising and job lists published orally or in writing, indexed or attached to the recorded job order (including the date it was received and the name of the employer representative or other business who gave it) for

each position advertised or listed, and records of the dates advertisements were run on publications issued; and

(4) Any records required by the Commissioner under regulations adopted pursuant to this Article. (1979, c. 780, s. 2.)

§ 95-47.30. Administration of this Article.

This Article shall be enforced under the general supervision of the Commissioner, who shall have the same powers and duties in the enforcement of this Article as in the enforcement of Article 5A of this Chapter. (1979, c. 780, s. 2.)

§ 95-47.31. Review of job listing services.

After the Commissioner receives written statements from two or more applicants complaining that the applicant failed to obtain employment as a result of the services of a job listing service, the Commissioner may contact other applicants who have paid a fee to the job listing service for the purpose of determining what percentage of such applicants obtain employment as a result of the services of the job listing service. After gathering information from such applicants and following the requirements of due process, the Commissioner shall place the survey results in the public records. (1979, c. 780, s. 2.)

§ 95-47.32. Severability.

If any provision of this Article or the application thereof to any person or circumstance is held invalid, such invalidity shall not affect other provisions or applications, and to this end the provisions of this Article are severable. (1979, c. 780, s. 2.)

Article 6.

Separate Toilets for Sexes.

§§ 95-48 through 95-53: Repealed by Session Laws 1993, c. 204, s.1.

Article 7A.

Uniform Boiler and Pressure Vessel Act.

§§ 95-54 through 95-69.7. Repealed by Session Laws 1981 (Regular Session, 1982), c. 1187, s. 1.

Article 7A.

Uniform Boiler and Pressure Vessel Act.

§ 95-69.8. Short title.

This Article shall be known as the Uniform Boiler and Pressure Vessel Act of North Carolina. (1975, c. 895, s. 1.)

§ 95-69.9. Definitions.

(a) The term "board" shall mean the North Carolina Board of Boiler and Pressure Vessel Rules.

(b) The term "boiler" shall mean a closed vessel in which water is heated, steam is generated, steam is superheated, or any combination thereof, under pressure or vacuum by the direct or indirect application of heat. The term "boiler" shall also include fired units for heating or vaporizing liquids other than water where these units are complete within themselves.

(b1) The term "Chief Inspector" shall mean the individual appointed by the Commissioner to hold the office of Chief of the Boiler Safety Bureau within the Department of Labor. The Chief Inspector serves as the North Carolina member on the National Board of Boiler and Pressure Vessel Inspectors.

(c) The term "Commissioner" shall mean the North Carolina Commissioner of Labor.

(d) Repealed by Session Laws 2005-453, s. 1.

(d1) The term "Deputy Inspector" shall mean any Boiler and Pressure Vessel Inspector who is employed by the Department of Labor and is subordinate to the Chief Inspector.

(e) The term "inspection certificate" or "certificate of inspection" shall mean certification by the Chief Inspector that a boiler or pressure vessel is in compliance with the rules and regulations adopted under this Article.

(f) The term "inspector's commission" shall mean a written authorization by the Commissioner for a person who has met the qualifications set out in this Article to conduct inspections of boilers and pressure vessels.

(f1) The term "National Board" shall mean the National Board of Boiler and Pressure Vessel Inspectors.

(f2) The term "person" shall mean any individual, association, partnership, firm, corporation, private organization, or the State of North Carolina or any political subdivision of the State or any unit of local government.

(g) The term "pressure vessel" shall mean a vessel in which the pressure is obtained from an indirect source or by the application of heat from an indirect source or a direct source, other than those included within the term "boiler". (1975, c. 895, s. 2; 1993, c. 351, s. 1; 2005-453, s. 1.)

§ 95-69.10. Application of Article; exemptions.

(a) This Article shall apply to all boilers and pressure vessels constructed, used, or designed for operation in this State including all new and existing installations unless specifically excluded by subsection (b) of this section.

(b) This Article shall not apply to:

(1) Boilers and pressure vessels owned or operated by the federal government, unless the agency in question has asked for coverage by this Article.

(2) Pressure vessels used for transportation or storage of compressed gases when constructed in compliance with the specifications of the United States Department of Transportation and when charged with gas marked, maintained, and periodically requalified for use, as required by appropriate regulations of the United States Department of Transportation.

(3) Portable pressure vessels used for agricultural purposes only or for pumping or drilling in an open field for water, gas or coal, gold, talc, or other minerals and metals.

(4) Boilers and pressure vessels which are located in private residences or in apartment houses of less than six families.

(5) Repealed by Session Laws 2007-231, s. 1, effective July 18, 2007.

(6) Air tanks located on vehicles licensed under the rules and regulations of other state authorities operating under rules and regulations substantially similar to those of this State and used for carrying passengers or freight within interstate commerce.

(7) Air tanks installed on right-of-way of railroads and used directly in the operation of trains.

(8) Any of the following pressure vessels that do not exceed the listed limitations if the vessel is not equipped with a quick actuating closure:

a. Five cubic feet in volume and 250 psig.

b. Three cubic feet in volume and 350 psig.

c. One and one-half cubic feet in volume and 600 psig.

d. An inside diameter of six inches with no limitation on pressure.

(9) Pressure vessels operating at a working pressure not exceeding 15 psig.

(10) Pressure vessels with a nominal water capacity not exceeding 120 gallons and containing water under pressure at temperatures not exceeding 120°F, including those containing air, the compression of which serves as a cushion.

(11) Boilers and pressure vessels on railroad steam locomotives that are subject to federal railway safety regulations pursuant to 49 C.F.R. § 230.

(12) Repealed by Session Laws 1985, c. 620, s. 2.

(13) Coil-type hot water supply boilers, generally referred to as steam jennies, where the water can flash into steam when released directly to the atmosphere through a manually operated nozzle and where adequate safety relief valves and controls are installed on them, provided none of the following limitations are exceeded:

a. There is no drum, header, or other steam space.

b. No steam is generated within the coil.

c. Maximum 1 inch tube size.

d. Maximum ¾ inch nominal pipe size.

e. Maximum 6 gallon nominal water storage capacity.

f. Water temperature of 350°F.

(14) Pressure vessels containing water at a temperature not exceeding 110 degrees fahrenheit except that this provision shall not exclude hydropneumatic pressure vessels from regulation.

(15) An air tank that does not exceed eight cubic feet in volume that is installed on a service vehicle.

(16) Autoclaves in medical offices and hospitals that are less than five cubic feet in volume, even if they are equipped with a quick actuating closure.

(17) Coil-type hot water supply boilers of the instantaneous type where adequate safety relief valves and controls are installed if none of the following limitations are exceeded:

a. There is no drum or header.

b. No steam is generated within the coil.

c. Maximum one-inch tube size.

d. Maximum three-quarter-inch nominal pipe size.

e. Maximum six-gallon nominal water storage capacity.

f. Water temperature not to exceed 250°F.

g. Maximum heat input does not exceed 400,000 Btu/hr or 110 kW.

h. Maximum pressure of 260 psig.

(18) Toy boilers, if all of the following apply:

a. The water containing volume of the boiler is less than one quart.

b. The operating pressure does not exceed 15 psig.

c. The maximum outside diameter of the shell is no greater than six inches.

d. The boiler is manually fired by solid fuels.

(19) Pressure vessels associated with electrical apparatus in electrical switchyards if the pressure vessels have proper pressure relief devices.

(20) Carbon dioxide tanks used in beverage dispensing service.

(c) The construction and inspection requirements established by the Department of Labor shall not apply to hot water supply boilers or water heaters which are directly fired with oil, gas, or electricity, or to hot water storage tanks heated by steam or any other indirect means, if they are equipped with ASME Code and National Board certified safety relief valves and do not exceed any of the following limitations:

(1) Heat input of 200,000 Btu/hr or 58.6 kW.

(2) Repealed by Session Laws 2005-453, s. 2.

(3) Nominal water capacity of 120 gallons.

(d) The construction requirements established by the Department of Labor shall not apply to pressure vessels installed in this State prior to December 31, 1981, if they are equipped with ASME Code and National Board certified safety relief valves and:

(1) Are of one-piece, unwelded, forged construction;

(2) Are constructed before January 1, 1981, and operating or could be operated, under the laws of any state or Canadian Province that has adopted one or more sections of the ASME Code;

(3) Are transferred into this State without a change of ownership; and

(4) Are determined by the Chief Inspector to be constructed under standards substantially equivalent to those established by the department at the time of transfer.

(e) The construction requirements established by the Department of Labor shall not apply to pressure vessels installed in this State prior to December 31, 1984, if they are equipped with ASME Code and National Board certified safety relief valves and:

(1) Are manufactured from gray iron casting material, as specified by the American Society for Testing and Materials, (ASTM) 48-60T/30;

(2) Are constructed before December 31, 1967, and operating or could be operated, under the laws of any state or Canadian Province that has adopted one or more sections of the ASME Boiler and Pressure Vessel Code;

(3) Are transferred into this State without a change of ownership; and

(4) Are determined by the Chief Inspector to be constructed under standards substantially equivalent to those established by the department at the time of transfer.

(f) The construction requirements established by the Department of Labor shall not apply to hydropneumatic tanks installed or operated by a community water system prior to January 1, 1986.

(g) The inspection requirements established by the Department of Labor shall not apply to pressure vessels used for transportation or storage of liquefied petroleum gas that are subject to inspection in accordance with the requirements established by the Department of Agriculture and Consumer Services. (1975, c. 895, s. 3; 1979, c. 920, ss. 1, 2; 1981, c. 591; 1983, c. 654; 1985, c. 620, ss. 1, 2; c. 629; 1993, c. 351, s. 2; 2005-453, s. 2; 2007-231, s. 1; 2011-366, ss. 1, 2, 3.)

§ 95-69.11. Powers and duties of Commissioner.

The Commissioner of Labor is hereby charged, directed, and empowered:

(1) To adopt, modify, or revoke rules governing the construction, operation, and use of boilers and pressure vessels, including, where necessary, requirements for fencing to prevent unauthorized persons from coming in contact with boilers and pressure vessels or the systems they are connected to.

(2) To delegate to the Chief Inspector any powers, duties, and responsibilities that the Commissioner determines will best serve the public interest in the safe operation of boilers and pressure vessels, and to supervise the Chief Inspector in the performance of those duties.

(3) To enforce rules adopted under authority of this Article.

(4) To inspect boilers and pressure vessels covered under this Article.

(5) To issue inspection certificates to those boilers and pressure vessels found in compliance with this Article.

(6) To enjoin violations of this Article in the civil and criminal courts of this State.

(7) To keep adequate records of the type, dimensions, age, conditions, pressure allowed upon, location, and date of the last inspection of all boilers and pressure vessels to which this Article applies.

(8) To require such periodic reports from inspectors, owners, and operators of boilers and pressure vessels as he deems appropriate in carrying out the purposes of this Article.

(9) To have free access, without notice, to any location in this State, during reasonable hours, where a boiler or pressure vessel is being built, installed, or operated for the purpose of ascertaining whether such boiler or pressure vessel is built, installed, or operated in accordance with the provisions of this Article.

(10) To investigate serious accidents involving boilers and pressure vessels to determine the causes of the accidents, and to have full subpoena powers in conducting the investigation.

(11) To establish reasonable fees for the inspection and issuance of inspection certificates for boilers and pressure vessels that are in use.

(12) To establish reasonable fees for the examination and certification of inspectors.

(13) To appoint qualified individuals to the Board of Boiler and Pressure Vessel Rules.

(14) To perform inspections and audits relating to the construction and repair of boilers and pressure vessels and to establish and collect fees for these activities.

(15) To order the payment of civil penalties provided by this section.

(16) To require that before any boiler or pressure vessel that is subject to this Article is transferred into the State, or is moved from one location to another within the State, the owner or the owner's authorized agent shall file with the Commissioner a written notice of intent to do so and the type of device involved and provide a copy of the specifications, previous inspection documents, or other information that the Commissioner deems necessary to determine whether the boiler or pressure vessel is in compliance with the provisions of this Article and the rules adopted under this Article.

(17) To grant exceptions from the requirements of the rules and regulations adopted under authority of this Article and to permit the use of other devices when such exceptions and uses will not expose the public to an unsafe condition likely to result in serious personal injury or property damage. (1975, c. 895, s. 4; 1985, c. 620, s. 3; 1993, c. 351, s. 3; 2005-453, s. 3; 2011-366, s. 4.)

§ 95-69.12. Boiler Safety Bureau established.

There is established a Boiler Safety Bureau within the Department of Labor. The Commissioner shall appoint a Chief Inspector of the Boiler Safety Bureau and any other employees that the Commissioner deems necessary to assist the Chief Inspector in administering the provisions of this Article and the rules adopted under this Article. (1975, c. 895, s. 5; 1981 (Reg. Sess., 1982), c. 1187, ss. 2, 3; 2005-453, s. 4.)

§ 95-69.13. Board of Boiler and Pressure Vessels Rules created; appointment, terms, compensation and duties.

(a) There is hereby created the North Carolina Board of Boiler and Pressure Vessels Rules consisting of nine members appointed by the Commissioner for a term of five years each. Of these nine appointed members, one shall be a representative of the owners and users of steam boilers within this State, one a representative of boiler manufacturers within this State, one a representative of boilermakers within this State who has had not less than five years' practical experience as a boilermaker, one shall be a representative of the owners or users of pressure vessels within the State, one shall be a representative of the pressure vessel manufacturers within the State, one a representative of boiler inspection and insurance companies authorized to insure boilers and pressure vessels within the State, one a representative of the antique boiler owners and operators in this State, one a contractor holding a Group I North Carolina Heating License, and one a mechanical engineer on the faculty of a recognized engineering college or a licensed professional engineer having boiler and pressure vessel experience. The Commissioner of Labor shall serve as chair. The Chief Inspector shall serve on the Board and in the absence of the Commissioner shall serve as chair.

(b) The Board shall meet at least twice annually and shall be responsible for:

(1) Studying and proposing rules and regulations, for adoption, modification or revocation by the Commissioner, governing the construction, installation, inspection, repair, alteration, use and operation of boilers and pressure vessels in this State. The rules and regulations so formulated shall conform as nearly as possible to the standards of the American Society of Mechanical Engineers.

(2) Devise and proctor examinations covering this Article and the rules adopted under this Article to applicants seeking a commission as inspectors of boilers and pressure vessels in this State.

(2a) Act as proctors during the administration of the National Board commissioning examination.

(3) Issue, suspend, or revoke inspector's commissions as inspectors of boilers and pressure vessels within this State. Whenever action is taken under this section to suspend or revoke a commission, the affected party shall be given notice of the availability of an administrative hearing and of judicial review in accordance with Chapter 150B of the General Statutes, the Administrative Procedure Act.

(c) The members of the Board shall serve without salary but shall be paid a subsistence and travel allowance as established in accordance with Chapter 138 of the General Statutes. (1975, c. 895, s. 6; 1977, c. 788; 1981 (Reg. Sess., 1982), c. 1187, s. 4; 1983, c. 717, s. 16; 1985, c. 620, s. 5; 2005-453, s. 5.)

§ 95-69.14. Rules and regulations governing the construction, operation and use of boilers and pressure vessels.

The Commissioner, after consultation with the Board, may adopt, modify, or revoke any rules and regulations governing the construction, installation, repair, alteration, inspection, use, and operation of boilers and pressure vessels as the Commissioner deems appropriate to insure the safe operation and avoidance of injury to person or property from boilers and pressure vessels. The rules and regulations will conform as nearly as possible to the standards of the American Society of Mechanical Engineers and the amendments and interpretations of those engineering standards.

The procedure for the adoption, modification, or revocation of the rules and regulations shall be in accordance with Chapter 150B of the General Statutes, the Administrative Procedure Act. (1975, c. 895, s. 7; 1985, c. 620, s. 4; 1987, c. 827, s. 1; 2005-453, s. 6.)

§ 95-69.15. Classification of inspectors; qualifications; examinations; inspector's commission.

(a)   There shall be three types of inspectors authorized to conduct inspections and report their findings to the Chief Inspector under this Article:

(1)   Boiler and Pressure Vessel Inspector or Deputy Inspector. - Shall be a qualified individual, employed by the Department of Labor and appointed by the Commissioner, to assist in conducting inspections under this Article and report on the suitability of boilers and pressure vessels so inspected.

(2)   Special Inspector or Insurance Inspector. - Shall be a qualified individual regularly employed by an insurance company authorized to insure in this State against injury to person or property or both from explosions and accidents involving boilers and pressure vessels. Special Inspectors shall not include employees of private contract inspection agencies.

(3)   Owner-User Inspectors. - Shall be a qualified individual employed on a full-time basis by a company operating pressure vessels for its own use and not for resale, and maintains an established inspection program for periodic inspection of pressure vessels owned or used by that company and where such inspection program is under the supervision of one or more engineers having qualifications satisfactory to the Commissioner.

(b)   Inspector's Commission. - Any company authorized to insure in this State against loss to person or property as a result of an explosion or accident involving boilers and pressure vessels or operating boilers or pressure vessels or both for its own use and not for resale, may apply for the issuance of an inspector's commission for an individual within its employ who has a commission from the National Board.

A North Carolina commission authorizes an inspector to make inspections on boilers and pressure vessels and report on the suitability of said boilers and pressure vessels to the Chief Inspector. Those inspectors holding commissions as special inspectors shall be limited to making inspections on boilers and pressure vessels insured by their employer. Owner-user inspectors shall be limited to conducting inspections on boilers and pressure vessels operated by their respective employers.

A person seeking a commission from this State to conduct in-service inspections of boilers and pressure vessels must take and pass an examination on this Article and the rules adopted pursuant to this Article prior to receiving the commission. Any person who has had a commission in this State but who has been inactive for more than one year must take or retake and pass the State examination before conducting further in-service inspections of boilers and pressure vessels.

(c)   Repealed by Session Laws 2007, c. 231, s. 2, effective July 18, 2007. (1975, c. 895, s. 8; 2005-453, s. 7; 2007-231, s. 2.)

§ 95-69.16. Inspection certificate required.

All boilers and pressure vessels subject to the provisions of this Article shall be inspected by a commissioned inspector. The Commissioner may determine both the frequency and the method of inspection. In determining the frequency of inspection, the Commissioner shall give due consideration to the hazard involved and the need for the protection of the public. The method of inspection must provide an adequate procedure to insure the safety of individuals likely to be injured by an explosion or accident involving a boiler or pressure vessel.

No boiler or pressure vessel may be operated without an inspection certificate, except pressure vessels being operated under an owner-user provision where administrative procedures of equal safety and competency have been approved by the Board and Commissioner. No more than 60 days grace period may be granted beyond the certificate expiration date. (1975, c. 895, s. 9; 1993, c. 351, s. 4; 2005-453, s. 8; 2007-231, s. 3.)

§ 95-69.17. Noncomplying devices; appeal.

(a)   If the Commissioner determines that a boiler or pressure vessel is subject to the provisions of this Article and that the operation of the boiler or pressure vessel is exposing the public to an unsafe condition likely to result in serious personal injury or property damage, the Commissioner may immediately order in writing that the use of the boiler or pressure vessel be stopped or limited until the Commissioner determines that the boiler or pressure vessel has been made safe for operation.

(b)   If the Commissioner determines that the provisions of this Article or the rules adopted pursuant to this Article have not been complied with, the Commissioner may refuse to issue or renew or may revoke, suspend, or amend an inspection certificate.

(c)   Whenever action is taken under this section, the affected party shall be given notice of the availability of an administrative hearing and of judicial review in accordance with Chapter 150B of the General Statutes, the Administrative Procedure Act. (1975, c. 895, s. 10; 1987, c. 827, s. 263; 1993, c. 351, s. 5; 2005-453, s. 9.)

§ 95-69.18. Operation without inspection certificate; operation not in compliance with this Article; operation after nonissuance or revocation of certificate.

(a)   No person may operate or permit to be operated any boiler or pressure vessel subject to the provisions of this Article without a valid inspection certificate unless the absence of a valid inspection certificate is the result of the Commissioner's failure to inspect the device.

(b)   No person may operate or permit to be operated any boiler or pressure vessel subject to the provisions of this Article other than in accordance with this Article and the rules adopted pursuant to this Article.

(c)   No person may operate or permit to be operated any boiler or pressure vessel subject to the provisions of this Article after the Commissioner has refused to issue or has revoked the inspection certificate for the boiler or pressure vessel. (1975, c. 895, s. 11; 1993, c. 539, s. 665; 1994, Ex. Sess., c. 24, s. 14(c); 2005-453, s. 10.)

§ 95-69.19. Violations; civil penalties; appeals.

(a)   Any person who violates G.S. 95-69.18(a) or (b) (operation without inspection certificate; operation not in accordance with Article or rules and regulations) shall be subject to a civil penalty not to exceed two hundred fifty dollars ($250.00) for each day each boiler or pressure vessel is so operated or used.

(b) Any person who violates G.S. 95-69.18(c) (operation after refusal to issue or after revocation of inspection certificate) shall be subject to a civil penalty not to exceed five hundred dollars ($500.00) for each day any such boiler or pressure vessel is so operated or used.

(c) In determining the amount of any penalty ordered under authority of this section, the Commissioner shall give due consideration to the appropriateness of the penalty with respect to the size of the business of the person being charged, the gravity of the violation, the good faith of the person, and the record of previous violations.

(d) The determination of the amount of the penalty by the Commissioner shall be final, unless within 15 days after receipt of notice thereof by certified mail with return receipt, by signature confirmation as provided by the U.S. Postal Service, by a designated delivery service authorized pursuant to 26 U.S.C. § 7502(f)(2) with delivery receipt, or via hand delivery, the person charged with the violation takes exception to the determination in which event the final determination of the penalty shall be made in an administrative proceeding and in a judicial proceeding pursuant to Chapter 150B of the General Statutes, the Administrative Procedure Act.

(e) The Commissioner may file in the office of the clerk of the superior court of the county where the violation occurred or where the person against whom a civil penalty has been ordered resides, or if a corporation is involved in the county where the corporation maintains its principal place of business, a certified copy of a final order of the Commissioner unappealed from, or of a final order of the Commissioner affirmed upon appeal. Upon filing of the final order, the clerk of superior court shall enter judgment in accordance with the order and notify the parties. The judgment shall have the same force and effect as a judgment by the superior court of the General Court of Justice. (2005-453, s. 11; 2007-231, s. 6.)

§ 95-69.20. Violations; criminal penalties.

(a) Any person who knowingly and willfully misrepresents himself as an authorized inspector administering or enforcing the provisions of this Article or the rules adopted pursuant to this Article shall be guilty of a Class 2 misdemeanor.

(b)   Any person knowingly making a material and false statement, representation, or certification in any application, record, report, plan, or any other document filed or required to be maintained pursuant to this Article or the rules adopted pursuant to this Article shall be guilty of a Class 2 misdemeanor. (2005-453, s. 12.)

§ 95-69.21: Reserved for future codification purposes.

§ 95-69.22: Reserved for future codification purposes.

§ 95-69.23: Reserved for future codification purposes.

§ 95-69.24: Reserved for future codification purposes.

§ 95-69.25: Reserved for future codification purposes.

§ 95-69.26: Reserved for future codification purposes.

§ 95-69.27: Reserved for future codification purposes.

§ 95-69.28: Reserved for future codification purposes.

§ 95-69.29: Reserved for future codification purposes.

Article 7B.

Historical Boilers.

§ 95-69.30. Safety Program for Operators and Apprentices.

The Department of Labor shall create and conduct a safety program for the purpose of providing instruction on how to properly care, maintain, operate, and exhibit historical boilers. The program shall also include instruction on how to train an apprentice to properly care, maintain, operate, and exhibit historical boilers. For purposes of this section, the term "historical boiler" means a steam boiler of riveted construction that is preserved, restored, or maintained for hobby or demonstration. (2013-360, s. 13.10(a).)

Article 8.

Bureau of Labor for the Deaf.

§§ 95-70 through 95-72: Repealed by Session Laws 1975, c. 412, s. 1.

Article 9.

Earnings of Employees in Interstate Commerce.

§ 95-73. Collections out of State to avoid exemptions forbidden.

No resident creditor or other holder of any book account, negotiable instrument, duebill or other monetary demand arising out of contract, due by or chargeable against any resident wage earner or other salaried employee of any railway corporation or other corporation, firm, or individual engaged in interstate business shall send out of the State, assign, or transfer the same, for value or otherwise, with intent to thereby deprive such debtor of his personal earnings and property exempt by law from application to the payment of his debts under the laws of the State of North Carolina, by instituting or causing to be instituted thereon against such debtor, in any court outside of this State, in such creditor's own name or in the name of any other person, any action, suit, or proceeding for the attachment or garnishment of such debtor's earnings in the hands of his employer, when such creditor and debtor and the railway corporation or other corporation, firm, or individual owing the wages or salary intended to be reached are under the jurisdiction of the courts of this State. (1909, c. 504, s. 1; C.S., s. 6568.)

§ 95-74. Resident not to abet collection out of State.

No person residing or sojourning in this State shall counsel, aid, or abet any violation of the provisions of G.S. 95-73. (1909, c. 504, s. 2; C.S., s. 6569.)

§ 95-75. Remedies for violation of § 95-73 or 95-74; damages; indictment.

Any person violating any provisions of G.S. 95-73 or 95-74 shall be answerable in damages to any debtor from whom any book account, negotiable instrument, duebill, or other monetary demand arising out of contract shall be collected, or against whose earnings any warrant of attachment or notice of garnishment shall be issued, in violation of the provisions of G.S. 95-73, to the full amount of the debt thus collected, attached, or garnisheed, to be recovered by civil action in any court of competent jurisdiction in this State; and any person so offending shall likewise be guilty of a Class 3 misdemeanor, punishable only by a fine of not more than two hundred dollars ($200.00). (1909, c. 504, s. 3; C.S., s. 6570; 1993, c. 539, s. 666; 1994, Ex. Sess., c. 24, s. 14(c).)

§ 95-76. Institution of foreign suit, etc., evidence of intent to violate.

In any civil or criminal action instituted in any court of competent jurisdiction in this State for any violation of the provisions of G.S. 95-73 and 95-74, proof of the institution or prosecution of any action, suit, or proceeding in violation of the provisions of G.S. 95-73, or the issuance of service therein of any warrant of attachment, notice, or garnishment or other like writ for the garnishment of earnings of the defendant therein, or of the payment by the garnishee therein of any final judgment rendered in any such action, suit, or proceeding shall be deemed prima facie evidence of the intent of the creditor or other holder of the debt sued upon to deprive such debtor of his personal earnings and property exempt from application to the payment of his debts under the laws of this State, in violation of the provisions of this Article. (1909, c. 504, s. 4; C.S., s. 6571.)

§ 95-77. Construction of Article.

No provision of this Article shall be so construed as to deprive any person entitled to its benefits of any legal or equitable remedy already possessed under the laws of this State. (1909, c. 504, s. 5; C.S., s. 6572.)

Article 10.

Declaration of Policy as to Labor Organizations.

§ 95-78. Declaration of public policy.

The right to live includes the right to work. The exercise of the right to work must be protected and maintained free from undue restraints and coercion. It is hereby declared to be the public policy of North Carolina that the right of persons to work shall not be denied or abridged on account of membership or nonmembership in any labor union or labor organization or association. (1947, c. 328, s. 1.)

§ 95-79. Certain agreements declared illegal.

(a)   Any agreement or combination between any employer and any labor union or labor organization whereby persons not members of such union or organization shall be denied the right to work for said employer, or whereby such membership is made a condition of employment or continuation of employment by such employer, or whereby any such union or organization acquires an employment monopoly in any enterprise, is hereby declared to be against the public policy and an illegal combination or conspiracy in restraint of trade or commerce in the State of North Carolina.

(b)   Any provision that directly or indirectly conditions the purchase of agricultural products or the terms of an agreement for the purchase of agricultural products upon an agricultural producer's status as a union or nonunion employer or entry into or refusal to enter into an agreement with a labor union or labor organization is invalid and unenforceable as against public policy in restraint of trade or commerce in the State of North Carolina. For purposes of this subsection, the term "agricultural producer" means any producer engaged in any service or activity included within the provisions of section 3(f) of the Fair Labor Standards Act of 1938, 29 U.S.C. § 203, or section 3121(g) of the Internal Revenue Code of 1986, 26 U.S.C. § 3121. (1947, c. 328, s. 2; 2013-413, s. 15.)

§ 95-80. Membership in labor organization as condition of employment prohibited.

No person shall be required by an employer to become or remain a member of any labor union or labor organization as a condition of employment or continuation of employment by such employer. (1947, c. 328, s. 3.)

§ 95-81. Nonmembership as condition of employment prohibited.

No person shall be required by an employer to abstain or refrain from membership in any labor union or labor organization as a condition of employment or continuation of employment. (1947, c. 328, s. 4.)

§ 95-82. Payment of dues as condition of employment prohibited.

No employer shall require any person, as a condition of employment or continuation of employment, to pay any dues, fees, or other charges of any kind to any labor union or labor organization. (1947, c. 328, s. 5.)

§ 95-83. Recovery of damages by persons denied employment.

Any person who may be denied employment or be deprived of continuation of his employment in violation of G.S. 95-80, 95-81 and 95-82 or of one or more of such sections, shall be entitled to recover from such employer and from any other person, firm, corporation, or association acting in concert with him by appropriate action in the courts of this State such damages as he may have sustained by reason of such denial or deprivation of employment. (1947, c. 328, s. 6.)

§ 95-84. Application of Article.

The provisions of this Article shall not apply to any lawful contract in force on the effective date hereof but they shall apply in all respects to contracts entered into thereafter and to any renewal or extension of any existing contract. (1947, c. 328, s. 7.)

Article 11.

Minimum Wage Act.

§§ 95-85 through 95-96: Repealed by Session Laws 1979, c. 839, s. 2.

Article 12.

Units of Government and Labor Unions, Trade Unions, and Labor Organizations, and Public Employee Strikes.

§ 95-97: Repealed by Session Laws 1998-217, s. 26.

§ 95-98. Contracts between units of government and labor unions, trade unions or labor organizations concerning public employees declared to be illegal.

Any agreement, or contract, between the governing authority of any city, town, county, or other municipality, or between any agency, unit, or instrumentality thereof, or between any agency, instrumentality, or institution of the State of North Carolina, and any labor union, trade union, or labor organization, as bargaining agent for any public employees of such city, town, county or other municipality, or agency or instrumentality of government, is hereby declared to be against the public policy of the State, illegal, unlawful, void and of no effect. (1959, c. 742.)

§ 95-98.1. Strikes by public employees prohibited.

Strikes by public employees are hereby declared illegal and against the public policy of this State. No person holding a position either full-or part-time by appointment or employment with the State of North Carolina or in any county, city, town or other political subdivision of the State of North Carolina, or in any agency of any of them, shall willfully participate in a strike by public employees. (1981, c. 958, s. 1.)

§ 95-98.2. Strike defined.

The word "strike" as used herein shall mean a cessation or deliberate slowing down of work by a combination of persons as a means of enforcing compliance with a demand upon the employer, but shall not include protected activity under Article 16 of this Chapter: Provided, however, that nothing herein shall limit or impair the right of any public employee to express or communicate a complaint or opinion on any matter related to the conditions of public employment so long as the same is not designed to and does not interfere with the full, faithful, and proper performance of the duties of employment. (1981, c. 958, s. 1.)

§ 95-99. Penalty for violation of Article.

Any violation of the provisions of this Article is hereby declared to be a Class 1 misdemeanor. (1959, c. 742; 1993, c. 539, s. 667; 1994, Ex. Sess., c. 24, s. 14(c).)

§ 95-100. No provisions of Article 10 of Chapter 95 applicable to units of government or their employees.

The provisions of Article 10 of Chapter 95 of the General Statutes shall not apply to the State of North Carolina or any agency, institution, or instrumentality thereof or the employees of same nor shall the provisions of Article 10 of Chapter 95 of the General Statutes apply to any public employees or any employees of any town, city, county or other municipality or the agencies or instrumentalities thereof, nor shall said Article apply to employees of the State or any agencies, instrumentalities or institutions thereof or to any public employees whatsoever. (1959, c. 742.)

Article 13.

Payments to or for Benefit of Labor Organizations.

§ 95-101. Definition.

As used in this Article, the term "labor organization" means any organization of any kind, or any agency or employee representation committee or plan, in which employee or employees participate and which exists for the purpose in whole or in part, of dealing with employers concerning grievances, labor disputes, wages, rates of pay, hours of employment, or conditions of work. (1963, c. 244.)

§ 95-102. Certain payments to and agreements to pay labor organizations unlawful.

It shall be unlawful for any carrier or shipper of property or any association of such carriers or shippers to agree to pay, or to pay, to or for the benefit of a labor organization, directly or indirectly, any charge by reason of the placing upon, delivery to, or movement by rail, or by a railroad car, of a motor vehicle, trailer, or container which is also capable of being moved or propelled upon the highways and any such agreement shall be void and unenforceable. (1963, c. 244.)

§ 95-103. Acceptance of such payments unlawful.

It shall be unlawful for any labor organization to accept or receive from any carrier or shipper of property, or any association of such carriers or shippers, any payment described in G.S. 95-102 above. (1963, c. 244.)

§ 95-104. Penalty.

Any person, firm, corporation, association or partnership which or who agrees to pay, or does pay, or agrees to receive, or does receive, any payment described in this Article shall be guilty of a Class 3 misdemeanor and shall only be fined not less than one hundred dollars ($100.00), nor more than one thousand dollars ($1,000) for each offense. Each act of violation, and each day during which such an agreement remains in effect, shall constitute a separate offense. (1963, c. 244; 1993, c. 539, s. 668; 1994, Ex. Sess., c. 24, s. 14(c).)

Article 14.

Inspection Service Fees.

§ 95-105: Repealed upon adoption of rule pursuant to G.S. 95-100.5(20), effective July 1, 2003.

§ 95-106: Repealed upon adoption of rule pursuant to G.S. 95-100.5(20), effective July 1, 2003.

§ 95-107. Assessment and collection of fees; certificates of safe operation.

The assessment of the fees adopted by the Commissioner pursuant to G.S. 95-69.11, 95-110.5, 95-111.4 and 95-120 shall be made against the owner or operator of the equipment and may be collected at the time of inspection. If the fees are not collected at the time of inspection, the Department must bill the owner or operator of the equipment for the amount of the fee assessed for the inspection of the equipment and the amount assessed is payable by the owner or operator of the equipment upon receipt of the bill. Certificates of safe operation may be withheld by the Department of Labor until such time as the assessed fees are collected. (1975, c. 777, s. 3; 1995, c. 217, s. 1; 2001-427, s. 11(c); 2005-347, s. 6; 2005-453, s. 13.)

§ 95-108. Disposition of fees.

All fees collected by the Department of Labor pursuant to G.S. 95-69.11, 95-110.5, 95-111.4 and 95-120 shall be deposited with the State Treasurer and shall be used exclusively for inspection and certification purposes. (1975, c. 777, s. 4; 2001-427, s. 11(d); 2005-347, s. 7; 2005-453, s. 14.)

§ 95-109. Repealed by Session Laws 1985 (Reg. Sess., 1986), c. 990, s. 3.

§ 95-110. Reserved for future codification purposes.

Article 14A.

Elevator Safety Act of North Carolina.

§ 95-110.1. Short title and legislative purpose.

(a) This Article shall be known as the Elevator Safety Act of North Carolina.

(b) The General Assembly finds that the use of unsafe and defective lifting devices imposes a substantial probability of serious and preventable injury to employees and the public exposed to unsafe conditions and that prevention of these injuries and protection of employees and the public from unsafe conditions is in the best interests and welfare of the people of the State. (1985 (Reg. Sess., 1986), c. 990, s. 1.)

§ 95-110.2. Scope.

This Article shall govern the design, construction, installation, plans review, testing, inspection, certification, operation, use, maintenance, alteration, relocation and investigation of accidents involving:

(1) Elevators, dumbwaiters, escalators, and moving walks;

(2) Personnel hoists;

(3) Inclined stairway chair lifts;

(4) Inclined and vertical wheelchair lifts;

(5) Manlifts; and

(6) Special equipment.

This Article shall not apply to devices and equipment located and operated in a single family residence, to conveyors and related equipment within the scope of the American National Standard Safety Standard for Conveyors and Related Equipment (ANSI/ASME B20.1) constructed, installed and used exclusively for the movement of materials, or to mining equipment specifically covered by the Federal Mine Safety and Health Act or the Mine Safety and Health Act of North Carolina or the rules and regulations adopted pursuant thereto. (1985 (Reg. Sess., 1986), c. 990, s. 1.)

§ 95-110.3. Definitions.

(a) The term "Commissioner" shall mean the North Carolina Commissioner of Labor or his authorized representative.

(b) The term "Director" shall mean the Director of the Elevator and Amusement Device Division of the North Carolina Department of Labor.

(c) The term "dumbwaiter" shall mean a hoisting and lowering mechanism equipped with a car or platform which moves in guides in a substantially vertical direction, the floor area of which does not exceed nine square feet, the total inside height of which, whether or not provided with fixed or removable shelves, does not exceed four feet, the capacity of which does not exceed 500 pounds, and which is used exclusively for carrying materials.

(d) The term "elevator" shall mean a hoisting and lowering mechanism equipped with a car or platform which moves in guides, and which serves two or more floors of a building or structure.

(e) The term "escalator" shall mean a power driven, inclined continuous stairway used for raising and lowering passengers.

(f) The term "inclined stairway chair lift" shall mean a hoisting and lowering mechanism with one or more chairs or a platform for one or more wheelchairs installed on a stairway for the purpose of transporting a physically disabled person.

(g) The term "inclined or vertical wheelchair lift" shall mean a powered platform-elevating device used to transport a physically disabled person in a wheelchair.

(h) The term "manlift" shall mean platforms or brackets and accompanying handholds, mounted on, or attached to, an endless belt operating vertically in one direction only and being supported by, and driven through, pulleys at the top and bottom and intended primarily for the conveyance of persons.

(i) The term "moving walk" shall mean a type of passenger carrying device on which passengers stand or walk and in which the passenger carrying surface remains parallel to its direction of motion and is uninterrupted.

(j) The term "operator" shall mean any person having direct control over the operation of any covered device or equipment.

(k) The term "owner" shall mean any person or authorized agent of such person who owns a device or equipment subject to regulation under this Article, or in the event the device or equipment is leased, the lessee. The term "owner" also shall include the State of North Carolina or any political subdivision thereof or any unit of local government.

(l) The term "person" shall mean any individual, association, partnership, firm, corporation, private organization, or the State of North Carolina or any political subdivision thereof or any unit of local government.

(m) The term "personnel hoist" shall mean an elevator installed inside or outside of buildings during construction, alteration or demolition and used primarily to raise and lower workers and other persons connected with or related to the building project.

(n) The term "special equipment" shall mean any permanently or semi-permanently located device, manually or power-operated, used for moving or lifting person or persons and materials but not considered as an elevator, escalator, dumbwaiter, moving walk, personnel hoist, inclined stairway chair lift, inclined or vertical wheelchair lift, or manlift. Special equipment shall include, but not be limited to, manhoists, lift bridges, elevators which are used only for handling building materials and workmen during construction, and stage and orchestra lifts. (1985 (Reg. Sess., 1986), c. 990, s. 1.)

§ 95-110.4. Elevator and Amusement Device Division established.

There is hereby created an Elevator and Amusement Device Division within the Department of Labor. The Commissioner shall appoint a director of the Elevator and Amusement Device Division and such other employees as the Commissioner deems necessary to assist the director in administering the provisions of this Article. (1985 (Reg. Sess., 1986), c. 990, s. 1.)

§ 95-110.5. Powers and duties of Commissioner.

The Commissioner of Labor is hereby empowered:

(1) To delegate to the Director of the Elevator and Amusement Device Division such powers, duties and responsibilities as the Commissioner determines will best serve the public interest in the safe operation of lifting devices and equipment;

(2) To supervise the Director of the Elevator and Amusement Device Division;

(3) To adopt, modify, or revoke such rules and regulations as are necessary for the purpose of carrying out the provisions of this Article including, but not limited to, those governing the design, construction, installation, plans review, testing, inspection, certification, operation, use, maintenance, alteration and relocation of devices and equipment subject to the provisions of this Article. The rules and regulations promulgated pursuant to this rulemaking authority shall conform with good engineering practice as evidenced generally by the most recent editions of the American National Standard Safety Code for Elevators, Dumbwaiters, Escalators and Moving Walks, the National Electrical Code, the American National Standard Safety Requirements for Personnel Hoists, the American National Standard Safety Code for Manlifts, the American National Standard Safety Standard for Conveyors and Related Equipment and similar codes promulgated by agencies engaged in research concerning strength of material, safe design, and other factors bearing upon the safe operation of the devices and equipment subject to the provisions of this Article. The rules and regulations may apply different standards to devices and equipment subject to this Article depending upon their date of installation. The rules and regulations for special equipment shall not adopt specifically any portion of the American National Standard Safety Code for Elevators, Dumbwaiters, Escalators and Moving Walks to inclined and vertical reciprocating conveyors;

(4) To enforce rules and regulations adopted under authority of this Article;

(5) To inspect and have tested for acceptance all new, altered or relocated devices or equipment subject to the provisions of this Article;

(6) To make maintenance and periodic inspections and tests of all devices and equipment subject to the provisions of this Article as often as every six months;

(7) To issue certificates of operation which certify for use such devices and equipment as are found to be in compliance with this Article and the rules and regulations promulgated thereunder;

(8) To have free access, with or without notice, to the devices and equipment subject to the provisions of this Article, during reasonable hours, for purposes of inspection or testing;

(9) To obtain an Administrative Search and Inspection Warrant in accordance with the provisions of Article 4A of Chapter 15 of the General Statutes;

(10) To investigate accidents involving the devices and equipment subject to the provisions of this Article to determine the cause of such accident, and he shall have full subpoena powers in conducting such investigation;

(11) To institute proceedings in the civil or criminal courts of this State, when a provision of this Article or the rules and regulations promulgated thereunder has been violated;

(12) To issue a limited certificate of operation for any device or equipment subject to the provisions of this Article to allow the temporary or restricted use thereof;

(13) To adopt, modify or revoke rules and regulations governing the qualifications of inspectors;

(14) To grant exceptions from the requirements of the rules and regulations promulgated under authority of this Article and to permit the use of other devices when such exceptions and uses will not expose the public to an unsafe condition likely to result in serious personal injury or property damage;

(15) To require that a construction permit must be obtained from the Commissioner before any device or equipment subject to the provisions of this Article is installed, altered or moved from one place to another and to require that the Commissioner must be supplied with whatever plans, diagrams or other data he deems necessary to determine whether or not the proposed construction is in compliance with the provisions of this Article and the rules and regulations promulgated thereunder;

(16) To prohibit the use of any device or equipment subject to the provisions of this Article which is found upon inspection to expose the public to an unsafe condition likely to cause personal injury or property damage. Such device or equipment shall be made operational only upon the Commissioner's determination that such device or equipment has been made safe;

(17) To order the payment of all civil penalties provided by this Article. Funds collected pursuant to a civil penalty order shall be deposited with the State Treasurer;

(18) To require that any device or equipment subject to the provisions of this Article which has been out-of-service and not continuously maintained for one or more years shall not be returned to service without first complying with all rules and regulations governing existing installations; and

(19) To coordinate enforcement and inspection activity relative to equipment, devices and operations covered by this Article in order to minimize duplication of liability or regulatory responsibility on the part of the employer or owner.

(20) To establish fees not to exceed two hundred dollars ($200.00) for the inspection and issuance of certificates of operation for all devices and equipment subject to this Article upon installation or alteration, for each follow-up inspection, and for annual periodic inspections thereafter. (1985 (Reg. Sess., 1986), c. 990, s. 1; 1995, c. 217, s. 2; 2001-427, s. 11(e).)

§ 95-110.6. Noncomplying devices and equipment; appeal.

(a) Whenever the Commissioner determines that a device or equipment is subject to the provisions of this Article, and that the operation of such device or equipment is exposing the public to an unsafe condition likely to result in serious personal injury or property damage, he may immediately order in writing that the use of the device or equipment be stopped or limited until such time as he determines that the device or equipment has been made safe for use by the public.

(b) Whenever the Commissioner determines that the provisions of this Article or the rules and regulations promulgated thereunder have not been complied with, he may refuse to issue or renew or may revoke, suspend or amend a certificate of operation.

(c) Whenever action is taken under this section, the affected party shall be given notice of the availability of an administrative hearing and of judicial review in accordance with Chapter 150B of the General Statutes, the Administrative Procedure Act. (1985 (Reg. Sess., 1986), c. 990, s. 1.)

§ 95-110.7. Operation without certificate; operation not in accordance with Article or rules and regulations; operation after refusal to issue or after revocation of certificate.

(a) No person shall operate or permit to be operated or use any device or equipment subject to the provisions of this Article without a valid certificate of operation unless the absence of a valid certificate is the result of the Commissioner's failure to inspect such device.

(b) No person shall operate or permit to be operated or use any device or equipment subject to the provisions of this Article otherwise than in accordance with this Article and the rules and regulations promulgated thereunder.

(c) No person shall operate or permit to be operated or use any device or equipment subject to the provisions of this Article after the Commissioner has refused to issue or has revoked the certificate of operation for such device or equipment. (1985 (Reg. Sess., 1986), c. 990, s. 1.)

§ 95-110.8. Operation of unsafe device or equipment.

No person shall operate, permit to be operated or use any device or equipment subject to the provisions of this Article if such person knows or reasonably should know that such operation or use will expose the public to an unsafe condition which is likely to result in personal injury or property damage. (1985 (Reg. Sess., 1986), c. 990, s. 1.)

§ 95-110.9. Reports required.

(a) The owner of any device or equipment regulated under the provisions of this Article, or his authorized agent, shall within 24 hours notify the Commissioner of each and every occurrence involving such device or equipment when:

(1)   The occurrence results in death or injury requiring medical treatment, other than first aid, by a physician. First aid means the one time treatment or observation of scratches, cuts not requiring stitches, burns, splinters and contusions or a diagnostic procedure, including examination and x-rays, which does not ordinarily require medical treatment even though provided by a physician or other licensed personnel; or

(2)   The occurrence results in damage to the device indicating a substantial defect in design, mechanics, structure or equipment, affecting the future safe operation of the device. No reporting is required in the case of normal wear and tear.

(b) The Commissioner, without delay, after notification and determination that an occurrence involving injury or damage as specified in subsection (a) has occurred, shall make a complete and thorough investigation of the occurrence. The report of the investigation shall be placed on file in the office of the division and shall give in detail all facts and information available. The owner may submit for inclusion in the file results of investigations independent of the department's investigation.

(c) No person, following an occurrence as specified in subsection (a), shall operate, attempt to operate, use or move or attempt to move such device or equipment, or part thereof, without the approval of the Commissioner, unless so as to prevent injury to any person or persons.

(d) No person, following an occurrence as specified in subsection (a), shall remove or attempt to remove from the premises any damaged or undamaged part of such device or equipment or repair or attempt to repair any damaged part necessary to a complete and thorough investigation. The department must initiate its investigation within 24 hours of being notified. (1985 (Reg. Sess., 1986), c. 990, s. 1.)

§ 95-110.10. Violations; civil penalties; appeals.

(a) Any person who violates G.S. 95-110.7(a) or (b) (Operation without certificate; operation not in accordance with Article or rules and regulations) shall be subject to a civil penalty not to exceed two hundred fifty dollars ($250.00) for each day each device or equipment is so operated or used.

(b) Any person who violates G.S. 95-110.7(c) (Operation after refusal to issue or after revocation of certificate) or G.S. 95-110.9(c) (Reports required) shall be subject to a civil penalty not to exceed five hundred dollars ($500.00) for each day any such device or equipment is operated or used.

(c) Any person who violates the provisions of G.S. 95-110.9(d) (Reports required) shall be subject to a civil penalty not to exceed five hundred dollars ($500.00).

(d) In determining the amount of any penalty ordered under authority of this section, the Commissioner shall give due consideration to the appropriateness of the penalty with respect to the size of the business of the person being charged, the gravity of the violation, the good faith of the person and the record of previous violations.

(e) The determination of the amount of the penalty by the Commissioner shall be final, unless within 15 days after receipt of notice thereof by certified mail with return receipt, by signature confirmation as provided by the U.S. Postal Service, by a designated delivery service authorized pursuant to 26 U.S.C. § 7502(f)(2) with delivery receipt, or via hand delivery, the person charged with the violation takes exception to the determination in which event the final determination of the penalty shall be made in an administrative proceeding and in a judicial proceeding pursuant to Chapter 150B of the General Statutes, the Administrative Procedure Act.

(f) The Commissioner may file in the office of the clerk of the superior court of the county wherein the person, against whom a civil penalty has been ordered, resides, or if a corporation is involved, in the county wherein the corporation maintains its principal place of business, or in the county wherein the violation occurred, a certified copy of a final order of the Commissioner unappealed from, or of a final order of the Commissioner affirmed upon appeal. Whereupon, the clerk of said court shall enter judgment in accordance therewith and notify the parties. Such judgment shall have the same effect, and all proceedings in relation thereto shall thereafter be the same, as though said judgment had been rendered in a suit duly heard and determined by the superior court of the General Court of Justice. (1985 (Reg. Sess., 1986), c. 990, s. 1; 2003-308, s. 3; 2007-231, s. 7.)

§ 95-110.11. Violations; criminal penalties.

(a) Any person who violates G.S. 95-110.8 (Operation of unsafe device or equipment) shall be guilty of a Class 2 misdemeanor.

(b) Any person misrepresenting himself as an authorized inspector administering or enforcing the provisions of this Article or the rules and regulations promulgated thereunder shall be guilty of a Class 2 misdemeanor.

(c) Any person knowingly making a material and false statement, representation or certification in any application, record, report, plan or any other document filed or required to be maintained pursuant to this Article or the rules and regulations promulgated thereunder shall be guilty of a Class 2 misdemeanor which may include a fine of up to five thousand dollars ($5,000). (1985 (Reg. Sess., 1986), c. 990, s. 1; 1993, c. 539, s. 669; 1994, Ex. Sess., c. 24, s. 14(c).)

§ 95-110.12. Legal representation.

It shall be the duty of the Attorney General of North Carolina, when requested, to represent the Department of Labor in actions or proceedings in connection with this Article or the rules and regulations promulgated thereunder. (1985 (Reg. Sess., 1986), c. 990, s. 1.)

§ 95-110.13. Authorization for similar safety and health federal-State programs.

Consistent with the requirements and conditions provided in this Article and the rules and regulations promulgated thereunder, the State, upon recommendation of the Commissioner of Labor, may enter into agreements or arrangements with appropriate federal agencies for the purpose of administering the enforcement of federal statutes and rules and regulations governing devices and equipment subject to the provisions of this Article. (1985 (Reg. Sess., 1986), c. 990, s. 1.)

§ 95-110.14. Confidentiality of trade secrets.

All information reported to or otherwise obtained by the Commissioner or his agents or representatives in connection with any inspection or proceeding under this Article or the rules and regulations promulgated thereunder which contains or might reveal a trade secret shall be considered confidential, except as to carrying out this Article and the rules and regulations promulgated thereunder, or when it is relevant in any proceeding under the same. In any such proceeding the Commissioner or the court shall issue such orders as may be appropriate to protect the confidentiality of trade secrets. (1985 (Reg. Sess., 1986), c. 990, s. 1.)

§ 95-110.15. Construction of Article and rules and regulations and severability.

This Article and the rules and regulations promulgated thereunder shall receive a liberal construction to the end that the welfare of the people may be protected. If any provisions of either or the application thereof to any person or circumstances is held to be invalid, such invalidity shall not affect those provisions or applications which can be given effect without the invalid provision or application, and to that end the provisions of this Article are severable. (1985 (Reg. Sess., 1986), c. 990, s. 1.)

§ 95-111. Reserved for future codification purposes.

Article 14B.

Amusement Device Safety Act of North Carolina.

§ 95-111.1. Short title and legislative purpose.

(a) This Article shall be known as the "Amusement Device Safety Act of North Carolina".

(b) The General Assembly finds that although most amusement devices are free from defect and operated in a safe manner, those which are not impose a substantial probability of serious and preventable injury to the public. Protection of the public from exposure to such unsafe conditions and the prevention of injuries is in the best interest and welfare of the people of the State.

(c) It is the intent of this Article that amusement devices shall be designed, constructed, assembled or disassembled, maintained, and operated so as to prevent injuries. (1985 (Reg. Sess., 1986), c. 990, s. 2.)

§ 95-111.2. Scope.

(a) This Article shall govern the design, construction, installation, plans review, testing, inspection, certification, operation, use, maintenance, alteration, relocation and investigation of accidents involving amusement devices.

(b) This Article shall not apply to any device which does not normally require the supervision or services of an operator. (1985 (Reg. Sess., 1986), c. 990, s. 2; 1991, c. 178, s. 1; 2003-170, s. 1.)

§ 95-111.3. Definitions.

(a) The term "amusement device" shall mean any mechanical or structural device or attraction that carries or conveys or permits persons to walk along, around or over a fixed or restricted route or course or within a defined area including the entrances and exits thereto, for the purpose of giving such persons amusement, pleasure, thrills or excitement. This term shall not include any of the following:

(1) Devices operated on a river, lake, or any other natural body of water.

(2) Wavepools.

(3) Roller skating rinks.

(4) Ice skating rinks.

(5) Skateboard ramps or courses.

(6)   Mechanical bulls.

(7)   Buildings or concourses used in laser games.

(8)   All terrain vehicles.

(9)   Motorcycles.

(10)   Bicycles.

(11)   Mopeds.

(12)   Rock walls that are in a fixed, permanent location.

(13)   Zip-lines.

(14)   Funhouses, haunted houses, and similar walk-through devices that are erected temporarily on a seasonal basis and do not have mechanical components.

(15)   Playground equipment, including but not limited to soft contained play equipment, swings, seesaws, slides, stationary spring-mounted animal features, jungle gyms, rider-propelled merry-go-rounds, and trampolines.

(b)   The term "amusement park" shall mean any tract or area used principally as a permanent location for amusement devices.

(b1)   The term "carnival area" shall mean any area, track, or structure that is rented, leased, or owned as a temporary location for amusement devices.

(c)   The term "Commissioner" shall mean the North Carolina Commissioner of Labor or his authorized representative.

(d)   The term "Director" shall mean the Director of the Elevator and Amusement Device Division of the North Carolina Department of Labor.

(e)   The term "operator" shall mean any person having direct control of the operation of an amusement device. The term "operator" shall not include any person on the device for the purpose of receiving amusement, pleasure, thrills, or excitement.

(f)   The term "owner" shall mean any person or authorized agent of such person who owns an amusement device or in the event such device is leased, the lessee. The term "owner" also shall include the State of North Carolina or any political subdivision thereof or any unit of local government.

(g)   The term "person" shall mean any individual, association, partnership, firm, corporation, private organization, or the State of North Carolina or any political subdivision thereof or any unit of local government.

(h)   The term "waterslide" shall mean a stationary amusement device that provides a descending ride on a flowing water film through a trough or tube or on an inclined plane into a pool of water. This term does not include devices where the vertical distance between the highest and the lowest points does not exceed 15 feet. (1985 (Reg. Sess., 1986), c. 990, s. 2; 1987, c. 864, s. 90(a); 1991, c. 178, s. 2; 2011-366, s. 5.)

§ 95-111.4. Powers and duties of Commissioner.

The Commissioner of Labor is hereby empowered:

(1)   To delegate to the Director of the Elevator and Amusement Device Division such powers, duties and responsibilities as the Commissioner determines will best serve the public interest in the safe operation of amusement devices;

(2)   To supervise the Director of the Elevator and Amusement Device Division;

(3)   To adopt, modify, or revoke such rules and regulations as are necessary for the purpose of carrying out the provisions of this Article including, but not limited to, those governing the design, construction, installation, plans review, testing, inspection, certification, operation, use, maintenance, alteration and relocation of devices subject to the provisions of this Article. The rules and regulations promulgated pursuant to this rulemaking authority shall conform with good engineering and safety standards, formulas and practices;

(4)   To enforce rules and regulations adopted under authority of this Article;

(5) To inspect and have tested for acceptance all new and relocated devices subject to the provisions of this Article. Relocated amusement devices shall be inspected upon reassembly at each new location within this State; provided that the Commissioner may provide for less frequent inspections when he determines that the device is of such a type and its use is of such a nature that inspection less often than upon each reassembly would not expose the public to an unsafe condition likely to result in serious personal injury or property damage;

(6) To inspect amusement devices which have been substantially rebuilt or substantially modified so as to change the original action, structure or capacity of the device;

(7) To make maintenance and periodic inspections and tests of all devices subject to the provisions of this Article. Devices located in amusement parks shall be inspected at least once annually;

(8) To issue certificates of operation which certify for use such devices as are found to be in compliance with this Article and the rules and regulations promulgated thereunder;

(9) To have reasonable access, with or without notice, to the devices subject to the provisions of this Article during reasonable hours, for purposes of inspection or testing;

(10) To obtain an Administrative Search and Inspection Warrant in accordance with the provisions of Article 4A of Chapter 15 of the General Statutes;

(11) To investigate accidents involving devices subject to the provisions of this Article to determine the cause of such accident, and he shall have full subpoena powers in conducting such investigation;

(12) To institute proceedings in the civil courts of this State, when a provision of this Article or the rules and regulations promulgated thereunder has been violated;

(13) To adopt, modify or revoke rules and regulations governing the qualifications of inspectors;

(14) To grant exceptions from the requirements of the rules and regulations promulgated under authority of this Article and to permit the use of other devices when such exceptions and uses will not expose the public to an unsafe condition likely to result in serious personal injury or property damage;

(15) To require that before any device subject to the provisions of this Article is erected in this State, or before any additions or alterations which substantially change such device are made, or before the physical spacing between such devices is changed, the owner or his authorized agent shall file with the Commissioner a written notice of his intention to do so and the type of device involved. Should circumstances necessitate, the Commissioner may require that such owner or his authorized agent furnish a copy of the plans, diagrams, specifications or stress analyses of such device before the inspection of same. When such plans, diagrams, specifications or stress analyses are requested by the Commissioner, he shall review them within 10 days of receipt, and upon approval, he shall authorize the device for use by the public;

(16) To prohibit the use of any device subject to the provisions of this Article which is found upon inspection to expose the public to an unsafe condition likely to cause personal injury or property damage. Such device shall be made operational only upon the Commissioner's determination that such device has been made safe;

(17) To order the payment of all civil penalties provided by this Article. The clear proceeds of funds collected pursuant to a civil penalty order shall be remitted to the Civil Penalty and Forfeiture Fund in accordance with G.S. 115C-457.2; and

(18) To coordinate enforcement and inspection activity relative to equipment, devices and operations covered by this Article in order to minimize duplication of liability or regulatory responsibility on the part of the employer or owner.

(19) To establish fees not to exceed two hundred fifty dollars ($250.00) for the inspection and issuance of certificates of operation for devices subject to this Article that are in use. (1985 (Reg. Sess., 1986), c. 990, s. 2; 1987, c. 635, s. 2; 1998-215, s. 110; 2001-427, s. 11(f).)

§ 95-111.5. Pre-opening inspection and test; records; revocation of certificate of operation.

(a) An owner of a device subject to the provisions of this Article, or his authorized agent, is hereby required to make a pre-opening inspection and test of such device, prior to admitting the public, each day such device is intended to be used.

(b) An owner of a device subject to the provisions of this Article, or his authorized agent, is hereby required to maintain for at least the previous 12 months a signed record of the required pre-opening inspection and test and such other pertinent information as the Commissioner may require by rule or regulation.

(c) The Commissioner is hereby empowered to revoke the certificate of operation for any device regulated by this Article upon failure by the owner or his authorized agent to make the required pre-opening inspection and test or to maintain the required record. (1985 (Reg. Sess., 1986), c. 990, s. 2; 2003-170, s. 2.)

§ 95-111.6. Noncomplying devices; appeal.

(a) Whenever the Commissioner determines that a device is subject to the provisions of this Article and the operation of such device is exposing the public to an unsafe condition likely to result in serious personal injury or property damage, he immediately may order in writing that the use of the device be stopped or limited until such time as he determines that the device has been made safe for use by the public.

(b) Whenever the Commissioner determines that the provisions of this Article or the rules and regulations promulgated thereunder have not been complied with, he may refuse to issue or renew or may revoke, suspend or amend a certificate of operation.

(c) Whenever action is taken under this section, the affected party shall be given notice of the availability of an administrative hearing and of judicial review in accordance with Chapter 150B of the General Statutes, the Administrative Procedure Act. (1985 (Reg. Sess., 1986), c. 990, s. 2.)

§ 95-111.7. Operation without certificate; operation not in accordance with Article or rules and regulations; operation after refusal to issue or after revocation of certificate.

(a) No person shall operate or permit to be operated or use any device subject to the provisions of this Article without a valid certificate of operation.

(b) No person shall operate or permit to be operated or use any device subject to the provisions of this Article otherwise than in accordance with this Article and the rules and regulations promulgated thereunder.

(c) No person shall operate or permit to be operated or use any device subject to the provisions of this Article after the Commissioner has refused to issue or has revoked the certificate of operation for such device. (1985 (Reg. Sess., 1986), c. 990, s. 2.)

§ 95-111.8. Location notice.

No person shall operate for the public or permit the operation for the public any device subject to the provisions of this Article after initial assembly or after reassembly at any location within this State without first notifying the Commissioner of the intention to operate for the public. Written notice of a planned schedule of operation or use shall be received at least 10 working days prior to the first planned date of operation or use. (1985 (Reg. Sess., 1986), c. 990, s. 2; 2003-170, s. 3; 2011-366, s. 6.)

§ 95-111.9. Operation of unsafe device.

No person shall operate, permit to be operated or use any device subject to the provisions of this Article if such person knows or reasonably should know that such operation or use will expose the public to an unsafe condition which is likely to result in personal injury or property damage. (1985 (Reg. Sess., 1986), c. 990, s. 2.)

§ 95-111.10. Reports required.

(a) The owner of any device regulated under the provisions of this Article, or his authorized agent, shall within 24 hours, notify the Commissioner of each and every occurrence involving such device when:

(1) The occurrence results in death or injury requiring medical treatment, other than first aid, by a physician. First aid means the one time treatment or observation of scratches, cuts not requiring stitches, burns, splinters and contusions or a diagnostic procedure, including examination and x-rays, which does not ordinarily require medical treatment even though provided by a physician or other licensed personnel; or

(2) The occurrence results in damage to the device indicating a substantial defect in design, mechanics, structure or equipment, affecting the future safe operation of the device. No reporting is required in the case of normal wear and tear.

(b) The Commissioner, without delay, after notification and determination that an occurrence involving injury or damage as specified in subsection (a) has occurred, shall make a complete and thorough investigation of the occurrence. The report of the investigation shall be placed on file in the office of the division and shall give in detail all facts and information available. The owner may submit for inclusion in the file results of investigations independent of the department's investigation.

(c) No person, following an occurrence as specified in subsection (a), shall operate, attempt to operate, use or move or attempt to move such device or part thereof, without the approval of the Commissioner, unless so as to prevent injury to any person or persons.

(d) No person, following an occurrence as specified in subsection (a), shall remove or attempt to remove from the premises any damaged or undamaged part of such device or repair or attempt to repair any damaged part necessary to a complete and thorough investigation. The department must initiate its investigation within 24 hours of being notified. (1985 (Reg. Sess., 1986), c. 990, s. 2.)

§ 95-111.11. Operators.

(a) Any operator of a device subject to the provisions of this Article shall be at least 18 years of age. An operator shall operate no more than one device at any given time. An operator shall be in attendance at all times the device is in operation.

(b) No person shall operate any amusement device equipment while under the influence of alcohol or any other impairing substance as defined by G.S. 20-4.01(14a). It shall be a violation of this subsection to knowingly permit the operation of any amusement device while the operator is under the influence of an impairing substance. (1985 (Reg. Sess., 1986), c. 990, s. 2; 2003-170, s. 4.)

§ 95-111.12. Liability insurance.

(a) No owner shall operate a device subject to the provisions of this Article, unless at the time, there is in existence a contract of insurance providing coverage of not less than one million dollars ($1,000,000) per occurrence against liability for injury to persons or property arising out of the operation or use of such device or there is in existence a contract of insurance providing coverage of not less than five hundred thousand dollars ($500,000) per occurrence against liability for injury to persons or property arising out of the operation or use of the amusement devices if the annual gross volume of the devices does not exceed two hundred seventy-five thousand dollars ($275,000); provided waterslides shall not be required to be insured as herein provided for an amount in excess of one hundred thousand dollars ($100,000) per occurrence. The insurance contract to be provided must be by any insurer or surety that is acceptable to the North Carolina Insurance Commissioner and authorized to transact business in this State; provided, however, that insurance for waterslides may be purchased under Article 21 of Chapter 58 of the General Statutes or under G.S. 58-28-5(b).

(b) No certificate of operation shall be issued by the Commissioner until such time as the owner or his authorized agent provides proof of the required contract of insurance.

(c) The Commissioner shall have the right to request from the owner of a device regulated by this Article, or his authorized agent, proof of the required contract of insurance, and upon failure of the owner or his authorized agent to provide such proof, the Commissioner shall have the right to prevent the commencement of or to stop the operation of the device until such time as proof is provided.

(d)   Operators of waterslides, as defined in G.S. 95-111.3(h), shall notify the Commissioner of all incidences of personal injury involving the waterslides, as required by G.S. 95-111.10(a). (1985 (Reg. Sess., 1986), c. 990, s. 2; 1987, c. 635, s. 1; c. 864, ss. 90(b), 91(a); 1989, c. 232; 1989 (Reg. Sess., 1990), c. 914; 1995, c. 517, s. 34.)

§ 95-111.13. Violations; civil penalties; appeal; criminal penalties.

(a)   Any person who violates G.S. 95-111.7(a) or (b) (Operation without certificate; operation not in accordance with Article or rules and regulations) shall be subject to a civil penalty not to exceed two hundred fifty dollars ($250.00) for each day each device is so operated or used.

(b)   Any person who violates G.S. 95-111.7(c) (Operation after refusal to issue or after revocation of certificate) or G.S. 95-111.10(c) (Reports required) or G.S. 95-111.12 (Liability insurance) shall be subject to a civil penalty not to exceed five hundred dollars ($500.00) for each day each device is so operated or used.

(c)   Any person who violates G.S. 95-111.8 (Location notice) shall be subject to a civil penalty not to exceed five hundred dollars ($500.00) for each day any device is operated or used without the location notice having been provided.

(d)   Any person who violates the provisions of G.S. 95-111.10(d) (Reports required) or knowingly permits the operation of an amusement device in violation of G.S. 95-111.11(a) (Operator requirements) shall be subject to a civil penalty not to exceed five hundred dollars ($500.00).

(e)   Any person who violates G.S. 95-111.9 (Operation of unsafe device) or G.S. 95-111.11(b) (Operation of an amusement device while impaired) shall be subject to a civil penalty not to exceed one thousand dollars ($1,000).

(f)   In determining the amount of any penalty ordered under authority of this section, the Commissioner shall give due consideration to the appropriateness of the penalty with respect to the size of the business of the person being charged, the gravity of the violation, the good faith of the person and the record of previous violations.

(g)   The determination of the amount of the penalty by the Commissioner shall be final, unless within 15 days after receipt of notice thereof by certified mail with return receipt, by signature confirmation as provided by the U.S. Postal Service, by a designated delivery service authorized pursuant to 26 U.S.C. § 7502(f)(2) with delivery receipt, or via hand delivery, the person charged with the violation takes exception to the determination, in which event final determination of the penalty shall be made in an administrative proceeding and in a judicial proceeding pursuant to Chapter 150B of the General Statutes, the Administrative Procedure Act.

(h)   The Commissioner may file in the office of the clerk of the superior court of the county wherein the person, against whom a civil penalty has been ordered, resides, or if a corporation is involved, in the county wherein the corporation maintains its principal place of business, or in the county wherein the violation occurred, a certified copy of a final order of the Commissioner unappealed from, or of a final order of the Commissioner affirmed upon appeal. Whereupon, the clerk of said court shall enter judgment in accordance therewith and notify the parties. Such judgment shall have the same effect, and all proceedings in relation thereto shall thereafter be the same, as though said judgment had been rendered in a suit duly heard and determined by the superior court of the General Court of Justice.

(i)   Any person who willfully violates any provision of this Article, and the violation causes the death of any person, shall be guilty of a Class 2 misdemeanor, which may include a fine of not more than ten thousand dollars ($10,000); except that if the conviction is for a violation committed after a first conviction of such person, the person shall be guilty of a Class 1 misdemeanor, which may include a fine of not more than twenty thousand dollars ($20,000). This subsection shall not prevent any prosecuting officer of the State of North Carolina from proceeding against such person on a prosecution charging any degree of willful or culpable homicide. (1985 (Reg. Sess., 1986), c. 990, s. 2; 2003-170, s. 5; 2003-308, s. 4; 2007-231, s. 8.)

§ 95-111.14. Denial of permission to enter amusement device.

The owner or amusement device operator may deny any person entrance to an amusement device if he or she believes such entry may jeopardize the safety of the person desiring entry, riders or other persons. (1985 (Reg. Sess., 1986), c. 990, s. 2.)

§ 95-111.15. Legal representation.

It shall be the duty of the Attorney General of North Carolina, when requested, to represent the Department of Labor in actions or proceedings in connection with this Article or the rules and regulations promulgated thereunder. (1985 (Reg. Sess., 1986), c. 990, s. 2.)

§ 95-111.16. Authorization for similar safety and health federal-State programs.

Consistent with the requirements and conditions provided in this Article and the rules and regulations promulgated thereunder, the State, upon recommendation of the Commissioner of Labor, may enter into agreements or arrangements with appropriate federal agencies for the purpose of administering the enforcement of federal statutes and rules and regulations governing devices subject to the provisions of this Article. (1985 (Reg. Sess., 1986), c. 990, s. 2.)

§ 95-111.17. Confidentiality of trade secrets.

All information reported to or otherwise obtained by the Commissioner or his agents or representatives in connection with any inspection or proceeding under this Article or the rules and regulations promulgated thereunder which contains or might reveal a trade secret shall be considered confidential, except as to carrying out this Article and the rules and regulations promulgated thereunder or when it is relevant in any proceeding under the same. In any such proceeding the Commissioner or the Court shall issue such orders as may be appropriate to protect the confidentiality of trade secrets. (1985 (Reg. Sess., 1986), c. 990, s. 2.)

§ 95-111.18. Construction of Article and rules and regulations and severability.

This Article and the rules and regulations promulgated thereunder shall receive a liberal construction to the end that the welfare of the people may be protected. If any provisions of either or the application thereof to any person or circumstances is held to be invalid, such invalidity shall not affect those provisions or applications which can be given effect without the invalid provision or application, and to that end the provisions of this Article are severable. (1985 (Reg. Sess., 1986), c. 990, s. 2.)

§§ 95-112 through 95-115. Reserved for future codification purposes.

Article 15.

Passenger Tramway Safety.

§ 95-116. Declaration of policy.

In order to safeguard life, health, property, and the welfare of this State, it shall be the policy of the State of North Carolina to protect its citizens and visitors from unnecessary mechanical hazards in the operation of ski tows, lifts, tramways and related devices to insure that reasonable design and construction are used, that accepted safety devices and sufficient personnel are provided for, and that periodic inspections and adjustments are made which are deemed essential to the safe operation of ski tows, ski lifts and passenger tramways. The primary responsibility for design, construction, maintenance, and inspection rests with the operators of such passenger tramway devices. The State, through the Commissioner of Labor, shall register all ski lift devices and passenger tramways and establish reasonable standards of design and operational practices, and cause to be made such inspections as may be necessary in carrying out this policy. (1969, c. 1021.)

§ 95-117. Definitions.

Each word or term defined in this Article has the meaning indicated in this section, unless a different meaning is plainly required by the context.

(1)   "Commissioner" means the Commissioner of Labor of the State of North Carolina.

(2)   "Industry" means activities of all those persons in the State who own, manage, or direct the operation of passenger tramways.

(3)   "Operator" means any person, firm, corporation, or organization which owns, manages, or directs the operation of a passenger tramway. "Operator" may apply to the State or any political subdivision or instrumentality thereof.

(4)   "Passenger tramway" means a device used to transport passengers uphill on skis, or in cars on tracks, or suspended in the air by the use of steel cables, chains or belts, or by ropes, and usually supported by trestles or towers with one or more spans. "Passenger tramway" shall include the following devices:

a.   "Chairlift," a type of transportation on which passengers are carried on chairs suspended in the air and attached to a moving cable, chain or link belt supported by trestles or towers with one or more spans, or similar devices;

a1.   "Conveyor," a type of transportation on which passengers are transported uphill on a flexible moving element (conveyor belt) that travels uphill on one path and generally returns underneath the uphill portion.

b.   "J bar, T bar or platter pull," so-called and similar types of devices or means of transportation which pull skiers riding on skis by means of an attachment to a main overhead cable supported by trestles or towers with one or more spans;

c.   "Multicar aerial passenger tramway," a device used to transport passengers in several open or in closed cars attached to, and suspended from, a moving wire rope or attached to a moving wire rope and supported on a standing wire rope, or similar device;

d.   "Rope tow," a type of transportation which pulls the skiers, riding on skis as the skier grasps the rope manually, or similar devices;

e. "Skimobile," a device in which a passenger car running on steel or wooden tracks is attached to and pulled by a steel cable, or similar device;

f. "Two-car aerial passenger tramway," a device used to transport passengers in two open or enclosed cars attached to, and suspended from, a moving wire rope or attached to a moving wire rope and supported on a standing wire rope or similar device. (1969, c. 1021; 2005-347, s. 1.)

§ 95-118. Registration required; application procedures.

(a) No person shall operate or permit to be operated or use any device subject to the provisions of this Article without a valid registration certificate.

(b) Operators of devices subject to the provisions of this Article shall apply to the Commissioner of Labor, on forms provided by the Commissioner, for registration of the devices that the operator owns or manages, or the operation of which the operator directs. The application shall contain information that the Commissioner may reasonably require in order for the Commissioner to determine whether the passenger tramway sought to be registered by the operator complies with the intent of this Article and the rules adopted by the Commissioner. (1969, c. 1021; 2005-347, s. 2.)

§ 95-119. Certification criteria; procedures; display of certificate.

(a) A registration certificate shall be issued annually when the Commissioner is satisfied that the facts stated in the application are sufficient to enable the Commissioner to fulfill his or her duties under this Article and that the device sought to be registered complies with the rules adopted pursuant to this Article.

(b) The Commissioner may conduct any inspections necessary to determine whether the device sought to be registered complies with the intent of this Article and the rules adopted pursuant to this Article.

(c) The registration certificate for each device subject to the provisions of this Article shall be displayed prominently at the place where passengers are loaded onto the device. (1969, c. 1021; 2005-347, s. 3; 2011-366, s. 7.)

§ 95-120. Powers and duties of the Commissioner.

In addition to all other powers and duties conferred and imposed upon the Commissioner by this Article, the Commissioner shall have and exercise the following powers and duties:

(1)   To adopt, modify, or revoke the rules necessary for carrying out the provisions of this Article, including those governing the design, construction, installation, operation, use, and maintenance of devices subject to the provisions of this Article. The rules adopted under this section shall conform as nearly as possible to the standards contained in the B77.1 - American National Standards Safety Requirements for Aerial Passenger Tramways and with good engineering and safety standards, formulas, and practices.

(1a)   To enforce the rules adopted under this Article.

(1b)   To grant exceptions from the requirements of the rules adopted under this Article and to permit the use of other devices when the exceptions and uses will not expose the public to an unsafe condition likely to result in serious personal injury or damage to property.

(2)   To hold hearings and take evidence in all matters relating to the exercise and performance of the powers and duties vested in the Commissioner, subpoena witnesses, administer oaths, and compel the testimony of witnesses and the production of books, papers and records relevant to any inquiry.

(3)   To approve, deny, revoke, and renew the registration certificates in accordance with the rules adopted pursuant to this Article.

(4)   To institute civil actions for injunctive or other relief against violators of this Article.

(5)   To cause the seal of the Commissioner of Labor to be affixed to all registrations issued by the Commissioner, and to employ, within the funds available to the Commissioner, and prescribe the duties of the personnel as the Commissioner may deem necessary in the administration of this Article.

(6)   To have reasonable access, with or without notice, to the devices subject to the provisions of this Article during reasonable hours, for the purposes of inspections and testing.

(7) To investigate accidents involving devices subject to the provisions of this Article to determine the cause of the accident. The Commissioner shall have full subpoena powers in conducting the investigations.

(8) To coordinate enforcement and inspection activity relative to equipment, devices, and operations covered by this Article in order to minimize duplication of liability or regulatory responsibility on the part of the operator, owner, or employer.

(9) To establish fees not to exceed one hundred thirty-seven dollars ($137.00) for the inspection and issuance of registration certificates for devices that are in use and subject to this Article. (1969, c. 1021; 2005-347, s. 4.)

§ 95-120.1. Liability insurance.

(a) No person shall operate a device subject to the provisions of this Article, unless at the time of operation, there is in existence:

(1) A contract of insurance providing coverage of not less than one million dollars ($1,000,000) per occurrence against liability for injury to persons or property arising out of the operation or use of the device; or

(2) A contract of insurance providing coverage of not less than five hundred thousand dollars ($500,000) per occurrence against liability for injury to persons or property arising out of the operation or use of the devices if the annual gross volume of the devices does not exceed two hundred seventy-five thousand dollars ($275,000).

The insurance contract to be provided must be made by an insurer or surety that is acceptable to the North Carolina Insurance Commissioner and authorized to transact business in this State.

(b) The Commissioner shall not issue a certificate of registration until the operator or the operator's authorized agent provides proof of the required contract of insurance.

(c) The Commissioner may request from the operator of a device subject to the provisions of this Article or the operator's authorized agent, proof of the required contract of insurance, and upon failure of the operator or authorized agent to provide proof of insurance, the Commissioner shall have the power to prevent the commencement of or to stop the operation of the device until such time as proof is provided. (2005-347, s. 5.)

§ 95-121. Inspections and reports.

The Commissioner may cause to be made such inspections of the construction, operation, and maintenance of passenger tramways as he shall deem to be reasonably necessary. If, as the result of an inspection, it is found that a violation of the Commissioner's rules and regulations exists, or a condition in passenger tramway construction, operation or maintenance exists, which endangers safety of the public, an immediate report shall be made to the Commissioner for appropriate investigation and order. (1969, c. 1021.)

§ 95-122. Emergency shutdown.

When facts are presented to the Commissioner tending to show that an unreasonable hazard exists in the continued operation of a passenger tramway, and after such verification of said facts as is practical under the circumstances and consistent with the public safety, the Commissioner may by an emergency order require the operator of said tramway forthwith to cease using the same for the transportation of passengers. Such emergency order shall be in writing, signed by the Commissioner, and notice thereof shall be served upon the operator or his agent immediately in control of said passenger tramway by a true copy of such order, with a return being made of such service and endorsed on the original order. Such emergency shutdown shall be effective for a period not to exceed 48 hours from the time of service. Immediately after the issuance of an emergency order, the Commissioner shall conduct an investigation into the facts of the case and shall take such action as may be appropriate and as provided by the provisions of this Article. (1969, c. 1021.)

§ 95-123. Orders.

If, after investigation, the Commissioner finds that a violation of any of his rules and regulations exists, or that there is a condition in passenger tramway construction, operation, or maintenance which endangers the safety of the public, the Commissioner shall forthwith issue his written order setting forth his findings, the corrective action to be taken, and fixing a reasonable time for compliance therewith. The order shall be sent to the affected operator by certified mail with return receipt, by signature confirmation as provided by the U.S. Postal Service, by a designated delivery service authorized pursuant to 26 U.S.C. § 7502(f)(2) with delivery receipt, or via hand delivery, and shall become final unless the operator contests the order by filing a petition for a contested case under G.S. 150B-23 within 20 days after receiving the order. The Commissioner shall have the power to institute injunctive proceedings in any court of competent jurisdiction of the district court district as defined in G.S. 7A-133 or superior court district or set of districts as defined in G.S. 7A-41.1, as the case may be, in which the passenger tramway is located for the purpose of restraining the operation of said tramway or for compelling compliance with any lawful order of the Commissioner. Judicial review of a final decision under this section may be obtained under Article 4 of Chapter 150B of the General Statutes. (1969, c. 1021; 1973, c. 1331, s. 3; 1987, c. 827, s. 264; 1987 (Reg. Sess., 1988), c. 1037, s. 106; 2003-308, s. 5; 2007-231, s. 9.)

§ 95-124. Suspension of registration.

If any operator fails to comply with the lawful order of the Commissioner as issued under this Article, and within the time fixed thereby, the Commissioner may suspend the registration of the affected passenger tramway for such time as he may consider necessary for the protection of the safety of the public. Any operator who shall be convicted, or enter a plea of guilty or nolo contendere, to operating a passenger tramway which has not been registered by the Commissioner, or after its registration has been suspended by the Commissioner, shall be guilty of a Class 1 misdemeanor. (1969, c. 1021; 1993, c. 539, s. 670; 1994, Ex. Sess., c. 24, s. 14(c).)

§ 95-125. Effective date of initial applications.

This Article shall take effect and become operative on July 30, 1969, provided that the initial applications for registration of passenger tramways shall be filed on or before November 1, 1969, and passenger tramways in existence on November 1, 1969, may be operated without registration until final action is taken by the Commissioner on the application for registration thereof. (1969, c. 1021.)

Article 16.

Occupational Safety and Health Act of North Carolina.

§ 95-126. Short title and legislative purpose.

(a) This Article shall be known as the "Occupational Safety and Health Act of North Carolina" and also may be referred to by abbreviations as "OSHANC."

(b) Legislative findings and purpose:

(1) The General Assembly finds that the burden of employers and employees of this State resulting from personal injuries and illnesses arising out of work situations is substantial; that the prevention of these injuries and illnesses is an important objective of the government of this State; that the greatest hope of attaining this objective lies in programs of research, education and enforcement, and in the earnest cooperation of the federal and State governments, employers and employees.

(2) The General Assembly of North Carolina declares it to be its purpose and policy through the exercise of its powers to ensure so far as possible every working man and woman in the State of North Carolina safe and healthful working conditions and to preserve our human resources:

a. By encouraging employers and employees in their effort to reduce the number of occupational safety and health hazards at the place of employment, and to stimulate employers and employees to institute new and to perfect existing programs for providing safe and healthful working conditions;

b. By providing that employers and employees have separate but dependent responsibilities and rights with respect to achieving safe and healthful working conditions;

c. By authorizing the Commissioner to develop occupational safety and health standards applicable to business giving consideration to the needs of employers and employees and to adopt standards promulgated from time to time by the Secretary of Labor under the Occupational Safety and Health Act of 1970, and by creating a safety and health review commission for carrying out adjudicatory functions under this Article;

d. By building upon advances already made through employer and employee initiative for providing safe and healthful working conditions;

e. By providing occupational health criteria which will assure insofar as practicable that no employee will suffer diminished health, functional capacity, or life expectancy as a result of his work experience;

f. By providing for training programs to increase the number and competence of personnel engaged in the field of occupational safety and health;

g. By providing an effective enforcement program which shall include a prohibition against giving advance notice of an inspection and sanctions for any individual violating this prohibition;

h. By providing for appropriate reporting procedures with respect to occupational safety and health which procedures will help achieve the objectives of this Article and accurately describe the nature of the occupational safety and health problem;

i. By encouraging joint employer-employee efforts to reduce injuries and diseases arising out of employment;

j. By providing for research in the field of occupational safety and health, by developing innovative methods, techniques, and approaches for dealing with occupational safety and health problems;

k. By exploring ways to discover latent diseases, establishing causal connections between diseases and work in environmental conditions, and conducting other research relating to health problems, in recognition of the fact that occupational health standards present problems often different from those involved in occupational safety;

l. By authorizing the Commissioner to enter into contracts with the Department of Health and Human Services, or any other State or local units, to the end the Commissioner and the Department of Health and Human Services and other State or local units may fully cooperate and carry out the ends and purposes of this Article.

m. The General Assembly of North Carolina appoints and elects the North Carolina Department of Labor as the designated agency to administer the Occupational Safety and Health Act of North Carolina. (1973, c. 295, s. 1; c. 476, s. 128; 1989, c. 727, s. 219(13); 1997-443, s. 11A.33; 2005-133, s. 2.)

§ 95-127. Definitions.

In this Article, unless the context otherwise requires:

(1) The term "Advisory Council" shall mean the Advisory Council or body established under this Article.

(2) The term "Commission" means the North Carolina Occupational Safety and Health Review Commission established under this Article.

(3) The term "classified service" means a position included in the State Merit System of Personnel Administration subject to the laws, rules and regulations of the North Carolina Human Resources Commission as administered by the Director of the Office of State Human Resources and as set forth in Chapter 126 of the General Statutes.

(4) The term "Commissioner" means the Commissioner of Labor of North Carolina.

(5) The term "days" shall mean a calendar day unless otherwise noted.

(6) The term "Department" means the Department of Labor of North Carolina.

(7) The term "Deputy Commissioner" means the Deputy Commissioner of the North Carolina Department of Labor, who is appointed by the Commissioner to aid and assist the Commissioner in the performance of his duties. The Deputy Commissioner shall exercise such power and authority as delegated to him by the Commissioner.

(8) The term "Director" means the officer or agent appointed by the Commissioner of Labor for the purpose of assisting in the administration of the Occupational Safety and Health Act of North Carolina.

(9) The term "employee" means an employee of an employer who is employed in a business or other capacity of his employer, including any and all business units and agencies owned and/or controlled by the employer.

(10) The term "employer" means a person engaged in a business who has employees, including any state or political subdivision of a state, but does not include the employment of domestic workers employed in the place of residence of his or her employer.

(11) The term "established federal standard" means any operative occupational safety and health standard established by any agency of the United States and presently in effect, or contained in any act of Congress in force on the date of enactment of this Article, and adopted by the Secretary of Labor under the Occupational Safety and Health Act of 1970.

(12) The term "federal act," as referred to in this Article, means the Occupational Safety and Health Act of 1970 (Public Law 91-596, 91st Congress, Act of December 29, 1970, 84 Stat. 1950).

(13) The term "imminent danger" means any conditions or practices in any place of employment which are such that a danger exists which could reasonably be expected to cause death, or serious physical harm immediately or before the imminence of such danger can be eliminated through the enforcement procedures otherwise provided by this Article.

(14) The term "issue" means an industrial, occupational or hazard grouping.

(15) The term "occupational safety and health standards" means a standard which requires conditions, or the adoption or use of one or more practices, means, methods, safety devices, operations or processes reasonably necessary and appropriate to provide safe and healthful employment and places of employment, and shall include all occupational safety and health standards adopted and promulgated by the Secretary which also may be and are adopted by the State of North Carolina under the provisions of this Article. This term includes but is not limited to interim federal standards, consensus standards, any proprietary standards or permanent standards, as well as temporary emergency standards which may be adopted by the Secretary, promulgated as

provided by the Occupational Safety and Health Act of 1970, and which standards or regulations are published in the Code of Federal Regulations or otherwise properly promulgated under the federal act or any appropriate federal agencies.

(16) The term "person" means one or more individuals, partnerships, associations, corporations, business trusts, legal representatives.

(17) The term "Secretary" means the United States Secretary of Labor.

(18) A "serious violation" shall be deemed to exist in a place of employment if there is a substantial probability that death or serious physical harm could result from a condition which exists, or from one or more practices, means, methods, operations, or processes which have been adopted or are in use at such place of employment, unless the employer did not know, and could not, with the exercise of reasonable diligence, know of the presence of the violation.

(19) The term "State" means the State of North Carolina. (1973, c. 295, s. 2; 1987, c. 282, s. 14; 2005-133, s. 3; 2013-382, s. 9.1(c).)

§ 95-128. Coverage.

The provisions of this Article or any standard or regulation promulgated pursuant to this Article shall apply to all employers and employees except:

(1) The federal government, including its departments, agencies and instrumentalities;

(2) Employees whose safety and health are subject to protection under the Atomic Energy Act of 1954, as amended;

(3) Employees whose safety and health are subject to protection under the Federal Coal Mine Health and Safety Act of 1969 (30 U.S.C. 801) and the Federal Metal and Nonmetallic Mine Safety Act (30 U.S.C. 725), or Subtitle V of Title 49 of the United States Code;

(4) Railroad employees whose safety and health are subject to protection under Subtitle V of Title 49 of the United States Code;

(5) Employees engaged in all maritime operations;

(6) Employees whose employer is within that class and type of employment which does not permit federal funding, on a matching basis, to the State in return of State enforcement of all occupational safety and health issues. (1973, c. 295, s. 3; 1998-217, s. 27.)

§ 95-129. Rights and duties of employers.

Rights and duties of employers shall include but are not limited to the following provisions:

(1) Each employer shall furnish to each of his employees conditions of employment and a place of employment free from recognized hazards that are causing or are likely to cause death or serious injury or serious physical harm to his employees;

(2) Each employer shall comply with occupational safety and health standards or regulations promulgated pursuant to this Article;

(3) Each employer shall refrain from any unreasonable restraint on the right of the Commissioner or Director, or their lawfully appointed agents, to inspect the employer's place of business. Each employer shall assist the Commissioner, the Director or the lawful agents of either or both of them, in the performance of their inspection duties by supplying or by making available information, any necessary personnel or necessary inspection aides;

(4) Any employer, or association of employers, is entitled to participate in the development of standards by submission of comments on proposed standards, participation in hearings on proposed standards, or by requesting the development of standards on a given issue under G.S. 95-131;

(5) Any employer is entitled, under G.S. 95-137, to review of any citation issued because of his alleged violation of any standard promulgated under this Article, or the length of the abatement period allowed for the correction of an alleged violation;

(6) Any employer is entitled, under G.S. 95-137, to a review of any penalty in the form of civil damages assessed against him because of his alleged violation of this Article;

(7) Any employer is entitled, under G.S. 95-132, to seek an order granting a variance from any occupational safety or health standard;

(8) Any employer is entitled, under G.S. 95-152, to protection of his trade secrets and other legally privileged communications. (1973, c. 295, s. 4.)

§ 95-130. Rights and duties of employees.

Rights and duties of employees shall include but are not limited to the following provisions:

(1) Employees shall comply with occupational safety and health standards and all rules, regulations and orders issued pursuant to this Article which are applicable to their own actions and conduct.

(2) Employees and representatives of employees are entitled to participate in the development of standards by submission of comments on proposed standards, participation in hearings on proposed standards, or by requesting the development of standards on a given issue under G.S. 95-131.

(3) Employees shall be notified by their employer of any application for a temporary order granting the employer a variance from any provision of this Article or standard or regulation promulgated pursuant to this Article.

(4) Employees shall be given the opportunity to participate in any hearing which concerns an application by their employer for a variance from a standard promulgated under this Article.

(5) Any employee who may be adversely affected by a standard or variance issued pursuant to this Article may file a petition for review with the Commissioner who shall review the matters set forth and alleged in the petition.

(6) Any employee who has been exposed or is being exposed to toxic materials or harmful physical agents in concentrations or at levels in excess of

that provided for by any applicable standard shall have a right to file a petition for review with the Commissioner who shall investigate and pass upon same.

(7) Subject to regulations issued pursuant to this Article any employee or authorized representative of employees shall be given the right to request an inspection and to consult with the Commissioner, Director, or their agents, at the time of the physical inspection of any work place as provided by the inspection provision of this Article.

(8) to (10) Repealed by Session Laws 1991 (Regular Session, 1992), c. 1021, s. 2.

(11) Any employee or representative of employees who believes that any period of time fixed in the citation given to his employer for correction of a violation is unreasonable has the right to contest such time for correction by filing a written and signed notice within 15 working days from the date the citation is posted within the establishment.

(12) Nothing in this or any other provision of this Article shall be deemed to authorize or require medical examination, immunization, or treatment for those who object thereto on religious grounds, except where such is necessary for the protection of the health or safety of others. (1973, c. 295, s. 5; 1991 (Reg. Sess., 1992), c. 1021, s. 2; 2011-366, s. 8.)

§ 95-131. Development and promulgation of standards; adoption of federal standards and regulations.

(a) All occupational safety and health standards promulgated under the federal act by the Secretary, and any modifications, revision, amendments or revocations in accordance with the authority conferred by the federal act or any other federal act or agency relating to safety and health and adopted by the Secretary, shall be adopted as the rules of the Commissioner of this State unless the Commissioner decides to adopt an alternative State rule as effective as the federal requirement and providing safe and healthful employment in places of employment as required by the federal act and standards and regulations heretofore referred to and as provided by the Occupational Safety and Health Act of 1970. Chapter 150B of the General Statutes governs the adoption of rules by the Commissioner.

(b), (c) Repealed by Session Laws 1991, c. 418, s. 8.

(d) Rules adopted under this section shall provide insofar as possible the highest degree of safety and health protection for employees; other considerations shall be the latest available scientific data in the field, the feasibility of the standard, and experience gained under this and other health and safety laws. Whenever practical the standards established in a rule shall be expressed in terms of objective criteria and of the performance desired. In establishing standards dealing with toxic materials or harmful physical agents, the Commissioner, after consultation and recommendations of the Department of Health and Human Services, shall set a standard which most adequately assures, to the extent possible, on the basis of the most available evidence that no employee will suffer material impairment of health or functional capacity even if such employee has regular exposure to the hazard dealt with by such standard for the period of his working life.

(e) The Commissioner may not adopt State standards, for products distributed or used in interstate commerce, which are different from federal standards for such products unless the adoption of such State standard, or standards, is required by compelling local conditions and does not unduly burden interstate commerce.

(f) Repealed by Session Laws 1991, c. 418, s. 8.

(g) Any rule, regulation, scope, or standard for agricultural employers adopted or promulgated prior to July 12, 1988, that differs from the federal rule, regulation, scope, or standard is repealed effective September 1, 1989, unless readopted pursuant to Chapter 150B of the General Statutes. (1973, c. 295, s. 6; c. 476, s. 128; 1975, 2nd Sess., c. 983, s. 81; 1987, c. 285, s. 17; 1987 (Reg. Sess., 1988), c. 1111, ss. 7, 8; 1989, c. 727, s. 219(14); 1991, c. 418, s. 8; 1997-443, s. 11A.34.)

§ 95-132. Variances.

(a) Temporary Variances. -

(1) The Commissioner may upon written application by an employer issue an order granting such employer a temporary variance from standards adopted by this Article or promulgated by the Commissioner under this Article. Any such

order shall prescribe the practices, means, methods, operations and processes which the employer must adopt or use while the variance is in effect and state in detail a program for coming into compliance with the standard.

(2)   An application for a temporary variance shall contain all information required as enumerated in 29 C.F.R. 1905.10(b) which is hereby incorporated by reference, as if herein fully set out.

(3)   Upon receipt of an application for an order granting a temporary variance, the Commissioner to whom such application is addressed may issue an interim order granting such a temporary variance, for the purpose of permitting time for an orderly consideration of such application. No such interim order may be effective for longer than 180 days.

(4)   Such a temporary variance may be granted only after notice to employees and interested parties and opportunity for hearing. The temporary variance may be for a period of no longer than required to achieve compliance or one year, whichever is shorter, and may be renewed only once. Application for renewal of a variance must be filed in accordance with provisions in the initial grant of the temporary variance.

(5)   An order granting a temporary variance shall be issued only if the employer establishes

a.   (i) That he is unable to comply with the standard by the effective date because of unavailability of professional or technical personnel or materials and equipment required or necessary construction or alteration of facilities or technology, (ii) that all available steps have been taken to safeguard his employees against the hazards covered by the standard, and (iii) that he has an effective program for coming into compliance with the standard as quickly as practicable, or

b.   That he is engaged in an experimental program as described in subsection (c) of this section as hereinafter stated.

(b)   Permanent Variances. -

(1)   Any affected employer may apply to the Commissioner for a rule or order for a permanent variance from a standard promulgated under this section. Affected employees shall be given notice of each such application and an opportunity to participate in a hearing. The Commissioner shall issue such rule

or order if he determines on the record, after opportunity for an inspection where appropriate and a hearing, that the proponent of the variance has demonstrated by a preponderance of the evidence that the conditions, practices, means, methods, operations, or processes used or proposed to be used by an employer will provide employment and places of employment to his employees which are as safe and healthful as those which would prevail if he complied with the standard.

(2)   The rule or order so issued shall prescribe the conditions the employer must maintain, and the practices, means, methods, operations, and processes which he must adopt and utilize to the extent they differ from the standard in question.

(3)   Such a rule or order may be modified or revoked upon application by an employer, employees, or by the Commissioner on his own motion, in the manner prescribed for its issuance under this subsection at any time after six months from its issuance.

(c)   Experimental Variances. - The Commissioner is authorized to grant a variance from any standard or portion thereof whenever he determines that such variance is necessary to permit an employer to participate in an experiment approved by him designed to demonstrate or validate new and improved techniques to safeguard the health or safety of workers. (1973, c. 295, s. 7; 1997-456, s. 27.)

§ 95-133. Office of Director of Occupational Safety and Health; powers and duties of the Director.

(a)   There is hereby created and established in the North Carolina Department of Labor a division to be known as the Occupational Safety and Health Division. The Commissioner shall appoint a Director to administer this division who shall be subject to the direction and supervision of the Commissioner. The Director shall carry out the responsibilities of the State of North Carolina as prescribed under the Occupational Safety and Health Act of 1970, and any subsequent federal laws or regulations relating to occupational safety and health, and this Article, as written, revised or amended by legislative enactment and as delegated or authorized by the Commissioner. The Commissioner shall make and promulgate such rules, amendments, or revisions in rules, as he may deem advisable for the administration of the office, he shall also accept and use the services, facilities, and personnel of any agency of the State or of any subdivision of State government, either as a free service or by reimbursement. The Director shall devote full time to his duties of office and shall not hold any other office. The Director, subject to the approval of the Commissioner, shall select a professional staff of qualified and competent employees to assist in the statewide administration of the Article. All of the employees referred to herein shall be under the classified service, as herein defined in G.S. 95-127, subdivision (3).

(b)   Subject to the general supervision of the Commissioner and Deputy Commissioner, the Director shall be responsible for the administration and enforcement of all laws, rules and regulations which it is the duty of the Division to administer and enforce. The Director shall have the power, jurisdiction and authority to:

(1)   Uniformly superintend, enforce and administer applicable occupational safety and health laws of the State of North Carolina;

(2)   Make or cause to be made all necessary inspections, analyses and research for the purpose of seeing that all laws and rules and regulations which the office has the duty, power and authority to enforce are promptly and effectively carried out;

(3)   Make all necessary investigations, develop information and reports upon conditions of employee safety and health, and upon all matters relating to the enforcement of this Article and all lawful regulations issued thereunder;

(4)   Report to the Federal Occupational Safety and Health Administration any information which it may require;

(5)   Recommend to the Commissioner such rules, regulations, standards, or changes in rules, regulations and standards which the Director deems advisable for the prevention of accidents, occupational hazards or the prevention of industrial or occupational diseases;

(6)   Recommend to the Commissioner that he institute proceedings to remove from his or her position any employee of the Office who accepts any favor, privilege, money, object of value, or property of any kind whatsoever or who shall give prior notice of a compliance inspection of a work place unless authorized under the provisions of this Article;

(7) Employ experts, consultants or organizations for work related to the occupational safety and health program of the Division and compensate same with the approval of the Commissioner;

(8) Institute hearings, investigations, request the issuance of citations and propose such penalties as he may in his judgment consider necessary to carry out the provisions of this Article;

(9) The Commissioner shall have the power and authority to issue all types of notices, citations, cease and desist orders, or any other pleading, form or notice necessary to enforce compliance with this Article as hereinafter set forth. The Commissioner is also empowered and authorized to apply to the courts of the State having jurisdiction for orders or injunctions restraining unlawful acts and practices prohibited by this Article or not in compliance with this Article and to apply for mandatory injunctions to compel enforcement of the Article, and the Commissioner is authorized, and further authorized by and through his agents, to institute criminal actions or proceedings for such violations of the Article as are subject to criminal penalties. The Director shall recommend to the Commissioner the imposition and amount of civil penalties provided by this Article, and the Commissioner may institute such proceedings as necessary for the enforcement and payment of such civil penalties subject to such review of the Commission as hereinafter set forth.

(10) The Director may recommend to the Commissioner that any person, firm, corporation or witness be cited for contempt or for punishment as of contempt, and the Commissioner is authorized to enter any order of contempt or as of contempt as he may deem proper and necessary, and any hearing examiner may recommend to the Commissioner that such order or citation for contempt be made.

(11) The Commissioner or the Director, or their authorized agents, shall have the power and authority to issue subpoenas for witnesses and for the production of any and all papers and documents necessary for any hearing or other proceeding and to require the same to be served by the process officers of the State. The Commissioner and the Director may administer any and all oaths that are necessary in the enforcement of this Article and may certify as to the authenticity of all records, papers, documents and transcripts under the seal of the Department of Labor.

(12) All orders, citations, cease and desist orders, stop orders, sanctions and contempt orders, civil penalties and the proceedings thereon shall be subject to

review by the Commission as hereinafter provided, including all assessments for civil penalties. (1973, c. 295, s. 8; 2005-133, s. 4.)

§ 95-134. Advisory Council.

(a) There is hereby established a State Advisory Council on Occupational Safety and Health consisting of 11 members, appointed by the Commissioner, composed of three representatives from management, three representatives from labor, four representatives of the public sector with knowledge of occupational safety and occupational health professions and one representative of the public sector with knowledge of migrant labor. The Commissioner shall designate one of the members from the public sector as chairman and all members of the State Advisory Council shall be selected insofar as possible upon the basis of their experience and competence in the field of occupational safety and health.

(b) The Council shall advise, consult with, and make recommendations to the Commissioner on matters relating to the administration of this Article. The Council shall hold no fewer than two meetings during each calendar year. All meetings of the Advisory Council shall be open to the public and a transcript shall be kept and made available for public inspection.

(c) The Director shall furnish to the Advisory Council such secretarial, clerical and other services as he deems necessary to conduct the business of the Advisory Council. The members of the Advisory Council shall be compensated for reasonable expenses incurred, including necessary time spent in traveling to and from their place of residence within the State to the place of meeting, and mileage and subsistence as allowed to State officials. The members of the Advisory Council shall be compensated in accordance with Chapter 138 of the General Statutes.

(d) In addition to its other duties, the Advisory Council shall assist the Commissioner in formulating and setting standards under the provisions of this Article. For this purpose the Commissioner may appoint persons qualified by experience and affiliation to present the viewpoint of the employers involved, persons similarly qualified to present the viewpoint of the workers involved, and some persons to represent the health and safety agencies of the State. The Commissioner for this purpose may include representatives or professional organizations of technicians or professionals specializing in occupational safety or health. Such persons appointed for temporary purposes may be paid such per diem and expenses of attending meetings as provided in Chapter 138 of the General Statutes. (1973, c. 295, s. 9; 1977, c. 806; 1983, c. 717, ss. 17, 18.)

§ 95-135. North Carolina Occupational Safety and Health Review Commission.

(a) The North Carolina Occupational Safety and Health Review Commission is hereby established. The Commission shall be composed of three members from among persons who, by reason of training, education or experience, are qualified to carry out the functions of the Commission under this Article. The Governor shall appoint the members of the Commission and name one of the members as chairman of the Commission. The terms of the members of the Commission shall be six years except that the members of the Commission first taking office shall serve, as designated by the Governor at the time of appointment, one for a term of two years, one for a term of four years, and the member of the Commission designated as chairman shall serve for a term of six years. Any vacancy caused by the death, resignation, or removal of a member prior to the expiration of the term for which he was appointed shall be filled by the Governor for the remainder of the unexpired term. The Governor shall fill all vacancies occurring by reason of the expiration of the term of any members of the Commission.

(b) The Commission shall hear and issue decisions on appeals entered from citations and abatement periods and from all types of penalties. Appeals from orders of the Director dealing with conditions or practices that constitute imminent danger shall not be stayed by the Commission until after full and adequate hearing. The Commission in the discharge of its duties under this Article is authorized and empowered to administer oaths and affirmations and institute motions, cause the taking of depositions, interrogatories, certify to official acts, and issue subpoenas to compel the attendance of witnesses and the production of books, papers, correspondence, memoranda, and other records deemed necessary as evidence in connection with any appeal or proceeding for review before the Commission.

(c) The Commission shall meet at least once each calendar quarter but it may hold call meetings or hearings upon at least three days' notice to each member by the chairman and at such time and place as the chairman may fix. The chairman shall be responsible on behalf of the Commission for the administrative operations of the Commission and shall appoint such hearing examiners and other employees as he deems necessary to assist in the performance of the Commission's functions and fix the compensation of such employees with the approval of the Governor. The assignment and removal of hearing examiners shall be made by the Commission, and any hearing examiner may be removed for misfeasance, malfeasance, misconduct, immoral conduct, incompetency, the commission of any crime, or for any other good and adequate reason as found by the Commission. The Commission shall give notice to such hearing examiner, along with written allegations as to the charges against him, and the same shall be heard by the Commission, and its decision shall be final. The compensation of the members of the Commission shall be on a per diem basis and shall be fixed by the Governor. The chairman of the Commission may be paid a higher rate of compensation than the other two members of the Commission. For the purpose of carrying out its duties and functions under this Article, two members of the Commission shall constitute a quorum and official action can be taken only on the affirmative vote of at least two members of the Commission. On matters properly before the Commission the chairman may issue temporary orders, subpoenas, and other temporary types of orders subject to the subsequent review of the Commission. The issuance of subpoenas, orders to take depositions, orders requiring interrogatories and other procedural matters of evidence issued by the chairman shall not be subject to review.

(d) Every official act of the Commission shall be entered of record and its hearings and records shall be open to the public. The Commission is authorized and empowered to make such procedural rules as are necessary for the orderly transaction of its proceedings. Unless the Commission adopts a different rule, the proceedings, as nearly as possible, shall be in accordance with the Rules of Civil Procedure, G.S. 1A-1. The Commission may order testimony to be taken by deposition in any proceeding pending before it at any stage of such proceeding. Any person, firm or corporation, and its agents or officials, may be compelled to appear and testify and produce like documentary evidence before the Commission. Witnesses whose depositions are taken under this section, and the persons taking such depositions, shall be entitled to the same fees as are paid for like services in the courts of the State.

(e) The rules of procedure prescribed or adopted by the Commission shall provide affected employees or representatives of affected employees an opportunity to participate as parties to hearings under this section.

(f) Any member of the Commission may be removed by the Governor for inefficiency, neglect of duty, or any misfeasance or malfeasance in office.

Before such removal the Governor shall give notice of hearing and state the allegations against the member of the Commission, and the same shall be heard by the Governor, and his decision shall be final. The principal office of the Commission shall be in Raleigh, North Carolina, but whenever it deems that the convenience of the public or of the parties may be promoted, or delay or expense may be minimized, the Commission may hold hearings or conduct other proceedings at any place in the State.

(g) In case of a contumacy, failure or refusal of any person to testify before the Commission, give any type of evidence, or to produce any books, records, papers, correspondence, memoranda or other records, such person upon such failure to obey the orders of the Commission may be punished for contempt or any other matter involving contempt as set forth and described by the general laws of the State. The Commission shall issue no order for contempt without first finding the facts involved in the proceeding. Witnesses appearing before the Commission shall be entitled to the same fees as those paid for the services of said witnesses in the courts of the State, and all such fees shall be taxed against the interested parties according to the judgment and discretion of the Commission.

(h) The Director shall consult with the chairman of the Commission with respect to the preparation and presentation to the Commission for adoption of all necessary forms or citations, notices of all kinds, forms of stop orders, all forms and orders imposing penalties and all forms of notices or applications for review by the Commission, and any and all other procedural papers and documents necessary for the administration of the Article as applied to employers and employees and for all procedures and proceedings brought before the Commission for review.

(i) A hearing examiner appointed by the chairman of the Commission shall hear, and make a determination upon, any proceeding instituted before the Commission and may hear any motion in connection therewith, assigned to the hearing examiner, and shall make a report of the determination which constitutes the hearing examiner's final disposition of the proceedings. A copy of the report of the hearing examiner shall be furnished to the Director and all interested parties involved in any appeal or any proceeding before the hearing examiner for the hearing examiner's determination. The report of the hearing examiner shall become the final order of the Commission 30 days from the date of the report as determined by the hearing examiner, unless within the 30-day period any member of the Commission had directed that the report shall be reviewed by the entire Commission as a whole. Upon application for review of any report or determination of a hearing examiner, before the 30-day period expires, the Commission shall schedule the matter for hearing, on the record, except the Commission may allow the introduction of newly discovered evidence, or in its discretion the taking of further evidence upon any question or issue. All interested parties to the original hearing shall be notified of the date, time and place of the hearing and shall be allowed to appear in person or by attorney at the hearing. Upon review of the report and determination by the hearing examiner the Commission may adopt, modify or vacate the report of the hearing examiner and notify the interested parties. The report of the hearing examiner, and the report, decision, or determination of the Commission upon review shall be in writing and shall include findings of fact, conclusions of law, and the reasons or bases for them, on all the material issues of fact, law, or discretion presented on the record. The report, decision or determination of the Commission upon review shall be final unless further appeal is made to the courts under the provisions of Chapter 150B of the General Statutes, as amended, entitled: "Judicial Review of Decisions of Certain Administrative Agencies."

(j) Repealed by Session Laws 1993, c. 300, s. 1. (1973, c. 295, s. 10; c. 1331, s. 3; 1985, c. 746, s. 1; 1985 (Reg. Sess., 1986), c. 955, ss. 6, 7; 1987, c. 827, s. 1; 1987 (Reg. Sess., 1988), c. 1111, s. 10; 1993, c. 300, s. 1; c. 474, s. 1; 2005-133, ss. 1, 5; 2006-203, s. 21.)

§ 95-136. Inspections.

(a) In order to carry out the purposes of this Article, the Commissioner or Director, or their duly authorized agents, upon presenting appropriate credentials to the owner, operator, or agent in charge, are authorized:

(1) To enter without delay, and at any reasonable time, any factory, plant, establishment, construction site, or other area, work place or environment where work is being performed by an employee of an employer; and

(2) To inspect and investigate during regular working hours, and at other reasonable times, and within reasonable limits, and in a reasonable manner, any such place of employment and all pertinent conditions, processes, structures, machines, apparatus, devices, equipment, and materials therein, and to question privately any such employer, owner, operator, agent or employee.

(3) The Commissioner or Director, or their duly authorized agents, shall reinspect any place of employment where a willful serious violation was found to exist during the previous inspection and a final Order has been entered.

(b) In making his inspections and investigations under this Article, the Commissioner may issue subpoenas to require the attendance and testimony of witnesses and the production of evidence under oath. Witnesses shall be reimbursed for all travel and other necessary expenses which shall be claimed and paid in accordance with the prevailing travel regulations of the State. In case of a failure or refusal of any person to obey a subpoena under this section, the district judge or superior court judge of the county in which the inspection or investigation is conducted shall have jurisdiction upon the application of the Commissioner to issue an order requiring such person to appear and testify or produce evidence as the case may require, and any failure to obey such order of the court may be punished by such court as contempt thereof.

(c) Subject to regulations issued by the Commissioner a representative of the employer and an employee authorized by the employees shall be given an opportunity to consult with or to accompany the Commissioner, Director, or their authorized agents, during the physical inspection of any work place described under subsection (a) for the purpose of aiding such inspection. Where there is no authorized employee representative, the Commissioner, Director, or their authorized agents, shall consult with a reasonable number of employees concerning matters of health and safety in the work place.

(d) (1) Any employees or an employee representative of the employees who believe that a violation of a safety or health standard exists that threatens physical harm, or that an imminent danger exists, may request an inspection by giving notice of such violation or danger to the Commissioner or Director. Any such notice shall be reduced to writing, shall set forth with reasonable particularity the grounds for the notice, and shall be signed by employees or the employee representatives of the employees, and a copy shall be provided the employer or his agent no later than at the time of inspection. Upon the request of the person giving such notice, his name and the names of individual employees referred to therein shall not appear in such copy of any record published, released or made available pursuant to subsection (e) of this section. If upon receipt of such notification the Commissioner or Director determines there are reasonable grounds to believe that such violation or danger exists, the Commissioner or Director or their authorized agents shall promptly make a special investigation in accordance with the provisions of this section as soon as practicable to determine if such violation or danger exists. If the Commissioner or Director determines there are not reasonable grounds to believe that a violation or danger exists he shall notify the employees or representatives of the employees, in writing, of such determination.

(2) Prior to, during and after any inspection of a work place, any employees or representative of employees employed in such work place may notify the inspecting Commissioner, Director, or their agents, in writing, of any violation of this Article which they have reason to believe exists in such work place. The Commissioner shall, by regulation, establish procedures for informal review of any refusal by a representative of the Commissioner or Director to issue a citation with respect to any such alleged violation and shall furnish the employees or representatives of employees requesting such review a written statement of the reason for the Commissioner's or Director's final disposition of the case.

(e) The Commissioner is authorized to compile, analyze, and publish, in summary or detailed form, all reports or information obtained under this section. Files and other records relating to investigations and enforcement proceedings pursuant to this Article shall not be subject to inspection and examination as authorized by G.S. 132-6 while such investigations and proceedings are pending, except that, subject to the provisions of subsection (e1) of this section, an employer cited under the provisions of this Article is entitled to receive a copy of the official inspection report which is the basis for citations received by the employer following the issuance of citations.

(e1) Upon the written request of and at the expense of the requesting party, official inspection reports of inspections conducted pursuant to this Article shall be available for release in accordance with the provisions contained in this subsection and subsection (e) of this section. The names of witnesses or complainants, and any information within statements taken from witnesses or complainants during the course of inspections or investigations conducted pursuant to this Article that would name or otherwise identify the witnesses or complainants, shall not be released to any employer or third party and shall be redacted from any copy of the official inspection report provided to the employer or third party. Witness statements that are in the handwriting of the witness or complainant shall, upon the request of and at the expense of the requesting party, be transcribed so that information that would not name or otherwise identify the witness may be released. A witness or complainant may, however, sign a written release permitting the Commissioner to provide information specified in the release to any persons or entities designated in the release. Nothing in this section shall be construed to prohibit the use of the name or statement of a witness or complainant by the Commissioner in enforcement proceedings or hearings held pursuant to this Article. The Commissioner shall make available to the employer 10 days prior to a scheduled enforcement hearing unredacted copies of: (i) the witness statements the Commissioner intends to use at the enforcement hearing, (ii) the statements of witnesses the Commissioner intends to call to testify, or (iii) the statements of witnesses whom the Commissioner does not intend to use that might support an employer's affirmative defense or otherwise exonerate the employer; provided a written request for the statement or statements is received by the Commissioner no later than 12 days prior to the enforcement hearing. If the request for an unredacted copy of the witness statement or statements is received less than 12 days before a hearing, the statement or statements shall be made available as soon as practicable. The Commissioner may permit the use of names and statements of witnesses and complainants and information obtained during the course of inspections or investigations conducted pursuant to this Article by public officials in the performance of their public duties.

(f)   (1)   Inspections conducted under this section shall be accomplished without advance notice, subject to the exception in subdivision (2) below this subsection.

(2)   The Commissioner or Director may authorize the giving to any employer or employee advance notice of an inspection only when the giving of such notice is essential to the effectiveness of such inspection, and in keeping with regulations issued by the Commissioner.

(g)   The Commissioner shall prescribe such rules and regulations as he may deem necessary to carry out his responsibilities under this Article, including rules and regulations dealing with the inspection of an employer's establishment. (1973, c. 295, s. 11; 1993, c. 317, ss. 1, 2; 1999-364, ss. 1, 2; 2003-174, s. 1.)

§ 95-136.1. Special emphasis inspection program.

(a)   As used in this section, a "special emphasis inspection" is an inspection by the Department's occupational safety and health division that is scheduled because of an employer's high frequency of violations of safety and health laws or because of an employer's high risk or high rate of work-related fatalities or work-related serious injuries or illnesses.

(b)   The Department shall develop and implement a special emphasis inspection program that targets for special emphasis inspection employers who:

(1)   Have a high rate of serious or willful violations of any standard, rule, order, or other requirement under this Article, or of regulations prescribed pursuant to the Federal Occupational Safety and Health Act of 1970, in a one-year period;

(2)   Have a high rate of work-related deaths, or a high rate of work-related serious injuries or illnesses, in a one-year period; or

(3)   Are engaged in a type of industry determined by the Department to be at high risk for serious or fatal work-related injuries or illnesses.

(4)   Repealed by Session Laws 1997-443, s. 17(b).

To identify an employer for a special emphasis inspection, the Department shall use the most current data available from its own database and from other sources, including State departments, divisions, boards, commissions, and other State entities. The Department shall ensure that every employer targeted for a special emphasis inspection is inspected at least one time within the two-year period following targeting of the employer by the Department. The Department shall update its special emphasis inspection records at least annually.

(c)   The Director shall make information about the special emphasis inspection program available prior to the date of implementation of the program.

(d)   The Department shall by March 1, 1995, and annually thereafter, report to the Joint Legislative Commission on Governmental Operations and the Fiscal Research Division of the General Assembly on the impact of the special emphasis inspection program on safety and health compliance and enforcement. (1991 (Reg. Sess., 1992), c. 924, s. 1; 1997-443, s. 17(b).)

§ 95-137. Issuance of citations.

(a)   If, upon inspection or investigation, the Director or his authorized representative has reasonable grounds to believe that an employer has not fulfilled his duties as prescribed in this Article, or has violated any standard, regulation, rule or order promulgated under this Article, he shall with reasonable promptness issue a citation to the employer. Each citation shall be in writing and shall describe with particularity the nature of the violation, including a reference to the provisions of the act, standards, rules and regulations, or orders alleged to have been violated. In addition, the citation shall fix a reasonable time for the abatement of the violation. The Director may prescribe procedures for the issuance of a notice in lieu of a citation with respect to de minimus violations which have no direct or immediate relationship to safety or health. Each citation or notice in lieu of citation issued under this section, or a copy or copies thereof, shall be prominently posted, as prescribed in regulations issued by the Director, at or near such place a violation referred to in the citation occurred.

(b)   Procedure for Enforcement. -

(1)   If, after an inspection or investigation, the Director issues a citation under any provisions of this Article, the Director shall, within a reasonable time after the termination of such inspection or investigation, notify the employer by certified mail with return receipt, by signature confirmation as provided by the U.S. Postal [Service], by a designated delivery service authorized pursuant to 26 U.S.C. § 7502(f)(2) with delivery receipt, or via hand delivery of any penalty, if any, the Director has recommended to the Commissioner to be proposed under the provisions of this Article and that the employer has 15 working days within which to notify the Director that the employer wishes to:

a.   Contest the citation or proposed assessment of penalty; or

b.   Request an informal conference.

Following an informal conference, unless the employer and Department have entered into a settlement agreement, the Director shall send the employer an amended citation or notice of no change. The employer has 15 working days from the receipt of the amended citation or notice of no change to notify the Director that the employer wishes to contest the citation or proposed assessment of penalty, whether or not amended. If, within 15 working days from the receipt of the notice issued by the Director, the employer fails to notify the Director that the employer requires an informal conference to be held or intends to contest the citation or proposed assessment of penalty, and no notice is filed by any employee or representative of employees under the provisions of this Article within such time, the citation and the assessment as proposed to the Commissioner shall be deemed final and not subject to review by any court.

(2) If the Director has reason to believe that an employer has failed to correct a violation for which a citation has been issued within the period permitted for its correction (which period shall not begin to run until the entry of a final order by the Commission in case of any review proceedings under this Article initiated by the employer in good faith and not solely for a delay or avoidance of penalties), the Director shall notify the employer by certified mail with return receipt, by signature confirmation as provided by the U.S. Postal Service, by a designated delivery service authorized pursuant to 26 U.S.C. § 7502(f)(2) with delivery receipt, or via hand delivery of such failure and of the penalty proposed to be assessed under this Article by reason of such failure and that the employer has 15 working days within which to notify the Director that the employer wishes to contest the Director's notification of the proposed assessment of penalty. If, within 15 working days from the receipt of notification issued by the Director, an employer fails to notify the Director that the employer intends to contest the notification or proposed recommendation of penalty, the notification and the proposed assessment made by the Director shall be final and not subject to review by any court.

(3) No citation may be issued under this section after the expiration of six months following the occurrence of any violation.

(4) If an employer notifies the Director that the employer intends to contest a citation issued under the provisions of this Article or notification issued under the provisions of this Article, or if, within 15 working days of the receipt of a citation under this Article, any employee or representative thereof files a notice with the Director alleging that the period of time fixed in the citation for the abatement of the violation is unreasonable, the Director shall immediately advise the Commission of such notification, and the Commission shall afford an opportunity for a hearing. The Commission shall thereafter issue an order, based on findings of fact, affirming, modifying, or vacating the Director's citation or the proposed penalty fixed by the Commissioner, or directing other appropriate relief, and such order shall become final 30 days after its issuance. Upon showing by an employer of a good faith effort to comply with the abatement requirements of a citation, and that an abatement has not been completed because of factors beyond the employer's reasonable control, the Director, after an opportunity for a hearing as provided in this Article, shall issue an order affirming or modifying the abatement requirements in such citation. The rules of procedure prescribed by the chairman of the Commission shall provide affected employees or representatives of affected employees an opportunity to participate as parties to hearings under this section.

(5)   Repealed by Session Laws 1993, c. 300, s. 2.

(6)   Each local unit of government shall report each violation for which it is issued a citation to its local governing board at its next public meeting and to its workers compensation insurance carrier or to the risk pool of which it is a member pursuant to Article 23 of Chapter 58 of the General Statutes. (1973, c. 295, s. 12; 1987 (Reg. Sess., 1988), c. 1111, s. 11; 1991 (Reg. Sess., 1992), c. 1020, ss. 2, 3; 1993, c. 300, s. 2; 2003-308, s. 6; 2005-133, ss. 6, 7; 2007-231, s. 10.)

§ 95-138. Civil penalties.

(a)   The Commissioner, upon recommendation of the Director, or the North Carolina Occupational Safety and Health Review Commission in the case of an appeal, shall have the authority to assess penalties against any employer who violates the requirements of this Article, or any standard, rule, or order adopted under this Article, as follows:

(1)   A minimum penalty of five thousand dollars ($5,000) to a maximum penalty of seventy thousand dollars ($70,000) may be assessed for each willful or repeat violation.

(2)   A penalty of up to seven thousand dollars ($7,000) shall be assessed for each serious violation, except that a penalty of up to fourteen thousand dollars ($14,000) shall be assessed for each serious violation that involves injury to an employee under 18 years of age.

(2a) A penalty of up to seven thousand dollars ($7,000) may be assessed for each violation that is adjudged not to be of a serious nature.

(3)   A penalty of up to seven thousand dollars ($7,000) may be assessed against an employer who fails to correct and abate a violation, within the period allowed for its correction and abatement, which period shall not begin to run until the date of the final Order of the Commission in the case of any appeal proceedings in this Article initiated by the employer in good faith and not solely for the delay of avoidance of penalties. The assessment shall be made to apply to each day during which the failure or violation continues.

(4) A penalty of up to seven thousand dollars ($7,000) shall be assessed for violating the posting requirements, as required under the provisions of this Article.

(b) The Commissioner shall adopt uniform standards that the Commissioner, the Commission, and the hearing examiner shall apply when determining appropriateness of the penalty. The following factors shall be used in determining whether a penalty is appropriate:

(1) Size of the business of the employer being charged.

(2) The gravity of the violation.

(3) The good faith of the employer.

(4) The record of previous violations; provided that for purposes of determining repeat violations, only the record within the previous three years is applicable.

(5) Whether the violation involves injury to an employee under 18 years of age.

The report of the hearing examiner and the report, decision, or determination of the Commission on appeal shall specify the standards applied in determining the reduction or affirmation of the penalty assessed by the Commissioner.

(c) The clear proceeds of all civil penalties and interest recovered by the Commissioner, together with the costs thereof, shall be remitted to the Civil Penalty and Forfeiture Fund in accordance with G.S. 115C-457.2. (1973, c. 295, s. 13; 1987 (Reg. Sess., 1988), c. 1111, s. 12; 1989 (Reg. Sess., 1990), c. 844; 1991, c. 329, s. 1; c. 761, s. 17; 1993, c. 474, s. 2; 1998-215, s. 111; 2004-203, s. 39(a); 2005-133, s. 8; 2006-39, s. 3; 2009-351, s. 4.)

§ 95-139. Criminal penalties.

(a) Any employer who willfully violates any standard, rule, regulation or order promulgated pursuant to the authority of this Article, and the violation causes the death of any employee 18 years of age or older, shall be guilty of a

Class 2 misdemeanor, which may include a fine of not more than ten thousand dollars ($10,000).

(b) Any employer who willfully violates any standard, rule, regulation, or order promulgated pursuant to the authority of this Article, and the violation causes the death of any employee under 18 years of age, shall be guilty of a Class 2 misdemeanor, which may include a fine of not more than twenty thousand dollars ($20,000).

(c) If an employer is convicted of more than one violation of subsection (a) or (b) of this section, the subsequent violation shall be penalized as follows:

(1) The employer shall be guilty of a Class 1 misdemeanor which may include a fine of not more than twenty thousand dollars ($20,000) if the subsequent violation results in the death of an employee 18 years of age or older.

(2) The employer shall be guilty of a Class 1 misdemeanor which may include a fine of not more than forty thousand dollars ($40,000) if the subsequent violation results in the death of an employee under 18 years of age.

(d) This section shall not prevent any prosecuting officer of the State of North Carolina from proceeding against such employer on a prosecution charging any degree of willful or culpable homicide. Any person who gives advance notice of any inspection to be conducted under this Article, without authority from the Commissioner, Director, or any of their agents to whom such authority has been delegated, shall be guilty of a Class 2 misdemeanor.

(e) Whoever knowingly makes any false statement, representation, or certification in any application, record, report, plan, or any other document filed or required to be maintained pursuant to this Article, shall be guilty of a Class 2 misdemeanor, which may include a fine of (i) not more than ten thousand dollars ($10,000) for falsifications pertaining to employees 18 years of age or older or (ii) not more than twenty thousand dollars ($20,000) for falsifications pertaining to employees under 18 years of age.

(f) Whoever shall commit any kind of assault upon or whoever kills a person engaged in or on account of the performance of investigative, inspection, or law-enforcement functions shall be subject to prosecution under the general criminal laws of the State and upon such charges as the proper prosecuting officer shall charge or allege. (1973, c. 295, s. 14; 1993, c. 539, s. 671; 1994, Ex. Sess., c. 24, s. 14(c); 2009-351, s. 5.)

§ 95-140. Procedures to counteract imminent dangers.

(a) The superior courts of this State shall have jurisdiction, upon petition of the Commissioner, to restrain any conditions or practices in any place of employment which are such that a danger exists, which could reasonably be expected to cause death or serious physical harm immediately or before the imminence of such danger can be eliminated through the enforcement procedures otherwise provided by this Article. Any order issued under this section may require such steps to be taken as may be necessary to avoid, correct, or remove such imminent danger and prohibit the employment or presence of any individual in locations or under conditions where such imminent danger exists, except those individuals whose presence is necessary to avoid, correct or remove such imminent danger or to maintain the capacity of a continuous process operation to assume normal operations without a complete cessation of operations, or where a cessation of operations is necessary to permit such to be accomplished in a safe and orderly manner.

(b) Upon the filing of any such petition the superior court shall, without the necessity of showing an adequate remedy at law, have jurisdiction to grant injunctive relief or temporary restraining order pending the outcome of an enforcement proceeding pursuant to this Article. The proceeding shall be as provided under the statutes and Rules of Civil Procedure of this State except that no temporary restraining order issued without notice shall be effective for a period longer than five days.

(c) Whenever and as soon as an inspector concludes that conditions or practices described in this section exist in any place of employment, he shall inform the affected employees and employers of the danger and that he is recommending to the Commissioner that relief be sought. If the Commissioner arbitrarily or capriciously fails to seek relief under this section, any employee who may be injured by reason of such failure, or the representative of such employee, may bring an action against the Commissioner in the superior court of the district in which the imminent danger is alleged to exist or the employer has its principal office or place of business, for a writ of mandamus to compel the Commissioner to seek such an order for such relief as may be appropriate. (1973, c. 295, s. 15.)

§ 95-141. Judicial review.

Any person or party in interest who has exhausted all administrative remedies available under this Article and who is aggrieved by a final decision in a contested case is entitled to judicial review in accordance with Article 4 of Chapter 150B of the General Statutes. The Commissioner may file in the office of the clerk of the superior court of the county wherein the person, firm or corporation under order resides, or, if a corporation is involved, in the county wherein the corporation maintains its principal place of business, or in the county wherein the violation occurred, a certified copy of a final order of the Commissioner unappealed from, or of a final order of the Commissioner affirmed upon appeal. Whereupon, the clerk of said court shall enter judgment in accordance therewith and notify the parties. Such judgment shall have the same effect, and all proceedings in relation thereto shall thereafter be the same, as though said judgment had been rendered in a suit duly heard and determined by the superior court of the General Court of Justice. (1973, c. 295, s. 16; c. 1331, s. 3; 1987, c. 827, s. 265.)

§ 95-142. Legal representation of the Department of Labor.

It shall be the duty of the Attorney General to represent the Department of Labor or designate some member of his staff to represent them in all actions or proceedings in connection with this Article. (1973, c. 295, s. 17.)

§ 95-143. Record keeping and reporting.

(a) Each employer shall make available to the Commissioner, or his agents, in such manner as the Commissioner shall require, copies of the same records and reports regarding his activities relating to this Article as are required to be made, kept, or preserved by section 8(c) of the Federal Occupational Safety and Health Act of 1970 (P.L. 91-596) and regulations made pursuant thereto.

(b) Each employer shall make, keep and preserve and make available to the Commissioner such records regarding his activities relating to this Article as the Commissioner may prescribe by regulation as necessary and appropriate for the enforcement of this Article or for developing information regarding the causes and prevention of occupational accidents and illnesses. In order to carry out the provisions of this section such regulations may include provisions requiring employers to conduct periodic inspections. The Commissioner shall also issue regulations requiring that employers, through posting of notices or other appropriate means, keep the employees informed of their protections and obligations under this Article, including the provisions of applicable standards. The Commissioner shall prescribe regulations requiring employers to maintain accurate records of, and to make reports at least annually on, work-related deaths, injuries and illnesses other than minor injuries requiring only first-aid treatment and which do not involve medical treatment, loss of consciousness, restriction of work or motion, or transfer to another job.

(c) The Commissioner shall issue regulations requiring employers to maintain accurate records of employee exposure to potentially toxic materials of [or] harmful physical agents which are required to be monitored or measured under this Article. Such regulations shall provide employees or their representatives with an opportunity to observe such monitoring or measuring, and to have access to the records thereof. Such regulations shall also make appropriate provisions for each employee or former employee to have access to such records as will indicate his own exposure to toxic materials or harmful physical agents. Each employer shall promptly notify any employee who has been or is being exposed to toxic materials or harmful physical agents in concentrations or at levels which exceed those prescribed by an applicable safety and health standard promulgated under this Article and shall inform any employee who is being thus exposed of the corrective action being taken.

(d) Any information obtained by the Commissioner or his duly authorized agents under this Article shall be obtained with a minimum burden upon employers, especially those operating small businesses. Unnecessary duplication of efforts in obtaining information shall be reduced to the maximum extent feasible. (1973, c. 295, s. 18; 1991 (Reg. Sess., 1992), c. 894, s. 1.)

§ 95-144. Statistics.

(a) In order to further the purposes of this Article, the Commissioner shall develop and maintain an effective program of collection, compilation, and analysis of occupational safety and health statistics. The Commissioner shall compile accurate statistics on work injuries and illnesses which shall include all disabling, serious or significant injuries or illnesses, whether or not involving loss of time from work, other than minor injuries requiring only first-aid treatment and which do not involve medical treatment, loss of consciousness, restriction of work or motion, or transfer to another job. On the basis of records made and kept pursuant to the provisions of this Article, employers shall file such reports with the Commissioner as he shall prescribe by regulations and as may be necessary to carry out his functions.

(b)   A listing of employment by area and industry of employers who have an assigned account number by the Division of Employment Security (DES) of the Department of Commerce of this State shall be supplied annually to the Commissioner by the DES. The listing of employment by area and industry shall contain at least the following: employer name; DES account number; indication of whether multiple or a single report unit; number of reporting units; average employment; establishment size code; geographical area; any four-digit code; and any other information deemed necessary by the Commissioner to meet federal reporting requirements. (1973, c. 295, s. 19; 2011-401, s. 5.1.)

§ 95-145. Reports to the Secretary.

(a) The Commissioner shall require employers in the State to make reports to the Secretary in the same manner and to the same extent as if the plan in force under this Article were not in effect, and

(b) The Commissioner shall make such reports to the Secretary in such form and containing such information as the Secretary from time to time shall require. (1973, c. 295, s. 20.)

§ 95-146. Continuation and effectiveness of this Article.

The Commissioner shall from time to time furnish to the Secretary information and assurances that this Article is being administered by adequate methods and by standards and enforcement procedures which are and will continue to be as effective as federal standards. (1973, c. 295, s. 21.)

§ 95-147. Training and employee education.

(a) The Commissioner, after consultation with appropriate departments and agencies of the State and subdivisions of government, shall conduct, directly or by grants or contracts, (i) education programs to provide an adequate supply of qualified personnel to carry out the purposes of this Article, and (ii) informational, educational and training programs on the importance of and proper use of adequate safety and health equipment to encourage voluntary compliance.

(b) The Commissioner is also authorized to conduct, directly or by grants or contracts, short-term training of personnel engaged in work related to the Commissioner's responsibilities under this Article.

(c) The Commissioner shall provide employers and employees programs covering recognition, avoidance and prevention of unsafe and unhealthful working conditions in places of employment and shall advise employers and employees, or their representatives, [of] effective means to prevent occupational injuries and illnesses. (1973, c. 295, s. 22.)

§ 95-148. Safety and health programs of State agencies and local governments.

It shall be the responsibility of each administrative department, commission, board, division or other agency of the State and of counties, cities, towns and subdivisions of government to establish and maintain an effective and comprehensive occupational safety and health program which is consistent with the standards and regulations promulgated under this Article. The head of each agency shall:

(1) Provide safe and healthful places and conditions of employment, consistent with the standards and regulations promulgated by this Article;

(2) Acquire, maintain, and require the use of safety equipment, personal protective equipment, and devices reasonably necessary to protect employees;

(3) Consult with and encourage employees to cooperate in achieving safe and healthful working conditions;

(4) Keep adequate records of all occupational accidents and illnesses for proper evaluation and corrective action;

(5)   Consult with the Commissioner as to the adequacy as to form and content of records kept pursuant to this section;

(6)   Make an annual report to the Commissioner with respect to occupational accidents and injuries and the agency's program under this section.

The Commissioner shall transmit annually to the Governor and the General Assembly a report of the activities of the State agency and instrumentalities under this section. If the Commissioner has reason to believe that any local government program or program of any agency of the State is ineffective, he shall, after unsuccessfully seeking by negotiations to abate such failure, include this in his annual report to the Governor and the General Assembly, together with the reasons therefor, and may recommend legislation intended to correct such condition.

The Commissioner shall have access to the records and reports kept and filed by State agencies and instrumentalities pursuant to this section unless such records and reports are required to be kept secret in the interest of national defense, in which case the Commissioner shall have access to such information as will not jeopardize national defense.

Employees of any agency or department covered under this section are afforded the same rights and protections as granted employees in the private sector.

This section shall not apply to volunteer fire departments not a part of any municipality.

Any municipality with a population of 10,000 or less may exclude its fire department from the operation of this section by a resolution of the governing body of the municipality, except that the resolution may not exclude those firefighters who are employees of the municipality.

The North Carolina Fire and Rescue Commission shall recommend regulations and standards for fire departments. (1973, c. 295, s. 23; 1983, c. 164; 1985, c. 544; 1989, c. 750, s. 3; 1991 (Reg. Sess., 1992), c. 1020, s. 1.)

§ 95-149. Authority to enter into contracts with other State agencies and subdivisions of government.

The Commissioner may enter into contracts with the Department of Health and Human Services or any other State officer or State agency or State instrumentality, or any municipality, county, or other political subdivision of the State, for the enforcement, administration, and any other application of the provisions of this Article. (1973, c. 295, s. 24; 1989, c. 727, s. 24; 1997-443, s. 11A.35.)

§ 95-150. Assurance of adequate funds to enforce Article.

The Commissioner shall submit to the General Assembly a budget and request for appropriations to adequately administer this Article which shall be sufficient to give satisfactory assurance that this State will devote adequate funds to the administration and enforcement of the standards herein provided and the proper administration of this Article as required by federal standards. (1973, c. 295, s. 25.)

Vision Books Order Form

Fax Orders: 1-980-299-5965

Phone Orders: 1-704-898-0770

E-mail Orders: www.visionbooks.org

Mail Orders: Vision Books, LLC
P.O. Box 42406
Charlotte, NC 28215

Shipp To:
Name_____
Address_____
City_____State_____Zip_____
Phone_____Fax_____
Email_____@_____

Bill To: We can bill a third party on your behalf.
Name_____
Address_____
City_____State_____Zip_____
Phone____(_____)_____Fax_____
Email_____@_____

Pamphlet Number ($15.00 Each)	Qty	Total Cost
_____	_____	_____
_____	_____	_____
_____	_____	_____
_____	_____	_____
_____	_____	_____
_____	_____	_____
_____	_____	_____
_____	_____	_____
_____	_____	_____
Full Volume Set 1-92	92 Pamphlets	1,380.00

Free Shipping Shipping & Handling on Full Volume Orders
Add $1.00 Shipping & Handling per pamphlet $_____

Total Cost $_____

Thank you for your support. Management!

DID YOU ENJOY THIS BOOK?

Vision Books, LLC would like to hear from you! If you or someone you know has been fasely imprisoned, we would like to hear your story. If the 'North Carolina Criminal Law and Procedure' has had an effect in your life or if you have suggestions, we would like to hear from you. Send your letters to:

Vision Books, LLC
Attn: Staff Writers
P.O. Box 42406
Charlotte, NC 28215
Email: staff@visionbooks.org

Order Additional Copies:

Fax Orders:	1-980-299-5965
Phone Orders:	1-704-898-0770
E-mail Orders:	www.visionbooks.org
Mail Orders:	Vision Books, LLC P.O. Box 42406 Charlotte, NC 28215

www.ingramcontent.com/pod-product-compliance
Lightning Source LLC
Chambersburg PA
CBHW051628170526
45167CB00001B/106